God and Reality

Essays on Christian Non-realism

Edited by Colin Crowder

MOWBRAY

Mowbray
A Cassell imprint
Wellington House
125 Strand
London
WC2R 0BB

127 West 24th Street
New York, NY 10011

First published 1997

British Library Cataloguing in Publication Data
A catalogue record for this book is available from the British Library.

ISBN 0–264–67392–1

Typeset by Keystroke, Jacaranda Lodge, Wolverhampton
Printed and bound in Great Britain by
Redwood Books, Trowbridge, Wiltshire

Contents

Foreword

It has not been particularly easy for the general public – not to mention the Christian public – to come to terms with what is involved in the debate which this book attempts to further. Headlines about 'atheist priests' create as much sheer puzzlement as anger; and some responses to the publications of those who have proclaimed themselves non-realists in their Christian commitment suggest that the question posed has been quite seriously misheard. Perhaps the problem could be put epigrammatically by saying that this question has been *heard* as a version of 'Does God exist?' whereas what is being asked is '*How* does God exist?'. The non-realist is proposing that most familiar ways of speaking about God do so in a style that implies a God existing in the way items exist in the world; and they rightly note that the Christian tradition itself witnesses to a deep unease about speaking of God as *a* being, as a substance or an object. But the non-realist also goes further, claiming (as I understand it) that the distinctively *religious* use of language about God, if we really grasp how it works, strictly requires us to let go of any suggestion that this language refers to some thing other than the contents of our minds and our language. To speak of God is to speak of the most radical dispossession that is thinkable, the most ultimate and unanswerable judgement imaginable; and this must be distinguished from any kind of encounter with another subject like myself and purified from any security that might lie in appeal to a grounding beyond myself. How this relates to the postmodernist idiom for which all language is stripped of the right to appeal to an 'outside' is a theme pursued in a variety of ways in these essays. But I take it that, postmodernism or no postmodernism, the important point for the most serious non-realists is indeed the religious requirement. A God who exists in the way that 'real' things are assumed to exist cannot save us, because such a God constantly slips over into being a presence that legitimizes instead of judging the integrity of the believer.

This is meant to be a foreword, not another essay. But I'll presume to offer five brief reflections that may be worth keeping in mind as this book is read, five reflections that may perhaps unsettle further the terms of the debate.

First: the non-realist insists that God is a reality constructed in language, an aspect of what we say and do; more specifically, a way of constructing (for example) an ideal unity of the values to which we are answerable. But a question in response might be to do with what it *means* to speak of a reality constructed in language, and with the variety of ways in which God does appear and function in speech. 'God is the imagined ideal unity of values'; 'God is a spirit of infinite power, wisdom and goodness'; 'Thou art God ineffable, incomprehensible, invisible, unsearchable, art ever, art alike'. Are these 'constructing' the same meanings? Arguably, the third of these idioms doesn't simply reduce to the first: the language of adoration *constructs* a reality, sure enough, but does so effectively only by pushing language to an extremity. What are we to say of language for God that insists on its own position at an edge of articulacy? as if pointing away? Can this be rendered without loss in functionalist terms, God as the verbal vehicle for aspirations on the part of speakers?

Second: this raises in turn a question discussed at one or two points in this book, a question about language itself. Does the realist/non-realist debate as set out here take for granted that the most interesting aspect of language is its *representational* work? To say 'Of course, it's not *about* anything' or (on the other hand) 'Of course religious language must *refer* to what it claims to refer to' may lead us astray. Language is something people do, it is a way of coping with an environment, of 'negotiating'. That is to say, it grows and changes in ways that no one chooses or plans, it shows signs of difficulty and strain, it encodes useful and unuseful ways of finding your way around. It 'represents' not as a straight spatial reproduction or even a diagrammatic structure, but as a set of guidelines for response, whose appropriateness is not tested simply by some supposed fidelity of 'picture' to 'original'. The non-realist is apparently saying that classical religious discourse may well be an appropriate response to the environment *in certain circumstances* – specifically, where issues about representation don't arise. The realist might reply that there are no circumstances where, ultimately, questions about language's representative force don't arise. But is there one simple and canonical *mode* of representation that religious language can be shown to possess or not to possess?

Third: the realist is always tempted to look for the *essence* of theological truth, so as to allow for the inevitable shifts in criteria of intelligibility between one culture and another. The so-called liberal may be as much (even more) of a realist than the conservative. But what the realist, liberal or not-so-liberal, may miss, and what the non-realist is often acutely aware of, is the way in which *how* something is said is significantly *part* of what is said; so that a shift in religious idiom may actually change the kind of claim being made in a doctrinal proposition. Opponents of liturgical reform sometimes say that there are theological truths that simply cannot be expressed in contemporary English, because contemporary English is the speech of a society in which certain 'registers' of language, particularly those connected with awe or veneration, are almost extinct. More widely: is it true that, when certain religious *practices* die, certain theological meanings die with them? If Catholics stop genuflecting to the Sacrament, are they still believing the same as their forebears? If we do move away from neat theories of representation, the question of how we talk truthfully of God becomes quite complex for the realist; the non-realist has an advantage in being able to point to the steady erosion of certain idioms and practices over the ages, concluding that there is a consistent drift towards an erosion of ontological claims of one kind and another, so that idioms and practices can be re-visioned as expressions of felt intensity or aspiration.

Fourth: the issue that *this* raises in turn is a particularly teasing one about the politics of realism and non-realism. Realism can act as a means of legitimizing the power of the Church's hierarchy. Anything written on this subject by a bishop is automatically and rightly suspect. But it is not at all clear that non-realism is politically innocent. The implicit claim (hinted at in the last paragraph) that non-realism represents the irreversible direction of human thinking is a powerfully political one; and the use of 'we' by the non-realist (or anyone else, of course), as in 'we can no longer believe that . . . ', is a claim to power and legitimacy of a kind. A non-realist may complain that the Church or the hierarchy, in disciplining or excluding people with particular views on this matter, displays its political and irreligious priorities: why should people be disadvantaged for their refusal not of a religious commitment or practice but of a metaphysical structure? But is the non-realist claim to do with the possible permissibility within the spectrum of belief of the non-realist 'option', or is it (para-doxically) another claim about *essences*, and, ultimately, a challenge to the legitimacy of anything other than non-realism? The robust claim that only the non-realist God can save sits uneasily with the bid for toleration as a recognized 'option'. And in this, the present debate is no different from doctrinal debates in the fourth and fifth centuries, where doctrine is consistently read as pertinent to salvation. If this is a contest over legitimacy of differing kinds, it is bound to be political; what would a *purely* religious disagreement look like?

Fifth and finally: this last observation is not meant cynically; there *is* a difficulty over the proposed isolation of the religious sphere, more particularly if the idioms used in this sphere are so analysed in other contexts as to qualify and restrict their meanings significantly. We are licensed to use words in the sphere of worship and reflection on our sustaining values; provided that we recognize that there is another court of instance in which we are reminded that no claim or implication can be admitted for such language that relates to the extra-mental or extra-linguistic. That court may be presided over by a familiar Kantian judge on a well-worn circuit, or by his revolutionary postmodernist successor; it may allow or disallow representational force in other linguistic contexts. But its verdict on religious language is consistent. And the problem this leaves is whether language remains in any sense usable in its 'religious' environment if it is subject to such a verdict. Can the functions of classical theological language actually survive the denial of ontological reference beyond the speaker? What is more, if the religious attitude or lifestyle is not simply an area of interest but a comprehensive vision and policy, as the non-realist often seems to insist, what exactly is being said if it is simultaneously spoken of as an area of discourse in which both expressions and attitudes are allowed that work quite differently from how they might work in other areas? This is, I grant, far more of a problem for the 'modernist' than for the 'postmodernist' strand of non-realism; that latter will see analogies across fields of discourse in which reference and representation are in any case non-issues. But the question is still there for any non-realist of how the discourse can function in the same way as hitherto (in the most important or central respects) without a continuing seriousness about those aspects of it which were noted in the first of these observations, the aspects of difficulty, extremity and self-subversion in order to point 'away'. In other words, is the concern to isolate and conserve the purity of the 'religious', and its independence of ontology, ultimately destructive of that very integrity, by subsuming it for other purposes under general rubrics of linguistic adequacy and declaring it eccentric by those conventions? This is a complex question, which I have not succeeded in putting very clearly; but I believe it is a serious one.

These reflections are only a few of the reactions generated by a remarkable collection of essays, all of them distinguished by moral and intellectual passion as well as lucidity and originality. I suspect my own position will have come into focus for the reader now: I still fail to see how what the non-realist advocates can be compatible in the long run with what I understand to be Christian belief. That failure may be hierarchical nervousness or intellectual cowardice; but I hope not, because I hope that what is here presented may be capable of moving the discussion on in the way it should move on — as a serious exchange of visions as to what religious language is like, and, more, as to what salvation from untruth might mean. In that task, we all have the freedom to question each other hard; as in these pages.

Rowan Williams
Bishop of Monmouth

Preface

Towards the end of 1994, Judith Longman, then of Cassell, approached me with the idea for a collection of essays on Christian non-realism. The idea had first been conceived at the Sea of Faith conference, a few months earlier, and a number of potential contributors had been identified at that time. Judith and I agreed that there was a need for a new kind of book on the non-realist debate, which would emphasize the internal diversity of Christian non-realism itself and of the critical response it has generated over the last few years.

The result is, I hope, the most wide-ranging contribution to the non-realist debate published to date. It is worth emphasizing, however, that non-realism is only one of the radical approaches to religious belief and practice which the Sea of Faith Network represents. Its distinctiveness makes a project like this legitimate, as I suggest in the Introduction; but I am conscious that there are important features of the contemporary theological landscape which, no matter how relevant to the non-realist approach, could not be explored at any length in this book.

I would like to express sincere thanks to Judith Longman, whose enterprise and enthusiasm initiated the project and sustained it in its early months, and to Ruth McCurry and Kathie Walsh, who have seen it through to publication. I am grateful to the contributors, of course, for their time and effort, and their generous response to editorial suggestions and to shifts in the schedule for production. I have been especially encouraged by my Durham colleagues Peter Selby (who first suggested me as a potential editor for this project) and Jeff Astley. I am also grateful to Alan Ford, for IT advice, and to Philip Knight, one of my PhD candidates, for the intellectual stimulus of his work on Christian non-realism in relation to the philosophical pragmatism of Richard Rorty. It seems to me that this is a good example of the kind of new thinking on non-realism which is now required, and which I hope these essays will help to foster.

Colin Crowder
Durham
June 1996

The contributors

Jeff Astley is Director of the North of England Institute for Christian Education, and an Honorary Lecturer in Theology and Education at the University of Durham. He is the author of *The Philosophy of Christian Religious Education* (SPCK, 1994), and a co-editor of several books on Christian education and on faith development.

Don Cupitt is Lecturer in the Philosophy of Religion at the University of Cambridge, Fellow of Emmanuel College, Cambridge, and an Anglican priest. He is the author of over twenty books, including, most recently, *What Is a Story?* (SCM Press, 1991), *The Time Being* (SCM Press, 1992), *After All* (SCM Press, 1994), *The Last Philosophy* (SCM Press, 1995) and *Solar Ethics* (SCM Press, 1995).

Anthony Freeman, an Anglican priest, was formerly Priest-in-Charge of St Mark's, Staplefield. He is the author of *God in Us: A Case for Christian Humanism* (SCM Press, 1993).

Daphne Hampson is Senior Lecturer in Divinity at the University of St Andrews. She is the author of *Theology and Feminism* (Blackwell, 1990) and *After Christianity* (SCM Press, 1996). A frequent lecturer and broadcaster, she has been foremost amongst those in Britain advocating a post-Christian spirituality.

David Hart, Anglican Chaplain to Loughborough University and Colleges, serves on the Steering Committee of the Sea of Faith Network.

He is the author of *Faith in Doubt: Non-realism and Christian Belief* (Mowbray, 1993), *One Faith? Non-realism and the World of Faiths* (Mowbray, 1995) and the forthcoming *Linking Up: Radical Christianity and Sexuality* (Arthur James, 1997).

Fergus Kerr OP of Blackfriars, Edinburgh, is an Honorary Senior Lecturer in Theology and Religious Studies at the University of Edinburgh. He is the author of *Theology after Wittgenstein* (Blackwell, 1986) and the forthcoming *Immortal Longings: Versions of Transcending Humanity* (SPCK, 1997), and is the editor of *New Blackfriars*.

Stephen Mitchell, Rector of Holy Trinity Church, Barrow-upon-Soar, and St Mary's Church, Walton-le-Wolds, is Chair of the Steering Committee of the Sea of Faith Network.

George Pattison is the Dean of Chapel at King's College, Cambridge. He is the author of *Art, Modernity and Faith: Towards a Theology of Art* (Macmillan, 1991), *Kierkegaard: The Aesthetic and the Religious* (Macmillan, 1992) and *Agnosis: Theology in the Void* (Macmillan, 1996). He is also the co-author, with Stephen Platten, of *Spirit and Tradition* (Canterbury Press, 1996), and the editor of *Modern Believing*.

Peter Selby is the William Leech Professorial Fellow in Applied Christian Theology at the University of Durham, and Honorary Assistant Bishop in the dioceses of Durham and Newcastle. He is the author of *BeLonging: Challenge to a Tribal Church* (SPCK, 1991) and *Rescue: Jesus and Salvation Today* (SPCK, 1995).

Graham Shaw, an Anglican priest, was formerly Chaplain of Exeter College, Oxford, and Rector of St Giles the Abbot, Farnborough. He is the author of *The Cost of Authority: Manipulation and Freedom in the New Testament* (SCM Press, 1983) and *God in Our Hands* (SCM Press, 1987).

Denys Turner is the H. G. Wood Professor of Theology at the University of Birmingham. He is the author of *Marxism and Christianity* (Blackwell, 1983), *The Darkness of God: Negativity in Christian Mysticism* (Cambridge University Press, 1995) and *Eros and Allegory: Medieval Exegesis of the Song of Songs* (Cistercian Publications, 1995).

Graham Ward is the Dean of Peterhouse, Cambridge. He is the author of

Barth, Derrida and the Language of Theology (Cambridge University Press, 1995) and *Theology and Contemporary Critical Theory* (Macmillan, 1996), and is a co-editor of *Literature and Theology*.

Colin Crowder is a Lecturer in Theology at the University of Durham. He has written on the philosophy of religion, and on ethical and social issues, and has co-edited books on religion and literature and on theology and education. He is also the reviews editor of *Literature and Theology*.

Introduction

Colin Crowder

The Sea of Faith

For Matthew Arnold, in his celebrated poem 'Dover Beach' (1867), the ebbing of the tide prompted the thought of the 'melancholy, long, withdrawing roar' of a sea once 'at the full' – 'The Sea of Faith'. Some writers have adopted this image to express their own sense of the way in which our world has changed, over the last two hundred years or so, as Christianity has been socially, culturally, and intellectually marginalized. The conventional shorthand for this historical process is 'secularization'; but for many of those who invoke the image of the sea of faith, retreating down the 'naked shingles of the world', what secularization amounts to is *desacralization*, which, no matter how inevitable, represents a profound loss. That 'long, withdrawing roar' is 'melancholy', indeed, and the disappointment lies in the disenchantment of the world.

This book is concerned with a movement in contemporary theology which sees things very differently. According to Christian non-realists, the tide can turn again, and if we are willing to lay aside some fixed ideas about belief, unbelief, and the difference between them we will be able to see it turn for ourselves. This is a point which is made by Don Cupitt, Lecturer in Philosophy of Religion in the University of Cambridge, and a Fellow of Emmanuel College, Cambridge, in his book *The Sea of Faith*, published in association with his ground-breaking television series of the same name in 1984:

1

It is those who are prepared to abandon their preconceptions and to become as ignorant and innocent as Socrates himself who will be able to see the tide returning. The sea of faith, in Matthew Arnold's great metaphor, flows as well as ebbs; but the tide that returns is not quite the same as the tide that went out.[1]

There is continuity, of course, but 'to expect the new to be the same as the old is to miss the point'.[2] Christianity has always transformed itself, and the New Testament itself is a record of the transformation of the earliest faith into something that could be comprehended within Graeco-Roman culture. The challenges presented by the modern world might be the most demanding that Christianity has ever had to face, but it is not unreasonable to believe that the faith can and will recreate itself once more. However, new meanings cannot be born unless the old ones die:

You have to go through inner turmoil; you have to descend into the primal chaos, into that nameless region in the depths of the human soul where all meanings are unmade and remade. There at the source of the creative energy that makes us and our world, you pass through a kind of death and rebirth. The more you lose, the more you will gain.[3]

The loss of faith, therefore, is not to be lamented, but celebrated: without it, there can be no living religion. Correspondingly, the sea of faith ebbs and flows, as it has always done, and the turning of the tide is the transformation of the faith. So to see it turn, 'we should be looking for signs of a profound mutation of Christianity, a reforging of all its meanings'.[4]

At the heart of this transformation is the recognition that 'religion is completely human, bound up with the cultures and the histories that it creates'.[5] But Cupitt insists that the philosophical revolution which we call the 'end of metaphysics' means that this is true not only of religion but of everything else as well:

We have come to see that there can be for us nothing but the worlds that are constituted for us by our own languages and activities. All meaning and truth and value are man-made and could not be otherwise. The flux of experience is continuous and has no structure of its own. It is we who impose shape upon it to make of it a world to live in.[6]

This perspective – 'radical humanism or anthropocentrism'[7] – is the moral of the story of modern thought which Cupitt narrates in *The Sea of Faith*, and to a greater or lesser extent it is found in the work of a number of writers who share Cupitt's interest in the human creation of religion.

Many of these are associated with the Sea of Faith Network, the aim of which is 'to explore and promote religious belief as a human creation'. This statement of intent is perhaps the only thing that unites the more than a thousand members of the Network, as these include not only Christians, but also members of other traditions, and of none. Taking its name from Don Cupitt's book, and much of its inspiration from his extensive writings, the Network has become an important focus of radical religious thinking since its inception in the late 1980s, and its annual conference and quarterly magazine reflect a range of debates about the future of religious belief and practice in the contemporary world. Nevertheless, the increasing visibility of the Network is as much as anything the result of the publication, in the early 1990s, of a series of highly accessible essays in Christian non-realism by clergymen of the Church of England: *Freeing the Faith: A Credible Christianity for Today*, by Hugh Dawes (SPCK, 1992), *Faith in Doubt: Non-Realism and Christian Belief*, by David A. Hart (Mowbray, 1993), and *God in Us: A Case for Christian Humanism*, by Anthony Freeman (SCM, 1993). The addition of these books to Graham Shaw's *God in Our Hands* (SCM, 1987), and, of course, to the work of Don Cupitt since *Taking Leave of God* (SCM, 1980), is indicative of the extent to which non-realism has become a significant challenge to more conventional understandings of the Christian faith not only in the academy but also in the church.

Realism and non-realism

I ought to stress, however, that many members of the Sea of Faith Network, and even some of the writers named above, are reluctant to be described as 'non-realists'. There are good reasons for this reluctance, but I cannot discuss them here, and it must suffice to note that many members of the Network prefer to think of themselves as 'radical Christians', 'Christian humanists', 'religious humanists', or even as 'post-Christian'. Much depends on the way in which these terms are interpreted by those who identify with them, but I think it is reasonable to detect a certain family resemblance, at least, and to expect a considerable overlap between some of the categories. What concerns me, in this context, is that they are all compatible with a broadly liberal understanding of religious belief as a human response to a transcendent reality – in other words, you can identify yourself in this way, and say that religion is a human creation, and yet stop short of saying that there is no God other than the God which we have made. It seems to me, looking in from the outside, that some of the people involved in the Network are religious radicals who still operate within an essentially 'realist' framework, and if asked would no doubt give good radical reasons for doing so. But this makes it all the more important to focus on the non-realist dimension of the Sea of Faith phenomenon, which is distinguished by its insistence that religion is, *without remainder*, a human creation.

Just as the Network is not a church, so non-realism is not a creed. There is, of course, an experimental edge to the work of some contemporary non-realists, but it is a mistake to think that non-realism is necessarily innovative at the level of religious beliefs and practices. It does not purport to offer a new religious language, but a new way of understanding the one which we already have, so that we can use it in an intellectually, morally and religiously responsible way. Non-realism, therefore, opposes realism as an *interpretation* of the Christian faith. Realism, which assumes that God is 'an actually-existing independent individual being'[8] or nothing at all, is natural enough, according to non-realist thinkers, but wrong. I think it is fair to say, however, that they tend to be far less interested in establishing the claim that theism (as understood by realists) isn't true than in arguing that *it doesn't work*. Anthony Freeman, for example, in his *God in Us*, sketches a critique of natural and revealed theology, but this comes across as incidental to his claim that 'I can still benefit from using God religiously, without believing in him as an objective and active supernatural person'.[9] In this respect, Freeman is following in the footsteps of Don Cupitt, in *Taking Leave of God*, whose philosophical criticisms of 'objective theism' are overtaken by a different kind of critique, essentially religious in character. Religious truth is not speculative or descriptive, but practical, existential, and necessarily subjective; what matters, then, is not theism, but spirituality. Yet Cupitt's understanding of spirituality for 'a fully-unified autonomous human consciousness'[10] is such that belief in an 'objective' God – the God of the realists – is not only surplus to religious requirements, but serves, in practice, to undermine them. 'An objective God cannot save.'[11]

The alternative, described in that context as 'expressivism', or 'subjectivism', is characteristic of what has subsequently become known as Christian non-realism:

> Belief in the God of Christian faith is an expression of allegiance to a particular set of values, and experience of the God of Christian faith is experience of the impact of those values in one's life.[12]

This takes us back to *The Sea of Faith*, where Cupitt argues that our religious beliefs 'are rules of life dressed up in pictures',[13] the symbolic expression of the spirituality of a community. His conclusions have been echoed by many non-realists:

> [R]eligion is our way of representing to ourselves, and renewing our commitment to, the complex of moral and spiritual values through which we shape our world, constitute ourselves, gain our identity and give worth to our lives.
>
> God (and this is a definition) is the sum of our values, representing to us their ideal unity, their claims upon us and their creative power.[14]

It is important to realize that Cupitt and other non-realists are not claiming that religious belief can still mean something, however minimal, to someone who considers realism to be intellectually untenable. The non-realist perspective is not meant to be the best that can be done in the circumstances, but the *right* way to interpret religious belief. *The Sea of Faith* remains significant not only for treating the issue of realism versus non-realism as 'the great undiscussed question underlying the whole development of modern religious thought', but for making a case for the thesis that 'the claims of theological realism and of religious seriousness now pull in opposite directions'.[15]

For many people, Christian non-realism is nothing but atheism in disguise – and not a very good disguise at that. The non-realists, who are understandably familiar with this charge, defend themselves in various ways, but commonly stress that the difference between non-realism and atheism is the difference between valuing and not valuing the resources – the words, images, stories, ideas, and rituals – which the Christian tradition makes available to us. Anthony Freeman, for example, says

> Our view of religion as a human creation – let us call it Christian humanism – still stands firmly in the Christian tradition and sees itself as a legitimate heir to the New Testament. We still find value in the Christian vocabulary, including the word God, and in the Christian stories, especially those of Jesus. A secular humanist, an atheist, has no place for such things.[16]

A similar point is made by Graham Shaw:

> Once we have recognized that all religion is man-made, instead of repudiating it with a misplaced sense of disappointment, we might still choose to affirm religious activity as something which enriches our lives and which like other forms of art is inextricably intertwined with human creativity and freedom.[17]

The atheist's mistake, according to Shaw, is to assume that religion cannot survive the recognition that it is a human creation. On the contrary, this recognition is at the heart of a 'responsible religion', and it is made possible by the testimony of the gospel itself to the intimacy of the relationship between the identity of the believer and the identity of God.[18]

On the basis of considerations such as these, some people are willing to accept that there is a genuine difference between Christian non-realism and atheism – even the 'Christian atheism' advocated by some of the 'death of God' theologians, in the 1960s, which tended to treat *any* kind of belief in God as something which had to be overcome for the sake of a new humanism, focused on the figure of Jesus. Christian non-realism doesn't do without God, in this sense, and therefore to identify it with atheism is, at the very least, unhelpful. Nevertheless, there is a common feeling that the God of the non-realists is such a pale reflection of the God of the realists that there is scarcely any point in continuing to use the traditional language – in other words, non-realism makes God somehow *unreal*. This suspicion is less specific than the accusation of atheism, but the non-realists are no less aware of it. Don Cupitt, for example, in *Taking Leave of God*, suggests that the difference between the 'real' and the 'unreal' varies from context to context, which means that 'the sense in which God is real is given in the language and practice of religion' and nowhere else.[19] Whether God is real *outside* of this context is another question altogether, and the first thing that must be said about it is that 'it is of no religious interest'. In fact, Cupitt's interpretation of the religious life (at this stage of his work) is such that he is inclined to say that 'religion forbids that there should be any extra-religious reality of God'.[20] But Cupitt's concluding reflections in *The Sea of Faith* show that there is something more fundamental and more positive to be said about the reality of God:

> The suggestion that the idea of God is man-made would only seem startling if we could point by contrast to something that has not been made by men. But since our thought shapes all its objects, we cannot. In an innocuous sense, all our normative ideas have been posited by ourselves, including the truths of logic and mathematics as well as all our ideals and values. How else could we have acquired them? Thus God is man-made only in the non-startling sense that everything is. That is modern anthropocentrism. But even on my account God is as real for us as anything else can be, and more primally authoritative than anything else is.[21]

The postmodern shift

By its own account, therefore, Christian non-realism does not so much reject the reality of God as radically reinterpret it. The quotation with which I concluded the preceding section is echoed by several other writers today, such as Hugh Dawes, who in arguing that non-realism is a corrective to common assumptions about what being 'real' amounts to, and not an attack on God's reality as such, maintains that 'God is as real as anything else in life'.[22] But Cupitt's conclusion in 1984 is sustained by a perspective which, even now, is not as evident in the work of some other Christian non-realists as one might expect it to be. I must say something about this, because I think that it presents us with a crucial insight into the character of contemporary non-realist thought.

In *The Sea of Faith*, Cupitt describes this perspective as 'anthropocentrism', or 'radical humanism', as we have already seen. These terms remind us of the claim that all meanings, and truths, and values, and not just the religious ones, are the product of *human* creativity. But it might help us to get a clearer sense of the philosophical issues if we switch the emphasis to human *creativity* and call this perspective 'constructivism'. Against the realist, who believes that The Truth Is Out There, the constructivist believes that our knowledge of the world is more a matter of *making* than of discovering. There are weaker and stronger versions of this perspective, and, in *The Sea of Faith*, Cupitt is advocating a strong version which draws on the thought of Kant, Marx, Nietzsche and Wittgenstein, among others. Since 1984, however, Cupitt's constructivism has become more radical still, in book after book, and not every non-realist has been able or willing to keep up with him.

I have focused on *The Sea of Faith* because of its connection with the Network of the same name, and because it remains an excellent point of entry into the non-realist world. Nevertheless, much of it belongs to a stage in Cupitt's development, associated with *Taking Leave of God*, which is now very much in the past. However, the radical constructivism to which I have drawn attention – or, in other words, the determination to be non-realist about *everything* – opens up the new horizons of the ten books which Cupitt has published in the last decade. Much of what he has to say in the early 1980s about Nietzsche and Wittgenstein, in particular, points forward to his more recent work. But the decisive shift occurs with Cupitt's appropriation of recent French thinkers, such as Derrida, whose writings have played a major role in shaping the 'postmodernism' of the present day.

Taking Leave of God is written under the shadow of Kant, and its themes, such as 'autonomy', 'internalization', and 'self-transcendence', bear witness to its investment in a distinctively *modern* concept of the human subject. It is this concept of subjectivity which Cupitt takes leave of, in the later 1980s, and almost every difference between his 'middle' and 'later' stages (so far!) can and must be related to this development. There is no doubt that there is a great difference between the individualism of the earlier work and the communitarian thinking of more recent writings. Similarly, the sheer austerity of the earlier work – its 'Christian Buddhism', its inter- pretation of religion as 'a severe inner discipline', and so on[23] – gives way to a celebration of the world, the body, and the passions which represents a different kind of spirituality altogether. There are many such shifts, and no one is more aware of them than Cupitt himself ('That's the story of my life – recantations'[24]); but the shift from a characteristically modern concept of the self to a distinctively *postmodern* one is fundamental.

I cannot hope to summarize the issues involved in the space available to me, but it is important to say something about developments in Cupitt's approach to language in the late 1980s. Postmodern philosophy, according to Cupitt, frees us from thinking that the function of words is to refer to the world, to a 'reality' beyond language. It teaches, instead, that the function of words is to refer to other words: so reference is 'horizontal' rather than vertical – a movement within language, rather than a move beyond it. This sense that reference is 'just another linguistic operation', which has no 'magic capacity to jump out of language',[25] should make us see the world as a world of words, a world of signs and stories. It is 'a world of difference, plurality, perspectives, ambiguity, play, squabbles, surfaces, mockery – in short, a fictional world'.[26] Like literature, the world is 'all metaphors, interpretations, deceptions';[27] 'a beginningless, endless, shimmering interplay of signs on a flat surface'.[28] In the postmodern era, 'there isn't much "reality" around',[29] or, alternatively, the line between the real and the fictional is no longer clear: 'in reality, reality is as impossibly plural, fictitious and feminine as Writing. The world is like a whole shelf of novels: that is postmodernism.'[30]

'It's a language-shaped world',[31] therefore, and seeing it in this way accentuates the constructivist perspective:

> Postmodernism is just the belated full realization that our knowledge is just human, a function of our contingent human conventions, capacities, needs and interactions, an imaginative construction which since it is perforce wholly carried in language, cannot help but be what language

is. That is all that postmodernism is – but, being that, it is more completely the death and dispersal of the old objective metaphysical God, with his masculine pronouns, than any previous philosophical movement has been.[32]

However, the postmodern shift entails the death and dispersal not only of the old God, but of the old humanity too – the free, autonomous individual of *Taking Leave of God*, for example. The self is no more and no less than a product of language, a construct of signs: there is now no question of 'internalizing' God, as there is nothing there in which God or anything else could be internalized. Cupitt still writes of 'an integral humanism, in which life, the body and the passions come first, and value is grounded in them'[33] – but there is more to this new humanism (or post-humanism?) than a reversal of values:

> Human knowledge has grown until we can't help recognizing that it is after all only our knowledge, only our world, only our morality, only our religion, only our rationality, our philosophy, our language . . . and after this 'anthropomonism' (*Only Human*, 1985) the next step is that we ourselves also are demythologized away, leaving only the flux of sign-formed events (*The Time Being*, 1992), and therefore an extremely lightweight world in which the self itself is only a transient 'literary' effect, somewhat as a *dramatis persona* is only a transient effect produced by the performance of a drama.[34]

We are not 'distinct individual substances', but 'our various interactions, relationships and roles'.[35] 'You are your life, and your life is the story of your life.'[36]

In the 1990s, Cupitt continues his endlessly creative explorations of postmodern non-realist Christianity. Our religion should be like art, 'in its capacity to revalue life by imaginatively transforming it',[37] and Christianity is the 'river of signs'[38] through which we live our lives. This 'river of signs' may seem a long way from the 'sea of faith', but some things haven't changed. Realism, castigated as 'idolatry and superstition' back in 1985,[39] remains the 'bogey'[40] – it still isn't true, and still doesn't work, and the charges against it are, I suspect, more serious than ever.[41] There are continuities between earlier and later descriptions of the alternative, as well, but it would be foolish to underestimate the difference between the conceptual framework of *Taking Leave of God* and the later invocations of 'outsidelessness', 'contingency', 'transience', 'expressionism' and so on. Only four years ago, Cupitt could summarize his religious vision in these terms:

> We must change the definition of what counts as religion, turning from God (the old metaphysical God, that is) to the fleeting, from eternity to time, from the long-term to the short-term, and from the inner to the outer. Religious thought has got to be not just secularized but temporalized, made immanent, mobile and expressive.[42]

> We need – don't we know it by now? – a religion without God, that is, a religion without absolutes, without perfection, without closure, without eternity. A religion of creativity and freedom must be a religion that says yes to time, contingency, open-endedness, transience.[43]

Since then, however, he has been exploring 'energetic Spinozism', 'poetical theology', 'Kingdom-religion', 'solar ethics', and much more besides – but all I can do here is to refer the reader to Cupitt's most recent books: *After All: Religion Without Alienation* (SCM, 1994), *The Last Philosophy* (SCM, 1995), and *Solar Ethics* (SCM, 1995). My point, in this context, is simply that Cupitt's postmodern non-realism is a long way from the non-realism of those who still take leave of God for the sake of the unreconstructed, undeconstructed human subject of modernity. Having said that, there are other writers, some of whom I mentioned earlier, who appear to come somewhere in between what it may be most appropriate to think of as the opposite ends of a spectrum. Christian non-realism, therefore, is a much more complex phenomenon than many of its critics – and even some of its advocates – would have us believe.

The future of the debate

The trouble with Christian non-realism is that there is scarcely a line in any of the works cited above which isn't open to one kind of criticism or another. Christian non-realists are, after all, committed to highly controversial interpretations of the life of the Church, of contemporary culture, of the sciences and the arts, of the Christian tradition and the other world religions, and of modern and postmodern philosophies. It is not surprising, therefore, that it has attracted serious criticism at these and various other levels, and that so many think that non-realism misinterprets everything it touches – not only Kant and Kierkegaard, Nietzsche and Wittgenstein, Derrida and Foucault, or any philosopher for that matter, but also the teaching of Jesus and the doctrines of the Church, morality and mysticism, psychology and painting, politics and prayer.

Much of this criticism is to be found in academic journals, and, in consequence, it is inaccessible for many people. There have been books, of course, but until recently they have tended to be published as 'refutations' of some specific academic or popular presentation of Christian non-realism. (Even the titles are characteristic of the genre, in echoing, to some extent, the titles of the books on the receiving end of the criticism.[44]) Other critics, in the last few years, have emphasized the developments in Cupitt's work, and in so doing have acknowledged that Christian non-realism is irreducibly diverse.[45] But what the debate has so far lacked, I think, is a book in which Christian non-realists *and* some of their critics can speak for themselves, and in such a way that they can do justice to some of the theological, philosophical, ethical and pastoral issues at stake.[46]

This book has been designed to fill the gap. *God and Reality* brings together, in a single collection of essays, five radical theologians widely associated with non-realism and seven of the most influential interpreters and critics of their work. The strength of this collection is its very diversity, and no attempt has been made to impose an artificial consistency of style or substance on either set of contributors. Exploring Christian non-realism from a variety of perspectives, *God and Reality* is intended to serve not only as an introduction to the contemporary debate, but as a contribution to its development in the future as a constructive theological dialogue. The non-realists, naturally, will always have harsh things to say about realism, and their critics can undoubtedly give as good as they get. But the accent must now be on dialogue, for the sake of fostering the kind of discussion of the future of religious belief and practice which is now urgently required. Something of the generosity which is needed in this context can be seen in the words of George Pattison, Dean of King's College, Cambridge, and a contributor to this volume, in an editorial for the special issue of the journal *Modern Believing* commemorating the tenth anniversary of the publication of *The Sea of Faith*:

> What is beyond doubt is that *The Sea of Faith* has both placed serious theological issues in the public arena in an almost unprecedented way, and, by virtue of the standpoint from which those issues have been addressed, provided a rare focus and catalyst for the shaping of the contemporary debate about religion.[47]

Moreover, the controversy surrounding the removal from his post of the Anglican priest Anthony Freeman, another contributor to *God and Reality*, ought to remind us that the non-realism debate is anything but marginal to the life of the Church:

The issues can no longer be dismissed as the ravings of off-beat academics who've spent too long locked up in their ivory towers. They are issues which the Church, and all who are concerned with the religious situation of our time, need to address.[48]

Notes

1 Don Cupitt, *The Sea of Faith* (BBC, 1984), p. 18.
2 *The Sea of Faith*, p. 18.
3 *The Sea of Faith*, pp. 16–17.
4 *The Sea of Faith*, p. 17.
5 *The Sea of Faith*, p. 19.
6 *The Sea of Faith*, p. 20.
7 *The Sea of Faith*, p. 20.
8 Don Cupitt, *Taking Leave of God* (SCM Press, 1980), p. 15.
9 Anthony Freeman, *God in Us* (SCM Press, 1993), p. 24.
10 *Taking Leave of God*, p. 9.
11 *Taking Leave of God*, p. 126.
12 *Taking Leave of God*, p. 69.
13 *The Sea of Faith*, p. 19.
14 *The Sea of Faith*, p. 269.
15 *The Sea of Faith*, pp. 55 and 54.
16 *God in Us*, p. 28.
17 Graham Shaw, *God in Our Hands* (SCM Press, 1987), p. xiv.
18 *God in Our Hands*, p. 177.
19 *Taking Leave of God*, p. 57.
20 *Taking Leave of God*, p. 96.
21 *The Sea of Faith*, pp. 270–1.
22 Hugh Dawes, *Freeing the Faith* (SPCK, 1992), p. 36.
23 *Taking Leave of God*, p. xii; *Only Human* (SCM Press, 1985), p. 200.
24 Don Cupitt, *Radicals and the Future of the Church* (SCM Press, 1989), p. 52.
25 Don Cupitt, *Creation Out of Nothing* (SCM Press, 1990), p. 80.
26 Don Cupitt, *What Is a Story?* (SCM Press, 1991), p. 130.
27 *Creation Out of Nothing*, p. 81.
28 Don Cupitt, *Life Lines* (SCM Press, 1986), p. 2.
29 *Radicals and the Future of the Church*, p. 79.
30 *Radicals and the Future of the Church*, p. 86.
31 *What Is a Story?*, p. 8.
32 *Radicals and the Future of the Church*, p. 86.
33 Don Cupitt, *The Long-Legged Fly* (SCM Press, 1987), p. 72.
34 Don Cupitt, *The Last Philosophy* (SCM Press, 1995), p. 112.
35 Don Cupitt, *The Time Being* (SCM Press, 1992), p. 26.
36 *The Time Being*, p. 145.
37 *Creation Out of Nothing*, p. 201.
38 *The Long-Legged Fly*, p. 146, *Radicals and the Future of the Church*, p. 55, etc.
39 *Only Human*, p. 212.
40 *What Is a Story?*, p. 82.
41 E.g. *The Time Being*, pp. 118–23.
42 *The Time Being*, p. 13.

43 *The Time Being*, pp. 81–2.

44 Keith Ward, *Holding Fast to God* (SPCK, 1982); Brian Hebblethwaite, *The Ocean of Truth* (Cambridge University Press, 1988); and (against Anthony Freeman's *God in Us*) Richard Harries, *The Real God* (Mowbray, 1994).

45 Scott Cowdell, *Atheist Priest? Don Cupitt and Christianity* (SCM Press, 1988); Stephen Ross White, *Don Cupitt and the Future of Christian Doctrine* (SCM Press, 1994); and Anthony C. Thiselton, *Interpreting God and the Postmodern Self: On Meaning, Manipulation and Promise* (T. & T. Clark, 1995).

46 The exception is the collection of essays and responses edited by Joseph Runzo, *Is God Real?* (Macmillan, 1993), but, unlike the present work, this investigates the issue almost entirely within the context of the philosophy of religion alone.

47 George Pattison, 'Editorial: *The Sea of Faith* – ten years after', *Modern Believing* XXXV (1994), p. 6.

48 'Editorial', p. 6.

1

Free Christianity

Don Cupitt

Christian non-realism is the first fully critical and entirely non-dogmatic style of religious thought to appear in the West. It has been around for some years now, and has even developed into something of a movement, both in Britain and overseas, and both within and on the outer fringes of the churches. It has arisen out of the way modern philosophy has developed since Kant, and out of the way theology has been developing since Rudolf Bultmann and the debate about demythologizing the Gospel. There are places overseas, such as the Harvard Divinity School, where a version of it is even considered respectable. Furthermore, there are parallels to it in other communities, such as Mordecai Kaplan's Jewish reconstructionism, and American Jewish humanism. Yet, in spite of all this evidence for its 'normality' non-realism makes only slow progress in Britain, and opposition to it remains fierce.

Why? Because there is a feeling that it has breached the final citadel. During the past century or so theologians have demythologized almost the whole cycle of Christian supernatural doctrine. In approximate ascending order of gravity, the main items are the virginal conception of Jesus, miracles in general, the bodily ascension of Christ, the bodily resurrection of Christ, life after death, the divinity of Christ and even (rather recently) God's absolute foreknowledge, and God's personality. All these doctrines, it seems, can be questioned, and perhaps reinterpreted in a non-realistic sense. If Christ is your Lord and comes first in your life, you may believe him ascended without thinking that he shot up in the air, and if you experience a new and risen sort of life in Christ, you may believe him risen without necessarily having to think that once upon a time his corpse was galvanized back to life just like Frankenstein's monster. But God's objective existence is another matter. Non-realistic theists preserve all that is of specifically *religious* value in the idea of God. God, they say, is a guiding spiritual ideal, a symbol of the ultimate unity of our values, and a focus of spiritual aspiration. But (they continue) we cannot give any coherent account of God as a supposed objectively-existing being, and we cannot prove God's existence. We have only this life, and only our human language about God, to go on. We are not and will never be in a position to compare our talk of God with God absolutely, to see if the description is accurate. So we should give up the old metaphysical dogmas completely, remembering that we have no absolute knowledge. All our knowledge is only human knowledge, fallible and limited by language. Religion is simply a lot of stories and symbols, values and practices, out of which you must now evolve your own religious life. Think of yourself not as a soldier, but as an artist who has chosen to work mainly within a particular tradition. That is faith, the production of one's own life as a work of religious art.

The sense of spiritual liberation that we feel when we grasp all this is astounding. Why the fury?

The main difficulty is that for many centuries religion has been seen as creed, and faith as intellectual submission. The believer assents to a set of supernatural doctrines, doctrines that are above reason but which are certified to us by the authority of the Bible and the Church – behind which of course stands the authority of God.

One philosophical doctrine is needed to support the whole system: metaphysical realism. No, it's not just a language-game, and it's not just poetry; it is considered vital to maintain the power of human language to jump right out of our everyday human world and express at least some true assertions about things transcendent and divine. Church leaders and fundamentalists alike are always 'objectivists', in the sense that they perceive very clearly that their supernatural beliefs have no chance of being true or even meaningful, unless metaphysical realism is true. Hence the striking fact that orthodoxy now perceives the essence of Christianity not as anything religious – in *that* department we non-realists do much better than our critics – but as a philosophical doctrine, realism.

Unfortunately, metaphysical realism was permanently demolished by Kant, who went on to develop the first interesting modern non-realist account of God. In Britain we have been slow to understand what is going on, partly because our philosophers were mostly raised on Plato and Aristotle and not on Kant and Hegel, and partly because at the beginning of the twentieth century Russell and Moore led the Anglo-Saxon world astray for generations by reintroducing a bizarre form of neo-realism (in Russell's case a realism of sense-data, and in Moore's even a naive realism about physical objects and our moral intuitions). But since the 1960s the tide has turned with a vengeance; and I am not talking only of linguistic philosophy, but of linguistics, of psychology and of the wholesale 'naturalizing of epistemology' that is now going on. The intellectual future is thoroughgoing naturalism. Metaphysical realism may still have a few surviving defenders in the older generation, but the young know that it is dead, even in the Anglo-Saxon world. Today, Christian non-realism offers the churches their last chance of a rational future (though so far all the signs are that they will prefer the alternative, which is fundamentalism, on the grounds that it will offer them a much, *much* bigger market).

Christian non-realism, then, is thoroughly naturalistic in outlook, seeing the whole system of supernatural doctrine as poetry to live by – or, as Wittgenstein put it, 'rules of life dressed up in pictures'. In Britain it can be traced back to Matthew Arnold in the nineteenth century, and more recently to the so-called 'non-cognitivism' of Richard Braithwaite and Richard Hare in the post-war years. I first described God as 'non-objective' in 1979, coined the phrase 'theological realism' in 1980, and introduced the term 'non-realism' in 1982. I thought I was inventing it, but I now find that Hilary Putnam had already used it in the late 1970s. Putnam is a major American philosopher of the analytical school. From 1975 he was finding very strong reasons for rejecting realism, but he didn't want to go back to realism's traditional alternative, idealism. So he used the term 'non-realism'. It is a cautious term, consciously undogmatic, which not only describes Wittgenstein's position accurately, but can be used to embrace almost all the leading schools of modern philosophy. The Americans talk about neo-pragmatism and post-analytical philosophy, the British talk about anti-realism and constructivism, and modern European philosophy has been well labelled 'superstructuralism'; but what is common to all these various movements is a reaction against a certain conception of the philosopher's task. Philosophers were supposed to justify knowledge, which meant justifying the objectivity of knowledge, which meant justifying realism. Even people like A. J. Ayer, Bernard Williams and Thomas Nagel have still felt that objective knowledge would be a good thing, and that realism does indeed occupy the high ground. It is what the philosopher should aspire after. But I'm using the term non-realism to embrace a wide variety of recent philosophical movements that want to get right away from those assumptions.

I'm saying, then, that I decline to be told that it's my job to justify knowledge, which means to prove its objectivity, which means to prove realism. And *that* is what I mean by non-realism – the refusal of a certain conception of the philosopher's task. I don't want to show how our knowledge copies an objective world; I only want to show what kind of a world our language gives us.

Let us spell out the contrast here in a little more detail. The difference between a realist and a non-realist is that a realist is a person who thinks that we have obviously got a ready-made world all laid on for us, whereas a non-realist is a person who says: 'Hang on. How could we ever know that? Surely we humans are always inside our own historically evolved vision of the world? Over the millennia we've slowly built up our own conventions, our own languages, our own knowledge, our own beliefs and values. This human cultural superstructure that we've laboriously developed is all of a piece, all our own; and our relationship with it is two-way. We made it, we use it to make our world – and it makes us, too. Man is the cultural animal, as Aristotle should have said. Culture is a system of conventional signs in motion, and by trading them back and forth we build our public world. So how are we ever going to learn that the world our culture opens up to us goes on, beyond the limits to which we ourselves have pushed it? Surely, so far as we are concerned all meanings are meanings of bits of our language, all truths are statements true in our language, and all values are humanly-posited values. We are the only makers of all these things, aren't we? Meaning and truth exist only where *we* have constituted them. So how can we imagine ourselves learning that they were somehow *pre-existent*, ready-made and waiting for us out there before we human beings came along and started to discover them?'

In this opening statement the non-realist is saying that whilst our human cultural forms – our language, our theories and so on – do indeed give us access to a world, the world they open up to us is inevitably just a humanly-constituted world. (Perhaps I should recall here that 'world' is *wer-ald*, the age of a man.) It is *our* world, but it cannot be *the* world. The realist nevertheless still says that we do have a fully-determinate world, a real mind-independent cosmos, already laid on for us, and with a single moral order built into it. The non-realist may claim that scientists *invent* the laws of nature; but the realist intends to go on saying that scientists are progressively *discovering* the laws of nature. The non-realist says that we must invent new moral guidelines to cover problems thrown up by developments in reproductive medicine; but the realist says that all questions of right and wrong have objective answers, anticipated and determined in the mind of God from all eternity. The realist refuses to admit that there are problems about language, because on the realist view the maker of the physical world and the maker of the moral order is also *our* maker, and he himself used language to build the world. The adequacy of language to copy the shape of reality is thus theologically guaranteed, and this brings us to the very heart of the realist case: the realist believes in a pre-established harmony between the structure of our language and the structure of reality, between thought and being, and between our moral constitution and the objective moral order of the world. On the realist view, the world was expressly made to be a home for us and a school of moral training, and we were made to fit into this home that God has set up for us. So there is no problem about language or about the objectivity of morality: the realist's belief in an objective metaphysical God is profoundly tied up with an optimistic and very homely cosmology. The old cosmologies were invented precisely in order to familiarize the terrible and cheer us up. That's why we have clung to them for so long: what really counts is not the evidence for them (it's nil) but our need of them.

Here then we come upon the region of sharpest conflict, because I can scarcely avoid the obvious corollary of the argument so far: a realist is a person who thinks that God made us and has himself taught us all we know about him, whereas a non-realist is a person who thinks we humans have ourselves developed all our ideas about our gods as *bonnes à penser*, and there's no way we could ever jump outside our own language and check whether our ideas about our gods correspond to the objective theological facts or not.

Indeed – and applying the present argument to the case of God – I'm arguing that from the non-realist point of view it is simply not the theologian's job to prove the objective existence of God, or even to ask what God is, but rather simply to ask what jobs the word 'God' does now, and in what ways we can use it in building our world and our lives. For the non-realist, God's world-building and our own coincide. In the narrative theology of the Bible and Christian doctrine, talk about God helps us to debate and to battle with the great questions of the coherence of our values, the unity of all value and the struggle between good and evil. But we are not talking metaphysics here, for these are human debates about human values, conducted within the conventions of a long-established literary genre. And, at a certain level, everybody is well aware that that is how it is.

A non-realist, then, thinks it obvious that we ourselves gradually evolved our own world-picture, our morality, and our religions; whereas a realist cordially dislikes 'humanism' and 'relativism' and insists that we owe everything to an objective God, who has himself settled all questions of truth and value from all eternity, before ever we were created. God has all the answers, and is indeed himself the whole Answer. In religion and morality a realist will tend to be a traditionalist, and probably also a revelationist. Religious authorities will also have to endorse realism because it sees Truth as objective and unchanging, and gives them clear credentials. They need it, therefore it is true – for them, at least.

So realists think we live in a ready-made and stable world, a divinely-created world of reassuringly authoritative and unchanging meanings, truths and values, whereas non-realists think that we live in a humanly-evolved world, *our* world, a world in which all meanings, truths and values depend on the current state of the (human) argument. Non-realism is like cosmic democracy: everything is seen as depending upon open debate, healthy institutions, and a human consensus refreshed by frequent injections of new metaphors, new valuations, new angles. If the price of liberty is eternal vigilance, the price of truth is endless openness to criticism and innovation. For the realist, what makes the Truth obviously true is its preservation unchanged; for the non-realist, what keeps truth true is the vividness with which it is re-imagined and re-expressed.

This new conception of truth as being everywhere only-human, democratic and lower-case sharply divides realists from non-realists. Will the religions remain locked into realism? If so, their future is already clear: it is fundamentalism. Alternatively, what new forms might religious thought take in response to the 'end of metaphysics' and the coming of the new post-realist world?

To see this question clearly, we need to kick away the ladder that we have just climbed. In order to state the argument so far, I have made a contrast between *our world* and *the world*. *Our world* is the world as we know it. Because all thought and communication are transacted in cultural signs, our world is always already a human world, coded into language, highly interpreted and therefore a world that we ourselves have built. We have contrasted our world, thus understood, with *the world*, the world that according to realism exists independently of our reading of it. And I seem to have argued that only *our world* exists; there is no *the world*. However if my argument is valid the initial contrast between *our world* and *the world* must have been meaningless, and should not have been made. Our world being radically outsideless, there is no sense in the suggestion that there could be something else to contrast it with. So there has been a certain reflexive difficulty in the argument so far, and that is why it is now necessary to kick away the ladder. As soon as we have managed to reach the new point of view we should immediately say to ourselves 'But it is outsideless!', and we should forget the false and misleading contrast that was earlier made in order to help us to get to this point. We haven't lost anything: everything is still *there*. But a deep philosophical shift has taken place.

Modern philosophy confuses us by using so many different vocabularies to describe the shift. 'We are always inside . . . ' Inside what? 'Our own experience', say the empiricists; 'The mind', say the idealists; 'Our own humanity and our practical needs', say the pragmatists; 'Language', or 'the flux of signs', say the modern linguistic philosophers and superstructuralists.

In very recent years I have perhaps added to the problem. I have been trying to restart philosophy, and get over the difficulty about reflexivity, by saying aloud: 'We do best to picture the world at large as a beginningless, endless and outsideless stream of language-formed events that continually pours forth and passes away – and this noise you hear is a typical bit of it.'

In developing this vision of the world I try to abolish the traditional contrasts between language and reality, between subjectivity and objectivity, between matter and mind, and between the merely-human and the super-natural or divine. The aim is to produce an effect of complete happiness on the basis of thoroughgoing religious naturalism and world-affirmation. I use the label 'energetic Spinozism' for this outlook, coupling it with what I call a 'poetical theology' and a 'solar (that is, expressivist) ethics'.

Such is one form that religious thought may take in our strange new world. Whereas the old medieval Christian universe (to which the churches are still committed) was very highly differentiated both vertically in space and horizontally in time, and elaborately scaled in degrees of being, rank and value, we try to undo the old distinctions and concertina everything down into the outpouring present. The result is (or at least, is intended to be) an effect of burning intensity. In the late 1980s I used the term 'active non-realism' for it: religion is no longer a theory of the world, but a practice of living, an art-like world-building activity. Now I prefer the term 'solar ethics', the sun being an object whose living and dying are one and the same. Kierkegaard, expounding the Sermon on the Mount, speaks of living eternally in the present moment, and of regaining immediacy after reflec-tion. When along these lines we undo the traditional binary oppositions and live in a way that fully unifies dying and living, time and eternity, the particular and the universal, immediacy and reflection, then human life and divine life have become each other. As that best of modern Christian writers, Nietzsche, puts it, 'It is not a "belief" which distinguishes the Christian: the Christian acts, he is distinguished by a *different* mode of acting . . . *evangelic practice alone* leads to God, it *is* God!' (*The Anti-Christ*, §33).

All this may help to explain the much-criticized 'belieflessness' of Christian non-realism. The non-realist Christian is a postmodern person who has lost all the old beliefs about finding the perfect, normative world elsewhere, either in the past, or in the world above, or in the future. The job of dogma was always to give us authoritative assurances that this present unsatisfactory world is only appearance: elsewhere there is a Real world which is free from all the limitations and miseries of this world.

The non-realist is a person who does not accept the old two-worlds doctrine, and therefore does not need dogmatic belief. There is only one world, the world that we have built up around ourselves, the world produced by our language. And non-realists argue that there is a practice of living by which we can find complete happiness in the here and now. Call it solar ethics, call it Love, call it eternal life.

* * *

So far in this discussion we have been sketching the philosophical and cultural context of Christian non-realism. We have limited ourselves to the West, but we should not leave this topic before noting that Mahayana Buddhism preserves a very rich tradition of non-realist philosophical and religious thought. Hence its great attractiveness to many younger Westerners today.

We turn now to consider briefly the *religious* context of non-realism, again limiting ourselves to the West. Let us begin from a feature of contemporary Anglo-Saxon societies – the mania for 'political correctness', and 'soundness'; the mania for sniffing out precisely where other people stand doctrinally and judging them accordingly. It is of course a legacy of Protestant doctrinal obsessions in particular, and more generally of the very long-standing use in our tradition of religious belief-systems as tools of social control. Our many creeds and confessions have usually appealed to the Bible for support.

Against this background, we begin by pointing out that the whole Bible, both Old and New Testaments, was written by Jews and that the Jews will themselves tell you that their faith is a practice-religion rather than a belief-religion. The contents and the literary forms of the biblical writings are so varied that although the Rabbis did develop a system of Jewish religious Law out of the Bible they did not similarly develop a system of orthodox religious doctrine. In any case, the Jews are so literary that the very idea that language can be used precisely to define and enforce religious truth is foreign to them.

Against this background, one can see why non-realists like Kant and Wittgenstein tell us to see religious truth as being 'regulative'. Its function is not to give us metaphysical information, but to shape the way we live. Non-realists, looking again to our Jewish origins, want to see practice preceding theory and the lived religious life coming before the holding of sound doctrines.

Religious thought in the Hebrew Bible is for the most part poetical and pre-philosophical, but here and there it does approach the philosophical style. This happens especially in Isaiah, chapters 40–55, where the writer reminds us a little of his contemporaries, the first Greek philosophers. The themes are similar, because he is ridiculing idolatry, thinking cosmologically, and insisting on the descriptive inadequacy of human language in speaking of God.

Here we see that modern non-realism represents the return in the critical period (the period since 1781, the date of Kant's first *Critique*) of very ancient themes in the Judaeo-Christian tradition. In its first two centuries or so Christian preaching to the Graeco-Roman world always began with an attack on idolatry, and thereafter for another millennium it was intellectually dominated by the Negative Theology. Christianity was a way rather than a set of correct doctrines and theology was not a university subject but rather guidance along the Way. You progressed by losing false and illusory beliefs, rather than by acquiring correct ones. In the Christian-Platonic mystical tradition the movement into God was a movement into Darkness and Nothingness, so that Christian spirituality could come to look and to sound surprisingly like the (non-theistic) spirituality of Buddhism; and it was strongly emphasized that the only human form under which God could be thought or represented was the human form of Christ. That is why Christ came to be portrayed as a cosmic, bearded figure: there was this Man, and behind him the dazzling darkness. That was all. Beautiful.

Modern Christian non-realists thus find much to admire in the old faith as it was until about 1200. But then things began to go badly wrong. Aristotle's thought suddenly became a great influence upon theology. It is very much more realistic than Plato's, and Aristotle's conception of metaphysics as the science of being led to a steadily worsening objectification of God. Theology became a science studied in the universities, and the Church became more and more a self-obsessed power-structure.

The preoccupation with power and hierarchy gradually displaced the old religion. Consider the way the crucifixion of Jesus was treated in the later Middle Ages. In major ecclesiastical buildings it becomes a symbol of the necessary submission of even the king to the pope. Christ, still a mature bearded man wearing the imperial crown, is crucified against the knees of the Father, who wears the papal tiara.

To a non-realist the crucifixion symbolizes the Negative Theology. Everything is made of signs, and all signs are fleeting. Everything must in the end be given up, even our very selves, even our idea of God. The crucifixion is an awesomely nihilistic image of the absolute nothingness from which we sprang, over which we dance, into which we return. Can we say Yes to it, can we say Yes to Christ in his death? Yes, the crucifixion is a seriously tough religious image, as tough as the Jain image of the saint as a hole, an absence, an empty outline cut out of a brass plate. Maybe even tougher: but in late medieval and Counter-Reformation times it became yet one more symbol of domination and submission to authority.

In this connection we should dwell for a moment on the non-realist reading of Jesus and his message. The sources are curious and varied, but I personally cite Kierkegaard's late *Christian Discourses* on texts from the Sermon on the Mount, Nietzsche's *Anti-Christ*, various works from the Bultmann school, and a number of excellent recent American writers, such as Sheehan, Breech and Crossan. Here is a brief résumé of Jesus' message as a non-realist reads it.

(1) *The world is passing away.* Most folk most of the time are well content to drift with their world and take their values from it. But what would you do if you suddenly found yourself at the end of your world, and obliged to choose absolutely?

(2) *The attack upon religious objectification.* Jesus criticizes the Temple, the religious professionals, tradition and externals. Like a Cynic, he is utterly indifferent to rank and hierarchy.

(3) *The hidden God.* Jesus appears to have no theology of universal human sinfulness and the need for expiation. He speaks of God in a very restrained and oblique style, using the 'divine passive' construction (as in 'they shall be comforted'). He privatizes or internalizes God. God is in the heart, hidden.

(4) *Forgetting the past and the future.* Jesus is uninterested in the sort of Grand Narrative religion that draws heavily upon the past for legitimation and on the future for vindication. He wants to concentrate all attention upon the here and now.

To non-realists it seems obvious that Christianity has during most of its history been drifting further and further away from Jesus. There has been only one Christian so far, says Nietzsche sourly, and he died on the cross. And Nietzsche felt, as a number of people feel now, that there are important and, as yet, largely unexplored possibilities in Jesus' teaching.

I return now in conclusion to the varieties of non-realism in the modern period, and the difficulty that such variety may be thought to present.

Casting one's mind back to the period around 1800 or so, a number of different forms of non-realism can already be discerned. There is a Kantian tradition of 'moral faith', which says things like 'Conscience is the voice of God', and 'Faith expresses a value-judgement', and which runs through German and Anglo-Saxon liberal protestantism up to modern times. There is an Hegelian, historicist version of non-realism, for which God is an awaited future totalization of the whole evolving world-process. There is a tradition stemming from the younger (and less orthodox) selves of Schleiermacher and Wordsworth that sees faith as a feeling-response of the heart to the living Whole in which we have our being. And there is a tradition of radical Christianity on the far left of the Reformed tradition that crops up memorably in William Blake, and intermittently in others since. It says, shortly, that God is known only through Christ – because Jesus Christ is the only God.

These four versions of non-realism demythologize God down into the moral demand, the goal of history, nature, and the man Christ Jesus respectively. I could name more, being conscious of having produced a number of distinct 'positions' myself during the past twenty-five years – four at least.

This protean quality of non-realism is exceedingly annoying to our orthodox critics, because they naturally wish to see us clearly defined and clearly condemned in the traditional and proper manner. They want us to stand still so that we can be shot, and they find our variety and mobility very frustrating. Why can't we keep still?

You will see by now why the difficulty arises. Orthodox realism inherits from Plato and Parmenides the belief in the ultimate unity of all truth and all values. The whole order of things is objectively coherent, both intellectually and morally, so that there is in the end One True Morality out there, which objectively coincides with the One Great Truth of all things out there. In which case every heresy ought surely to be easily definable as a minor blemish or spot on the face of the vast realist vision, and treatable accordingly.

Unfortunately, things are not as the realists would wish. Nobody has succeeded in totalizing either the history of philosophy, or the history of religions, or the history of ethics along the lines demanded by their theory. The evidence of the history of philosophy, of religions, and of moralities suggests rather that all these things are like art-products, and they cannot be finally totalized for the same reason that we cannot either finalize the definition of art or totalize its history. The very notions of orthodoxy, system and heresy belong only to the realist vision. (Come to think of it, the very notion of 'the high ground' is also realist.) So we non-realists somehow cannot help being mobile, errant.

2

Non-realism and the life of the Church[1]

Anthony Freeman

A number of commentators[2] have claimed that a non-realist interpretation of Christianity may be acceptable in a faculty of theology but not in a parish. I believe this view to be profoundly mistaken. In matters of spirituality, and not least in the area of understanding their faith, the Church of England has always denied any division between professional theologians, parochial clergy, and the laity. All Christians, according to their ability, are expected to hold their faith *spiritu et mente*, with the heart and with the understanding also. That is why we have the vernacular Bible. That is why we have a Book of Common Prayer. In principle at least, every member of the Church, 'from Archbishop to ploughboy', is nourished on the same daily prayers, the same Scripture readings, the same sacraments. No one pretends this ideal has ever obtained in practice, but it remains the ideal and should be jealously guarded. The alternative view, that the faithful should be protected (in effect prevented) from opening their religion to the intellectual and critical world of their day, leads straight to two results: superstition and manipulation among those within the religious community, and an abandonment of religious faith and practice altogether by those outside. Both these results are manifest today in historically Christian countries. The extent to which, against the trend, 'a reasonable, holy and lively' Christianity is still found, is the extent to which the ideal of a rational faith – open to the cultural and philosophical winds of today – has been upheld.

It may well be that 'postmodernism' and 'non-realism' are passing fashions. I would certainly never choose to apply these particular labels to myself. However, there are many people in the country who are exploring their faith and the meaning of their lives under the influence of these movements. Are they to be told that for Christians this is not allowed? Are they to be told, in effect, that you have to become a follower of Plato before you can become a follower of Christ? The chances are they know nothing of Platonism or non-realism or any other '-ism'. They simply know in their bones what does and what does not feel authentic. And if they are made to accept a religious foundation which they feel is not authentic, then the whole edifice will be built on shifting sand and not solid rock. What follows is an attempt to describe what it means for the Church to be open to non-realism as a permitted starting point – not something to be imposed, but something to be allowed for those who find themselves at that position. In the space available the treatment cannot be comprehensive. The topics touched on have been chosen because they have emerged as matters of particular concern to both friend and foe alike where the question of non-realism in the life of the Church has been addressed.

A general word before looking at matters in detail. None of the topics dealt with here could be called easy. Few honest Christians could say that they have no problems with the creed, or prayer, or the meaning of the sacraments, or in comforting of the bereaved. The question to be asked of non-realism is not therefore 'Can it wave a magic wand and solve problems which have puzzled and divided Christians for two thousand years?' The question, rather, is whether a non-realist approach to these practical and theological questions has a creative contribution to make within the life of the Church and the ongoing Christian pilgrimage.

Believing in God

We are concerned with non-realism and the life of the Church, and the corporate life of the Church centres on its public liturgy, including the recitation of the creed. So the question inevitably arises, 'Can a non-realist Christian say with integrity "I believe in God"?' Many critics – both orthodox Christians and professed atheists – answer 'No'. This effectively denies non-realists any place in the Church beyond that of enquiring guests who may one day feel able to embrace the faith and join the family. On the other hand, no less a figure than the Regius Professor of Divinity in the University of Oxford can write:

When believers say, in a liturgical situation, 'I believe in God . . . ', *they are not assenting to some philosophical theory or factual proposition*. They are saying, 'I commit myself to membership of the community which shapes its life on this story, as a disclosure of God and a summons to personal redemptive action in the world'.[3]

Coming from the author of *Holding Fast to God* (the book written to refute Don Cupitt's non-realist manifesto *Taking Leave of God*) this is a remarkable testimony to the subtlety and complexity of what Keith Ward himself calls 'The Problem of Saying the Creeds'. Believers who espouse non-realism find that it provides a way of handling that problem. It is an aid to saying the creed honestly. Their opponents see it as a denial of Christian faith. One distinguished bishop, writing on behalf of the most senior clergy and laity of his diocese, put it like this:

We all find it difficult to understand how anyone who now refuses to believe in the existence of God as an objective being, not dependent solely upon human imaginings, can be regarded as holding the historic belief of the Christian Church.[4]

So what does it take to be a Christian and to recite the creed with integrity? Is it a matter of holding a particular historic belief? In which case who decides upon the boundaries of that belief? Or is it a matter of committing oneself to a particular community? In which case, who decides upon the boundaries of that community? It is a sobering reflection – which those who think of themselves as orthodox believers might find deeply worrying if they dared to think about it – that every Christian in the world *officially believes as crucial to salvation* some doctrine which the majority of those who call themselves Christians believe to be untrue. And every Christian in the world is *officially out of communion* with the majority of those who call themselves Christians. And they all say the creed, believing themselves to hold the one faith and to belong to the one Church! Such is the consequence of divided Christendom. Christianity survives in this ludicrous situation because in practice very few among the laity (or even among the clergy) are much bothered by their Church's official doctrine or ecclesiology. If you are trying to live a decent life and you choose to associate yourself in some way with the Christian tradition, then for most people that makes you a Christian. Another way of putting this is to say that many – perhaps most – Christians are what might be called 'practical non-realists'. On the one hand (in theory) they would hold that the creed, at least in its major doctrines, is in some sense descriptively true. Yet on the other (in practice), they are happy to live with theological contradictions which their 'theoretical realism' ought to make intolerable.

This is quite a simple point, but it needs spelling out in some detail because our very familiarity with the situation can easily blind us to its significance. It is an undeniable fact that different Christian communities hold 'the historic faith' in different forms. If, as the hymn tells us, there is but 'one Church, one faith, one Lord', this diversity needs to be explained. We can safely agree that the teaching of different churches reflects the varying human circumstances in which the tradition has developed and grown. Beyond that, opinions differ. The thoroughgoing non-realist will say that the various traditions are all that we have. If we choose to interpret this variety of communities and beliefs in terms of a single Church and its faith, there is nothing wrong with that. But they are theoretical ideals, not really existing entities, and their boundaries – who counts as belonging to the one Church, what counts as being part of the one faith – are determined by ourselves. Everyone else, disagreeing with the non-realists, will say that there really do exist, in the mind of God if nowhere else, a 'true Church' and a 'true faith' which set the absolute standards, the blueprints, against which any earthly expressions of Christian faith or community should be judged.

Christians opposed to non-realism may take one of two basic stances in relation to these blueprints. The ecumenical approach is to look for common ground within the existing faith and order of the churches. Each church is asked what it believes and what it practises, and where it falls short of its own ideals. Out of the responses a picture gradually builds up of those elements valued by Christians. That picture becomes the basis for a united Christian life and message. Such a process has an inevitable tendency to compromise and to play down what is distinctive in each tradition. It has been unkindly, but not entirely inaccurately, caricatured as 'Everybody giving up something they do believe in for the sake of something none of them believes in'. The alternative approach to the ecumenical is the chauvinistic. The opening assumption is that one's own particular brand of Christianity is the true one and that all the rest are to be judged by it. The Roman Catholic Church has traditionally been associated with this attitude, but it is by no means alone. Indeed, we should find it slightly curious if certain individuals – never mind a whole Christian community or tradition – were to say that they believed their own church to be in significant error.

The lesson to be drawn from these observations is that all Christians, non-realists, ecumenical realists and chauvinistic realists alike, are living in a situation where they (or the churches to which they belong) find themselves having to make a choice. They have to choose not only between various competing versions of Christianity, but also to decide upon the criteria by which they will make their choice! Further, they are having to decide whether or not to acknowledge as truly 'Christian' the versions they do not choose. And the extent to which they are willing to do this, and so to live with mutually contradictory teachings about God and his dealings with the world, is the extent to which they are 'practical non-realists'. That is, they are managing to avoid the negative consequences which would follow from their strict acceptance of religious language as descriptively true of the person and work of God.

For all that, the non-realist view that God exists only in relation to ourselves, and not independently 'out there', is counter-intuitive and causes great conceptual problems. If we have indeed 'created' God in our human minds, then it seems that one of the ingredients we have included is the need to feel that God is 'over against us', both challenging and sustaining us, and that this should be a reality and not just an idea. We may disallow a crudely material concept of God. We may accept, following the existentialists, that God is not a particular being but rather the Ground of Being. We may go all the way with the theologians of the *via negativa*, the apophatic tradition of the Pseudo-Dionysius and *The Cloud of Unknowing*, which says that we must set aside every image and all language in our approach to God. We may do all of this, and yet still − in spite of everything − the demand for there to be 'something out there' is most insistent. If non-realism is to find open acceptance in the Church, it has to overcome this conceptual block.

A major obstacle is the word 'God' itself. It is generally assumed that there is a single agreed meaning of the word, at least when spelled with a capital 'G', and certainly when used in a Christian context. This is not the case. Keith Ward again:

> One person can say, 'I believe in God', and mean that there is a person looking after them. Another can mean that an ineffable infinite reality of supreme value underlies all things. Strange as it may seem, the latter will be closer to the main theological discourse of the Christian church.[5]

So there already exist within the Church many different (and in some cases barely compatible) understandings of the term 'God'. Among them is the non-realist definition given by Don Cupitt: 'God . . . is the sum of our values, representing to us their ideal unity, their claims upon us and their creative power.'[6] Why should this way of talking about God have been singled out in particular as unacceptable? Part of the answer at least has to do with the central religious activity of prayer.

Prayer

'If you do not believe in a personal and independently existing God, then to whom are you praying?' is a regular taunt directed at non-realist Christians. It is probably the principal concern of those who are opposed to allowing non-realism among the clergy. The answer is, that we are taking seriously the fact that all religious language has the character of metaphor and analogy. The use of an icon or a crucifix to help focus the eyes during prayer does not entail the notion that the worshipper is praying to the physical image. Similarly, the use of an idea of God to focus the mind should not entail the notion that one is praying to the mental image. Many Christians would accept this, but would go on to assert that behind both the physical and the mental images there must be some reality of which both images are human expressions. Non-realists are saying that this assertion carries us further than we can legitimately go. Some would deny altogether the possibility of there being such a reality; others would deny simply the possibility of our having any access to such a reality. This does not prevent us from praying. Consider the four classic elements of prayer:[7]

Adoration is the prayer in which we rejoice in God for his own sake. Its importance (and what distinguishes it from thanksgiving) is that it directs us completely away from ourselves to that which is utterly beyond us. John Macquarrie, writing about the prayer of adoration, has expressed it in this way:

> Mystical writers have declared God to be more than power, more than goodness, more than beauty, and this is their way of saying that although these qualities do point us to God, when they are raised to the absolute they transcend our understanding. . . . The human being has a need to adore, to relate to that which is incomparable and absolute.[8]

Opponents claim that non-realism denies all this by bringing God down to our level, reducing him to the sum of human values. This argument can easily be turned around. It is the more traditional believers – such as the bishop quoted above – who by their insistence on 'the existence of God as an objective being' are effectively refusing to allow God to 'transcend our understanding' in the way required by pure adoration. The moment we insist on saying of the absolute that 'It must exist', we are limiting it and so paradoxically denying its unique character. Thus the following declaration, with which Macquarrie closes the article already quoted, would not only be endorsed by many non-realist Christians, but it actually coheres better with their concept of God than with the more common notions approved by the churches:

> It is exposure to the absolute in adoration that helps to draw human beings out of their own pettiness, stretching them to a fuller stature in which they will be fit to live in communion with God and in true community with one another.[9]

Contrition (incorporating confession of sin) is the second element of prayer. There is little doubt that the ability to handle failure and guilt is one of the life skills essential to healthy integrated living, and for this the prayer of contrition, grounded in the assurance of forgiveness in Christ, has been an invaluable tool for many Christians. The undoubted religious abuses in this area should not be allowed to detract from the enormous benefits. And precisely here, it might be felt, is an unquestionable need for an 'external' God who can stand over against us and pronounce us forgiven. This is something we cannot do for ourselves. But is this so? Central to this aspect of the Gospel message is the teaching that our own forgiveness depends above all else on our willingness to forgive others (Matt 18.23–35). This is frequently interpreted, not as an arbitrary decree by God, but as a reflection of the psychological truth that the capacity for receiving forgiveness is bound up with the ability to bestow it. This in turn is bound up with the capacity for love (Luke 7.36–50). So we may quite properly ask 'Does the practical truth of all this depend upon a realist personal God?' Surely not. Forgiving one another in love, and receiving forgiveness with humility and gratitude, are central to the Christian life and they are never easy. The variety of spiritual exercises which come under the umbrella title of the prayer of contrition provides a useful – even an essential – support for this dimension of Christian living. And this is as true for non-realists as for anyone else.

Thanksgiving is the prayer of gratitude. Traditionally it is praising God for his goodness in his works, especially where we ourselves are the beneficiaries, so it complements the prayer of adoration in which we praise God for what he is in himself. Can thanksgiving survive in the non-realist climate? Yes, it can. The old injunction to 'count your blessings' is still wise advice. More generally 'an attitude of gratitude', as it has been called, is a remedy against many spiritual and emotional ills. Conscious thankfulness for what we do have can help to relieve anxiety or inordinate longing for what we do not have, and it is hard to be envious of someone else's good fortune or talents at the same time as we are giving thanks for them. For the non-realist, there is an acknowledgement here of all that is 'given' in our lives, of all that is not of our own making. It need not entail belief in a supernatural provider in order to fulfil its role in shaping our lives and attitudes.

Supplication (embracing both petition and intercession) concludes the four-part division of prayer represented by the familiar mnemonic ACTS. It provides the most obvious challenge to non-realists, since of all the kinds of prayer it is the one which most apparently demands that God be an independent agent able to respond to requests. At the same time it is an aspect of prayer which creates difficulties for all who take its implications seriously. How can a God who is both almighty and all-good so often appear to deny his petitioners their legitimate requests? Why should God, 'who knows our necessities before we ask and our ignorance in asking', nonetheless require such asking to be done? If nature is governed by God's 'laws which never can be broken', how can God intervene in answer to prayer without self-contradiction? It is with these well-known problems in mind that the non-realist contribution to the debate is approached, not because non-realism can supply all the answers, but in order to put any inadequacies it may display into context.

One way of understanding supplication is to imagine the worshipper trying to persuade a reluctant monarch to act in the petitioner's favour. This is probably how the matter has been interpreted through much of Christian history. Certainly in the Middle Ages, the pattern of the earthly court is likely to have shaped thinking about the heavenly court, each having its monarch and its courtiers of varying ranks, whose aid was essential if one's requests were to reach the throne itself. If such a picture were the only permissible one for a Christian, then non-realists would certainly be in trouble. But it is not. Indeed, it is fashionable even in orthodox circles to pour scorn on this picture as unworthy of both God and his supplicants. Few Christians of any sophistication would hold to it without at least some modification. One such alteration is to transform the picture of God as almighty but reluctant, into one of him as desirous of helping us but deliberately limiting himself to working with us rather than overriding us. The role of prayer is then a matter of the human will being aligned with the divine will in order to enable the joint desire to be accomplished. On this model, 'Thy will be done' is not a passive resignation to the inevitable, but a co-operative venture. 'Thy will' and 'my will' are not assumed to be at variance, but trusted to be in ultimate conformity.

With an interpretation of prayer along these lines, the move to non-realism is much more feasible. The creative human role in both the input and the outcome of petition and intercession is affirmed.

Eucharist

A special instance of prayer is provided by the eucharist. Here we have been taught to understand that God plays an active role. He not only receives and responds to the prayer, he makes it. When Christians celebrate the eucharist they are brought into a special association with Christ's pleading of his own 'full, perfect, and sufficient sacrifice, oblation, and satisfaction, for the sins of the whole world', which he made once for all upon the cross. It is nothing less than the perfect prayer of God the Son to God the Father in the unity of the Holy Spirit. Furthermore, at the eucharist God is believed to intervene in a unique way to bring about the fulfilment of Christ's words over the bread at the Last Supper: 'This is my body.' Much of the bewilderment felt by opponents of Christian non-realism finds articulation here. Surely, they say, when you give a moment's thought to the doctrine of the eucharist, it becomes self-evident that non-realism and Christianity are mutually inconsistent.

To answer this challenge we need to look at the way in which the problem of eucharistic doctrine has been tackled previously. First, it has always been insisted that the physical properties of the sacramental bread and wine remain intact. Popular Catholic piety and Protestant propaganda may sometimes have claimed otherwise, but no reputable theologian or Church body has ever denied it. Secondly, it has always been insisted that at the eucharist Christ is present in some way associated with the bread and wine. The method of his being present and the purpose for his being present have been hotly debated, but the fact of his being present has not. Only in the minds of ecclesiastical opponents has any Christian truly believed in a doctrine of the 'real absence' of Christ from the eucharist. Catholics have tended to associate the divine presence more closely with the physical elements, as in the words of Thomas Aquinas: 'Wine is poured and bread is broken, but in either sacred token Christ is here by power divine.'[10] Protestants have tended to speak rather of the presence of Christ in the hearts of the communicants, as in the words of administration from the 1552 Book of Common Prayer: 'Take and eat this in remembrance that Christ died for thee, and feed on him in thy heart by faith with thanksgiving.' Neither has denied Christ's presence altogether.

Traditional theology has had to face two questions in relation to these beliefs. First, how is the sacramental body of Christ at the eucharist related to the glorified body of Christ sitting at the right hand of the Father in heaven? And second, how is the sacramental presence of Christ in the eucharist related to the physical presence of the bread and wine? Christians have never come up with an agreed solution to these questions. It may be that the root of the problem has been that traditional theology has started in the wrong place, with the central (but ultimately hypothetical) entity called the body of Christ. A non-realist will wish to start with the worshipping congregation and the bread and wine. What change takes place in them? What change actually and observably takes place in the course of the service? The answer is that there is a change in the attitude of the worshippers towards the bread and wine, and this change has come about as a direct result of the elements having had the memorial of Christ's death read over them and their having then been eaten 'in remembrance of him'. Even the most extreme Protestant, who would strongly deny any special treatment to the remains of the blessed bread, would accept that the bread which was actually ceremonially eaten had become in some sense holy by the use to which it had been put. By refusing to speculate on hypothetical answers to questions about Christ's body, the non-realist may well be able to open a way to heal some of the divisions between Christians on these matters.

The analogy is often drawn between the sacramental bread and a bank note. The paper money is never physically more than paper and ink, but when issued by the authority of the bank it may be used as if it were silver or gold coin. It becomes money. For all practical purposes it is coinage. In a similar way, the consecrated bread is never physically more than bread, but when prayed over and presented by the Church in the person of its authorized minister it may be treated as if it were the body of Christ. For all practical purposes it is the body of Christ. In theory, the bank has enough precious metal in its vaults to redeem the value of every bank note in circulation. In practice it usually does not. The system nonetheless works very well so long as everybody acts as though it did, and does not test the system by presenting all the notes at one time. If that does happen, or looks as though it might happen, then the currency collapses. Confidence has been destroyed, and the bank with it. Opponents of non-realism would say that a non-realist eucharist would be the equivalent of issuing bank notes while admitting that the vaults were empty. But that is the whole point. It is a fiction that the Bank of England has enough gold to buy all its own bank notes. We all know it is. But we still use the currency because we find it a useful way of doing business, and it works so long as we all accept the value of the notes. People may once have accepted the currency because they trusted that there was gold in the vault. Now they do so because they trust that the convenience of the system guarantees its survival. So with the eucharist. Its spiritual value may once have been grounded in the belief that it actually did put the worshipper in direct contact with an otherwise absent bodily presence of Christ. Now we can say that the rites and ceremonies have proved to have a spiritual value of their own, independent of any theory of Christ's body.

There already exists within the Church of England a situation where eucharistic doctrine is so contentious that what some members of the Church hold to be the essence of the sacrament is denied totally by others. Yet anyone can safely receive communion at the hands of a priest whose doctrine they abhor, since the failings of the minister do not detract from the effect of the sacrament.[11] It seems strange that the holding of non-realist views, which in theory could pave the way to greater doctrinal tolerance, should have proved the one exception to this general rule, and been deemed to render a priest unfitted to officiate at the altar.

Funerals

There is a poetic appropriateness in ending this brief survey with ministry at the time of death. But that is not the only reason for ending with this topic. Funerals have at least three qualities which make them a good subject with which to draw together the themes of our investigation into non-realism in the life of the Church. First, they are still a point of pastoral contact with most people in this country, even those who would never associate with the Church in other circumstances, and thus involve the Church in its most public aspect. Second, they touch the central doctrines of the faith – death and resurrection, judgement and redemption. And third, they involve ritual and liturgy of every kind, from the open and formal to the intensely private and personal. Perhaps, in view of the diverse nature of the subject, it is best to consider three actual bereavement situations involving parish priests of known non-realist views.[12]

The Smith family did not live or worship in the parish concerned in the first example, but had a long-standing association with it and were known personally to the vicar, Father Michael. Mrs Smith was a devout Anglo-Catholic; her husband and sons (young adults) were agnostic. She died in tragic circumstances and her family turned instinctively to Father Michael both to take her funeral and to help them cope with a complex bereavement. Personalities undoubtedly played a part, but the priest's theological stance was also a key factor in enabling him to meet their needs. They would not have been helped – indeed they felt strongly that their already painful situation would have been made harder – by 'off the shelf' Christian assurances based on a way of believing which was not theirs. Yet they also felt strongly that Mrs Smith's own faith must be affirmed by the style and content of her funeral. Father Michael was the priest to whom they spontaneously turned. His own Anglo-Catholic background gave him a community of interest with the wife and mother whose faith they wished to respect; at the same time his well-known espousal of the Sea of Faith cause gave them confidence that he would appreciate their own agnosticism and make available to them the resources of the Christian tradition in a way that was accessible to them and which would respect their own beliefs.

In the second example the situation with the family was the reverse of the first. Alan was a non-believer whose personality and attitude to life were nonetheless a classic expression of Christian living in its peculiarly English dress. He was committed to integrity at work, to family life, to helping those less fortunate than himself, and to the avoidance of any hint of hypocrisy. His wife and family were in varying degrees conventional members of the Church of England. When Alan died suddenly and without any warning, his family wanted a church funeral service which would celebrate and commemorate Alan's life, and reflect their own faith, without appearing to attribute to him beliefs which he was known not to hold. They turned for advice to a priest friend whose non-realist views had commended her to Alan as someone whose ministry he could receive with integrity. Amidst many tears, and the floor strewn with piles of hymn books, prayer books and Bibles, two evenings were spent creating an appropriate funeral liturgy, firmly based on the authorized order of service and subsequently conducted by the family's own vicar in their parish church.

A final story illustrates a situation where the vicar's holding non-realist views presented difficulties for the bereaved family. John and his family were personal friends and neighbours of the priest concerned, so there was a potential for embarrassment and ill-feeling. In the event, when John died after a long and distressing illness, the pastoral care of the family was, by mutual consent, put in the hands of a neighbouring minister who also conducted the funeral, but in John's own church. The non-realist priest attended the service as a family friend, and as vicar he welcomed the congregation and the visiting minister to the service, but took no part in leading it. All was done decently and in order, and the whole process felt 'right'. Would that all the hazards of ministry could be negotiated as happily as that one.

These examples show how with pastoral sensitivity there need be no problem with non-realist clergy in relation to funerals. With regard to the service itself, so long as a priest is willing and able to use the authorized liturgy, whether for funerals or at other times, then the basic rights of the parishioners are safeguarded. It might even be argued that, at parish level, ordinary parishioners who wish to find the rites of passage administered willingly, and in accordance with the rites and ceremonies of the Church of England, are more likely to find their needs met by the clergy of the non-realist persuasion than by some of their more orthodox colleagues. When it comes to the interpretation of the tradition represented in the prayers and readings, undertaken in the pastoral visits before and after the ceremony itself, that of course is another matter. But the non-realist minister is in no worse case here than any others. There are many instances in which clergy of all ecclesiastical backgrounds have had to temper their personal beliefs and preferences in the face of mourners' attitudes and wishes. It must often be very hard, for example, for conservative ministers to serve with integrity those bereaved people who neither have nor desire to have an orthodox faith, and yet whose spiritual and emotional needs the Church is committed to meeting. This highlights the significance of our first two examples, where the non-realist priest was able to meet a pastoral need where a more orthodox minister would have been handicapped.

Open Christianity

The dispute within the Church over non-realism is a particular example of a recurring debate within its life. Is the Church to be a closed élite, a chosen few, the storm-troops of the kingdom? Or is it to be a mixed bag, a motley assortment of the good, the bad and the indifferent, all trying in their different ways to make something of their lives in the shadow of the Galilean? At its best, the Church has managed to contain the legitimate insights of both these approaches by keeping its general membership as open as possible, while offering within its fellowship opportunities for those who feel the need to embrace a more rigorous way.[13] The present small number of 'non-realists' are in themselves something of a theologically austere group, and can easily give the appearance of élitism. Yet their aim for the whole Church is the very opposite: to keep its doors open to all, and not to put up unnecessary barriers in the form of world-views and philosophical outlooks which claim to be the only possible ones for Christians. And this openness must extend to the ranks of the parish clergy and not just to the laity or academic priests. A Church which is open rather than narrowly 'confessional' needs priests who can stand alongside their flocks in their questioning of received understandings of Christian teaching.

Notes

1 This essay is written from the standpoint of a priest in the Church of England. The practical examples and the theological arguments reflect that background, and should not be taken to limit the discussion to one denomination.

2 For example, Paul Goodman in the *Sunday Times* (31 July 1994).

3 Keith Ward, *A Vision to Pursue: Beyond the Crisis in Christianity* (SCM Press, 1991), p. 3 (my emphasis).

4 Private correspondence in the hands of the author.

5 *A Vision to Pursue*, p. 3.

6 Don Cupitt, *The Sea of Faith* (BBC, 1984), p. 269.

7 See, for example, John Macquarrie, Gordon S. Wakefield, Michael Hollings, George Appleton and A. M. Ramsey, 'Prayer' in Gordon S. Wakefield (ed.), *A Dictionary of Christian Spirituality* (SCM Press, 1983), pp. 307–13.

8 'Prayer', p. 307.

9 'Prayer', p. 308.

10 From the proper for the Feast of Corpus Christi.

11 See Article XXVI.

12 The names have been changed to preserve anonymity.

13 The classic account of this remains that of Kenneth E. Kirk, *The Vision of God* (Longmans, Green and Co., 1931).

3

Non-realism and the universe of faiths

David Hart

Until the last century, the encounter of the faiths was not by dialogue. In 1845, in his Boyle Lectures, F. D. Maurice opened up an exciting new area of comparative theology which he entitled 'The religions of the world and their relations to Christianity'.[1] Throughout the nineteenth century the debate within theology was that between the modern world, as investigated by science and history, and the Christian faith, which was taken to be the central bedrock of Western intellectual life and civilization. Much of the focus of interpretation was inevitably then centred on understandings of Scripture and the discussion of how the created order came into being. The focus therefore remained on an understanding of Christianity that was in keeping with a modern critical understanding. At the same time, within the areas of colonial Africa, India, and the Far East, Christianity had been exported as a commodity from the beginning of the century (the Church Missionary Society was founded in 1799). Emphasizing the propagation rather than the exploration of the faith appropriate to such an exercise, it remained until after the colonial withdrawal for any real assessment of its impact upon indigenous populations and religions to be made.[2]

Only in recent times has there been any real opportunity for the faiths to enter into dialogue and to compare themselves one to another on an equal footing, where questions of political hegemony were not around to obscure the issue. Nonetheless, there is a line of development in Western thought which non-realists would claim prepares the ground for an understanding of all religions, their rituals and myths, as a human creation.

A seminal figure in this development was the German theologian, or rather sociologist of religion, Ernst Troeltsch. He argued that a genuine understanding of Christianity could only be given alongside a conception of its place within the developing history and society in which it was located. Since there was no exterior reference point provided by which the veracity of its doctrines could be tested, they could be evaluated only by the general criteria that were applicable to an analysis of history. These were to include *criticism*, as a careful and scientific method of inquiry into the events of the past; *analogy*, as our assumption that human experience remains essentially continuous between past and present, so that what we would expect to find in one period is also likely to be found in another (and thereby he argues, for example, that the concept of miracle would be problematic for the modern mind); and *correlation*, as an understanding that any particular event can be highlighted and explained in relation to other events in the historical series, since events are causal and inter-connected and no single event can be described in any way as standing outside the historical process. As Christians, we can only assess Christianity as an historical religion in these terms and as it has come down to us. Although we value it highly, and may regard it as the highest religious development for humanity, we are not in a position to make any absolute claims for it in relation to other existing or possible belief systems. It is final and unconditional *for us*, because we have nothing else. But this does not preclude the possibility that other racial groups, living under entirely different cultural conditions, may experience their contact with the divine life in quite a different way. Troeltsch left open the question of what this way might be, but his idealist background led him to imply that the presence of God as an immanent spiritual force is accessible in all religious traditions, although Christianity may have evolved as the highest under-standing of the spiritual life that humankind has reached. It has to be said that Troeltsch did not take his insights significantly further in relating critical thought to traditions other than Christianity. But he did face squarely for the first time in modern theology the problem of placing Christianity in any way at the centre (either temporal or geographical) of the world's spiritual stage:

With every advance in history of religions research into the origins of Christianity we see so many related yet originally independent religious and ethical forces flowing together, that it is quite impossible to treat Christian faith as something absolutely separate. Christianity is by no means the product of Jesus alone. Plato, the Stoa and immeasurable popular religious forces from the ancient world are involved in it. This also seems to make the consequence impossible – calling the Christian community the eternal absolute centre of salvation for the whole span of humanity. Of course nothing certain can be said here; but it is not probable. Man's age upon earth amounts to several hundred thousand years or more. His future may come to still more. It is hard to imagine a single point of history along this line, and that the centre-point of our own religious history, as the sole centre of all humanity. That looks far too much like the absolutising our own contingent area of life [*sic*]. That is in religion what geocentricism and anthropocentricism are in cosmology and metaphysics. The whole logic of Christocentricism places it with these other centricisms.[3]

This problem was faced again later in the twentieth century by the Jesuit theologian Karl Rahner. In his attempt to attach the broadest of theological panoramas to the philosophical phenomenology provided by Martin Heidegger, under whom he had studied, Rahner needed in his voluminous *Theological Investigations* to provide a convincing account of the existence of holy and faithful living outside the household of those who have joined the covenant of Abrahamic promise. Many people appear to live saintly lives on the basis of a non-Christian or even a non-theistic interpretation of life, and Rahner suggested a bold initiative for affirming their virtues and their stance independent of confessional Christianity. He suggested that in their lives and thinking they should be described as 'anonymous Christians'. Since Christ was known by Christians as 'the light of the world', anyone whose life shared such a quality of illumination as his offered must perforce be at one with him, even if not known to him. This theology is in the spirit of the text 'he that is not against us is for us' (Mark 9.40). Thereby Rahner challenged the common Catholic assumption, enunciated from Cyprian onwards, that *extra ecclesiam nulla salus* – 'outside the Church there is no salvation'.[4]

Rahner was not alone among Catholic theologians who, in the 1960s, attempted to influence the spirit of the Second Vatican Council towards a more open acceptance of believers in traditions other than Christianity. Heretofore we have confined ourselves largely to European thinkers and thought, but in this decade the influence was also felt of two writers very much outside this arena. The monk Thomas Merton left the confines of his native North America in the interests of dialogue with the religious life, particularly of the Far East. Before he could contribute much to an area that increasingly dominated his own spiritual thinking, he died in a tragic accident while attending an interfaith colloquium at Bangkok. At much the same time, another Jesuit, of mixed Iberian and Indian parentage, Raimundo Pannikar, attempted above all in his book *The Unknown Christ of Hinduism* (1964) to show how Hindu religion, whilst being unconscious of the history of Jesus, revealed within its teaching much of the spiritual reality of the Logos who is the pre-existing Christ of the Johannine gospel. Again, Pannikar insisted that where the spirit of Christ is, there also is his name by implication, and the full resources of salvation are accessible within that tradition.

These theological ideas were certainly at variance with the traditional Catholic position of the necessity of the conversion of other faiths – not only argued for but actively prosecuted, especially by the Jesuit order, out of the ranks of which two of these radical thinkers had emerged. The spirit of the 1960s was an open embrace of change and Pope John XXIII was prepared to give his blessing to this theological sea of change, and the Vatican document *On the Relation of the Church to Non-Christian Religions* is arguably the most radical departure of the conciliar documents to emerge from Vatican II. Meanwhile, on the Protestant side, there was movement too, although not surprisingly perhaps this was not as warm a movement towards other traditions as Catholicism felt able to offer at this period in its development. Much of twentieth-century Protestant thought in this area was affected by the position taken by the Neo-orthodox theology, as most fully articulated in the *Church Dogmatics* (1932–68) of Karl Barth. Barth specifically opposed Troeltsch's position by arguing that the main difference between Christian and other faiths was centred on the question of the initiative of the impulse: was it from God or from man? He argued that the main problem with nineteenth-century Protestant thought was that it had not dissociated itself sufficiently from philosophical idealism, and in its dominant thinkers, such as Schleiermacher and Ritschl, it appeared simply to articulate the quest of the human imagination for God, laying on one side the biblical initiative of the incarnation of God in the person and acts of Jesus Christ. In the viewpoint of Christian faith, the decisive initiative had taken place within this tradition, rendering any other logically inferior, with the maximal possible status of a *praeparatio evangelica*, and thereby privileging Judaism in particular among the other faiths. Such a re-emphasis on revelation, rather than on religion and reason, was shared by other mid-century writers, such as Emil Brunner and Hendrik Kraemer, but in retrospect it made little advance on pre-critical Protestant theology. While it admitted the validity of biblical criticism, it did not take on board the full implications of such an exercise. Once the documents of any faith are understood and reviewed as human creations, no single idea to be found within them can be accorded the type of unique status that Barth still attempted to afford the doctrine of the incarnation. It is within the text as a dogmatic idea, but cannot be read as critically determinative of the whole text. Thus Barth's attempt to discover a *biblical* view of divine revelation was really a cul-de-sac, since its basic premise, the decisive action of God in Christ, is a pre-critical dogmatic position, rendered suspicious by the detailed work of the biblical critics.

A more positive contribution to the Protestant understanding of the relation of the world faiths has been provided in the work of John Hick. He argued that the incarnation should be construed not in substantial terms but in an understanding informed by *agapē* – a dynamic model allowing the experience of salvation through Christ. In renaming an earlier book, *Christianity at the Centre*, as *The Centre of Christianity*, he himself underwent a dramatic shift in his understanding of theology which he took to be parallel to the shift in astronomy from a Ptolemaic picture of the universe, with our earth at the centre, to the Copernican view that our planet is merely one of many that revolves around the sun as its centre:

> [T]he needed Copernican revolution in theology involves an equally radical transformation in our conception of the universe of faiths and the place of our own religion within it. It involves a shift from the dogma that Christianity is at the centre to the realisation that it is *God* who is at the centre, and that all the religions of mankind, including our own, serve and revolve around him.[5]

But this was not the most radical shift that Hick was to make in his own writings. In *An Interpretation of Religion*, he developed the strongly Kantian theory that at the centre of all religion lies not God but the transcendental *Real* as the foundation of all existence. According to Hick, it is beyond our knowledge and impersonal in itself, but can be experienced in a manner analogous to the way in which we experience the world, not *in re*, but filtered through our minds. Hick's theory here gives us an epistemology which we can use in the evaluation of any faith, even naturalist humanism. And this criterion is based on 'the transformation of human existence from self-centredness to Reality-centredness'.[6]

The great advantage of Hick's interpretation is that in his adoption of the term 'the Real' he enables himself to make assessments free from the narrow confines of the monotheistic faiths, and to explore other traditions, including those which major on a metaphysical *impersona*, whether it be called Brahman, the Tao, or the Dharmakaya. The interpretation allows for a truly universal discourse. But its problem is its lack of philosophical rigour. Hick acknowledges that the basis of his epistemology of religion is the 'Kantian insight' in Thomas Aquinas that *cognita sunt in cognoscente secundum modum cognoscentis* (things known are in the knower according to the mode of the knower).[7] But in a truly Kantian epistemology the Real can never be experienced either by filter or any other means. It is a necessary category of thought (together with time and space), but its existence in the natural world is not a subject of speculation for Kant. The 'transcendental something = X' is only conceivable as a mental category. To allow it external linguistic sense analogous to that previously given by religions to God is not a step that the Kantian project allows for. Hick is too sanguine in his use of Kant to establish what he takes to be an objective being outside and beyond our world of thought, our mental constructions of reality.

Here is the point at issue. For non-realists would follow Wittgenstein in their contention that there is no exit from the confines of the human linguistic world. Our socially constructed language does not allow us even to postulate an existence that continues alongside or beyond our human existence. Hick realizes the absoluteness of the divide, and also the significance of the issues at stake: 'The debate between realist and non-realist understandings of religious language exposes the most fundamental of all issues in the philosophy of religion today.'[8] Hick criticizes non-realist religion as being 'welcome news for the few which is at the same time grim news for the many'.[9] By this, he means that a faith that has no place for an objective external deity or, by implication, a life beyond death, has no theory of salvation, which is a key concept in what he calls 'post-axial' religion. This perspective 'sees ordinary human existence as radically defective: as a fallen life in a fallen world, or as immersed in egocentric illusion and pervasively subject to *dukkha*'.[10] Hick seems to believe that non-realists can find no way out of the brevity and the corruption which is the life that 95 per cent of humanity seems to experience.

But a non-realist would wish to point out here the inadequacy of Hick's own account of the analysis he suggests is offered by post-axial religion. Since non-realism questions the existence of any given objective Reality, either outside or inside the human spirit, it would wish to reject any single expanation of 'how the world is'. It would point out that each religious faith offers a diversity of ideas and perspectives on how the world came into being and what the human destiny is under God. The 66 books of the Bible, for instance, each have a different nuance on these existential questions. It is not true to suggest that a biblical view centres on fallen life in a fallen world. This is the sort of Barthian error we have already exposed as inconsistent with a critical approach. It *may* be true of the Book of Genesis, although the American writer Matthew Fox has convincingly argued in his *Original Blessing* (1983) that a positive evaluation of the created order can just as emphatically be derived from the Jewish accounts of creation as the later doctrine of original sin. And although both Hinduism and Buddhism may be seen to concentrate on this world as what Keats called 'the vale of soul-making', through their doctrines of monism and Nirvana, they each offer a positive and joyful message to the believer as much as they emphasize the constrictions of the present – both elements co-exist in their doctrines of Karma. The point of a non-realist perspective is that it is neither descriptive nor propositional. The world cannot be described as (a) or (b) at all. Rather, we tell different stories of our experiences as humans of being and living in a world of contradictions, and how we construct our stories shows us the sort of world which we are constructing as we enact our lives in a temporal series of responses and choices. The creativity of the religious imagination is not thereby élitist in the way that Hick fears in his *Interpretation*. Wherever one's place in the social spectrum, one has an innate religious imagination that one can use to interpret the world of experience or curtail and ignore in preference for dogmatic or materialist concerns. Life, in an image developed by Cupitt, should be viewed as the sun, whose waxing and waning are part of the same movement and curve.[11] So are each of our births and deaths as individuals, and the successes and failures that make up the substance of what lies in between.

Within a non-realist perspective, new horizons become opened up for believers to leave go the intellectual and emotional agonies of trying to square commitment to their own religious culture with valid recognition of the stories, liturgies and lifestyles offered by others. If the question is not one of dogmatic truth but rather of attempts to picture an ethical ideal, many of the boundaries disappear with an ease that may still astonish the realist believer. For, as with the Berlin Wall, the connections of the edifice meant that once certain bricks were removed it was easy to see how the whole barrier had been rendered superfluous as a structure. Trespass across the divide at first appears audacious and earth-shattering, but as many incursions become made, to and fro, it becomes less significant as a marker than other geographical distinctions that are still seen as pertaining.

I wish to conclude my analysis of ways that the religious traditions might view one another and relate in a more mutual and positive fashion than previously by suggesting ways in which members of different faith-traditions can 'cross over' the boundaries between them with impunity, to borrow from one another, and to discover some benefit in attempting to live in one another's stories of faith. Christianity has always argued against syncretism, but the time has come to practise it. In eschewing fixed metaphysical definitions in favour of ethical actions, non-realists encourage believers into practical exercises of faith which will have their integrity discovered within the realm of religious experience. We recall an earlier debate during which the mathematician, Blaise Pascal, after agonizing over contradictory evidence for the existence of God, counselled to take holy water and attend masses. So today we should adopt (without hesitating over whether they fit into the theories) such practices as we find in other religions which are either missing entirely or neglected within our own. Christians in great numbers have taken up yoga as a form of prayerful meditation. It has not strictly been necessary within Christian realist orthodoxy, since Catholicism stressed the Mass as the acceptable prayerful offering and Protestantism advised simple and spontaneous prayer in the form of words, petitions and requests, as sufficient dialogue with God. As another example, Jews could enter with Muslims in the prostrations that are part of their daily routine of prayer, commended in the Koran. If they removed from their mental image the suggestion that obeisance alongside gentiles was the equivalent of idolatry, they might come to experience the force of this powerful image of solidarity with other worshippers, and an understanding of submission as social respect for the high ethical ideals in life. If a humanist listens to a Hindu speak of how Lord Krishna became blue after ingesting part of the Ganges, he will no longer need to accept that as part of the scientific account of how the earth came to be, but can listen sympathetically to a myth and discover what it is in the way the world is constructed that such a story is trying to highlight in our common human experience – and it may help in this exercise to recall that the Hindus do not have a specific doctrine of the creation of the world at a particular point in time, since they believe both worlds and gods are eternal, and that there is a never-ending cycle of self-perpetuating existence in our universe.

There are different models of how the traditions can meet and how the boundaries can be removed. The American theologian John S. Dunne speaks of 'passing over' from one faith to another, with the implication that one can normally return to one's own faith fortified by the extra insights attained. But it could be passage of a rather more permanent nature. So Bede Griffiths, a Benedictine monk who left the comfort of an ancient British religious house to set up an ashram in South India, used the somewhat more personal and pertinently also more permanent image of 'the marriage of East and West': 'The Hindu, the Buddhist, the Muslim, the humanist, the philosopher, the scientist, have all something to give and something to receive. The Christian, to whatever church he may belong, cannot claim to have the monopoly of the Truth.'[12] Griffiths completed his life by adopting the vesture, eating the food, and adapting to the ritual of the Hindu culture he had chosen. He was non-realist enough to recognize that the eucharist was not the only embodiment of the divine–human encounter, and its perceptions of the mystic Christ within could be as compelling within another tradition that he had chosen to adopt as his own. In this monk-turned-*sadhu* have we perhaps an example of the fulfilment of the logic which Thomas Merton had begun to exercise in his journey to Bangkok?

Perhaps Dom Bede saw his own journey to India as some type of response to the reciprocal journey that had been made by Mahatma Gandhi, who attempted to live by the best of the principles he perceived from whichever tradition they happened to emanate. More personal even than the title of Bede Griffiths' work was the chosen title of Gandhi's autobiography, *The Story of My Experiments with Truth*. For Gandhi, truth consisted of tips that one picked up in the course of life that gave one an indicator of value or meaning in what one was doing. In the same way, the concept 'God' does not for him have the status of a metaphysical Absolute either imparted by the Vedas or locatable in the sky. He uses a more creative and pragmatic definition, which is forged only in the human path of personal spiritual discovery in the vicissitudes of an individual's life: 'To me God is Truth and Love; God is ethics and morality; God is fearlessness; God is the source of light and life, and yet he is above and beyond all these. God is conscience.'[13] Because he adopted a non-realist stance on faith, Gandhi was able to forge a spirituality in quite a unique way, not only for his own familial life but also for his nation at a creative time at which they were called to produce an identity of their own beyond their colonial past. Within this spirituality, he managed to harness much of the Christian pacifist insight, as encapsulated in Jesus' sermon on the mount, alongside the Hindu stress on *ahimsa*, the way of non-violence in a situation of conflict. And the appeal he was able to make to these terms from each of the traditions helped him to gain the respect he needed both from Britain and his own country, to exercise untrammelled influence as the holy man who was at the same time the acknowledged political leader of his people at the time of their imminent independence from colonial rule.

Whereas realism is fitting for a society based on hierarchy, such as a colonial power, non-realism is a more appropriate theory for a society interconnected by forces of free exchange and commerce, loosened from political restraint. This may well explain the relative contemporary absence on the global scene of non-realist theology in some areas where the debate has been elsewhere – South Africa would be one such case. But it is present now in societies such as Britain today where free markets and relative lack of political restraint have led whole communities to import their faiths. Where these can now attempt to live in amicable co-existence, non-realists believe that by removing the metaphysical 'charge' of truth-claims, and by emphasizing the telling and hearing of stories of the inter-connections between our gods, our spirits, and our human ideals, we can learn God together more meaningfully than before. We may even be able to come to worship together when we realize that God is not a reality external to our lives but is that burning desire within to create a more just and a more harmonious world for our children. Human(e) ideals personified in theological form enable us to bend our knees together to all that is loving and pure and to attempt to extirpate what would keep us from reaching our common goals. Non-realism as the polar opposite of fundamentalism enables us to value the goals not just of our like-minded group but of the traditions of our global village, to which we now have greater and easier access than at any time in the past.

Notes

1 F. D. Maurice, *The Religions of the World and Their Relations to Christianity* (6th edn; Macmillan, 1886).

2 Cf. Arun Shourie, *Missionaries in India: Continuities, Changes, Dilemmas* (ASA Publications, 1994), who argues that outside the Dalit community Christianity made little real impact on the population.

3 *Ernst Troeltsch: Writings on Theology and Religion*, trans. and ed. Robert Morgan and Michael Pye (Duckworth, 1977), p. 189.

4 Karl Rahner, 'Christianity and the non-Christian religions', *Theological Investigations*, vol. 5, trans. Karl-H. Kruger (Darton, Longman and Todd, 1966), pp. 115–34, and 'Anonymous Christians', *Theological Investigations*, vol. 6, trans. Karl-H. and Boniface Kruger (Darton, Longman and Todd, 1969), pp. 390–8.

5 John Hick, *God and the Universe of Faiths* (Macmillan, 1973), p. 131.

6 John Hick, *An Interpretation of Religion* (Macmillan, 1989), p. 14.

7 John Hick, 'A response to Gerard Loughlin', *Modern Theology* 7 (1990), p. 64.

8 John Hick, 'Religious realism and non-realism: defining the issue' in Joseph Runzo (ed.), *Is God Real?* (Macmillan, 1993), p. 3.

9 *An Interpretation of Religion*, p. 207.

10 'Religious realism and non-realism: defining the issue', p. 11.

11 Don Cupitt, *After All* (SCM Press, 1994), p. 109.

12 Bede Griffiths, *The Marriage of East and West* (Collins, 1982), p. 202.

13 *The Selected Works of Mahatma Gandhi*, ed. S. Narayan (Gitendra T. Desai Navajivan Trust, 1968), vol. 6, p. 102.

4

All in the mind?

Stephen Mitchell

When Anthony Freeman published a clear, straightforward and popular account of a shift in his Christian belief – from a belief in a supernatural God to a non-supernatural version of Christianity – the popular press were equally clear and straightforward in their verdict: Anthony Freeman was a godless vicar sacked for losing his faith.

Theological reflections do not translate easily into newspaper reports but those reports can be very revealing. In the months following the publication of *God in Us*,[1] one phrase in particular came to be used by the press in their attempt to describe Freeman's position – God exists only in the mind. The phrase seems to have first appeared in a *Guardian* feature by Walter Schwarz, commenting on the state of belief in the Church and the retirement of the Bishop of Durham, David Jenkins:

> The debate about God is breaking out again, more seriously and more radically than in the sixties, when John Robinson of Woolwich liberated many would-be Christians from the straitjacket of a literalist belief in physical miracles.
>
> This time, Christians – and priests at that – are saying God does not exist (because nothing exists) except in human minds.[2]

The same phrase was taken up by Richard Harries, the Bishop of Oxford, to launch an attack on Freeman and the Sea of Faith: 'One of the weaknesses of the Sea of Faith group of Christians who argue that God exists only in their minds is that they fail to respect atheism.'[3] According to Christopher

Mordaunt, the Bishop and the press were justified in equating the belief that God exists only in the mind with atheism:

> . . . (leaving aside the question of whether minds exist) that is an unhappy turn of phrase, because it is generally used to refer to something that doesn't exist. 'It exists in his mind' suggests pink elephants or the bloodstains on Lady Macbeth's hands – things that are not really there.[4]

There were further criticisms. If God existed only in the mind of the believer, God was purely subjective and of no public good. If nothing exists except in human minds, then everything is subjective. Everyone is locked into their own imaginings and communication is impossible. Individualism is taken to extremes and the Sea of Faith followers are simply solipsists.

This was the nub of Harries' argument in *The Real God*, published as an equally accessible response to *God in Us*. The paragraph is worth quoting in full:

> First, God exists outside my mind, as the circumference of a circle exists outside its centre. My mind, and every mind, is the centre of a sphere whose radius is infinite. From time to time there arise people who think that everything that exists is simply a product of their imagination, a dream; a view technically known as solipsism. If I say that you are part of my dream and you reply 'But I am not, here I am speaking to you', a solipsist can always reply that your response is also part of my mind's projection or dream. Solipsism is notably difficult to refute philosophically, except by Dr Johnson's common-sense recourse of stubbing his foot against a stone. Nevertheless it is a fundamental assumption for most of us that there is indeed a world outside our minds, that other people exist and that we can discern aspects of this world which can be judged more or less true or more or less false. In a similar way a realist view of God asserts that there is a spiritual milieu, in which we live and move and have our being, but which is not confined to or limited by the language which we use about it.[5]

The passage is highly significant. Harries describes a position which is far removed from that intended by Freeman or the non-realists. Something has gone seriously wrong. Something vital has been omitted from the argument.

Radicals have failed to make clear the connection between their understanding of God and their understanding of the self, between the study of God and the study of the mind. Mordaunt, in the passage quoted, gives it away when he writes, in parentheses, 'leaving aside the question of whether minds exist'. The question of the mind cannot be left on one side, for there is a vital relationship between God and self. As Don Cupitt wrote in *The Leap of Reason* in 1976: 'The self is the fundamental analogy of God.'[6] His followers have been reluctant to examine both sides of the equation. Scott Cowdell, in a lecture given at the second Sea of Faith Conference in 1989, did, however, see this as the main distinction between modern liberal and postmodern radical theologies: 'Such was the age of liberal theology, the modern period. The old God of revealed theology might be dead, but the modern self was very much alive. The postmodern episteme however brings the death of the self as well.'[7]

It is not difficult to see why there should be a reluctance to pursue this radical programme in place of Freeman's more liberal strategy. Proclaiming the death of God is one thing, proclaiming the death of the self another.

But failure to get rid of dualist ways of thinking, both about God and the self, leaves radicals open to the charge of inconsistency. This is exactly the argument Richard Harries puts forward in the passage already quoted. So he argues that beyond our different views of the world, beyond our changing theories and explanations, stands the real world itself. Beyond the many different views we have of ourselves, beyond our changing personalities and the roles we play in life, are real persons. Why then should we not say that beyond the many different manifestations of faith is the real God? Only when all dualist ways of talking about the world and the self are abandoned will dualist theologies seem redundant.

At first the prospects of abandoning talk of a real self do not seem good. Dualist talk is deeply engrained in us. Going to view the body of a friend prepared for burial, the overwhelming conviction is that this is not the person we knew so well. The warmth, personality, spirit, mind and consciousness of our friend have gone. People must be more than their bodies. During a moment of quiet meditation we become aware of our remarkable capacity for self-reflection and the experience of our own private thoughts. Consciousness must be more than the activity of the brain. But in what sense is the mind *more than* the activity of the brain? What *more* makes the body a person?

From Plato in the fourth century BCE to Descartes in the seventeenth century CE, dualism gave sense to these aspects of human experience. For Plato, the soul was the vital element of the human person. In *Phaedo*, for example, he describes the soul, the essence of our humanity and individuality, as immortal, unchanging and indestructible in contrast to the body which is subject to death and decay. The soul and the body each has its own home in a separate world. However, for the few years of our earthly lives, our souls are imprisoned in our bodies, determining all our thoughts and actions until finally being released at death.

Whether or not this account can be made coherent, there are good reasons for us to reject it. Interested as we are in the ways we have changed throughout the different periods of our lives, aware of the many facets to our personalities, playing many different roles within our communities and driven by strong biological instincts, unchanging, immortal and incorporeal souls have very little appeal.

Even worse, Plato would have us despise much that we would regard as important and valuable. With attention firmly fixed on the immortal soul, Plato's philosopher and his pupils attempt to disregard their bodies, abstain from physical and sexual pleasures, free themselves from the distractions of the senses and avoid, as much as they can, all physical contacts and associations. The body is said to fill us with a great deal of nonsense, is the cause of war and greed, interrupts, disturbs and distracts us and prevents us from getting a glimpse of the truth. Thus, thoroughly dissatisfied with the body, and longing for their souls to be independent of it, Plato's philosophers find death a happy release.

There are, no doubt, times when we echo this last sentiment. When our friends are racked with pain and their bodies are consumed by disease, we might well pray for, or even want to work towards, hastening death. But that does not signal a *general* dissatisfaction with the body, only a desire to bring relief from particular pains in particular circumstances.

For Descartes, the vital distinction was made between mind and matter. As a mathematician, impressed by the certainty of mathematical knowledge, he sought to find equally clear and indubitable certainties in all areas of knowledge. Doubting anything that could be doubted, he was led to believe in the certainty of his own thinking and in the being and nature of the thinking being that was having those thoughts. A human being was essentially a conscious mind.

But again, our interests do not coincide with his. Without pursuing further his understanding of mind and matter, and the many problems of relating the mind to the body, two features in particular make his method unappealing to us. First, for Descartes, reason stands in sharp contrast to custom and example. If, therefore, we are to be free of error, we must escape from our culture. The very historical processes which enable us to mature are corrupting. Ancient cities which have taken shape over time are said to be ill laid out in comparison to new towns. So too, our own reasoning would be far better had we been mature at birth. Childhood is a time when we acquire a thousand prejudices. Reason and culture stand in opposition to one another.

Second, his method is highly individualistic. The foundation for reforming his opinions is, he says, wholly his own. Nothing is to be trusted. Everything is to be doubted. Only his own private self-consciousness can provide a starting point to lay down foundations for truth.

To those who value the interdependence of human life, and glory in the variety of human culture and experience, to those who recognize a continuity between human life and animal life, the method of Descartes is not going to be their starting point. For them the question has to be asked, 'Is it helpful to talk of minds independent of culture and historical change?'

There is another argument that may persuade us to reject the dualisms that require us to speak of the mind and the body as two independent substances occupying different worlds. This centres around the question as to whether we can even talk coherently about the identity of persons without speaking about their bodies. Do there have to be physical bodies for there to be persons? A series of papers by Bernard Williams has provoked much discussion around this and related questions, and the conclusion that 'a person is a material body which thinks'.[8]

Suppose we are persuaded by the arguments to abandon dualist ways of speaking about the self. We are then confronted with the task of building up a biological, cultural and historical account of the self, the mind and consciousness. But if dualism is unattractive, so too is the view that our conscious mental processes are no more than physical events in the brain. While we may readily acknowledge that physical activity causes pleasure or pain, that alterations to our nervous systems or brain chemistry can cause changes even to our personalities, that some of our mental activity can be mimicked by artificial intelligence machines, we may be reluctant to adopt a fully determinist account of human behaviour.

When Colin Blakemore, for example, sums up the central thesis of his book *The Mind Machine* in three sentences, we are uneasy: 'The human brain is a machine, which alone accounts for all our actions, our most private thoughts, our beliefs. It creates the state of consciousness and the sense of self. It makes the mind.'[9] To say that we are machines, albeit wonderfully sophisticated machines, seems to leave questions about the self and the mind unanswered. What is the nature of the mind and the self that the brain makes? What is the nature of its making?

It is worth pausing to note that Christians, whether of a realist or a non-realist persuasion, are likely to agree in wanting to reject both dualist and determinist ways of talking about the self. The immortality of the soul has never been a Christian doctrine. The creeds and traditional teaching prefer to speak of the resurrection of the body. So, for example, Richard Harries in *The Real God* tells us that we are physical beings in a physical world – a physical world, moreover, which 'makes itself from the bottom upwards in ever more complex forms of life, until *we* emerge, as part of that physical universe'.[10] We are, he says, so rooted in this world that we have no immediate or overwhelming knowledge of any other world. Nor is it necessary, he says, 'to believe that we have a soul that is a kind of box within a box. Modern science, like the Hebrews of old, stresses that we are psychosomatic unities, body, mind and spirit all bound up together.' And while soul-language may be important, we do not have to believe that the soul 'is an isolatable thing'.[11] In discussing human fulfilment, the question of the self is clearly important to Harries. (Perhaps more important to him than to Freeman, who makes no comment at all upon the self.) 'What' he asks 'is the self which we are to discover, express and fulfil? It is not simply the product of genetic inheritance or our childhood influences.'[12]

So a liberal, like Harries, when talking about the self, seems to agree with the radical in rejecting both dualism and a simple physicalism or materialism. But then the question has to be asked, 'How *is* the liberal going to talk about the self?' What answer is Harries going to give to his own question? Can the radical persuade him to go further and admit that a non-realist view of the self is at least a credible option? And if such a view is at least admitted as a possibility, then we have a non-realist analogy of the self with which to speak of God.

In his book *Making the Human Mind*, Professor Sharpe puts forward one such view of the self, and the idea that 'the human conscious mind is itself a human creation, brought about through linguistic behaviour'.[13] In the last chapter he provides a speculative history as to how this might have come about.

When we talk about creatures who have minds, he argues, we are talking about creatures who are self-conscious, able to think about themselves and reflect upon what they do and believe. How might this have come about? Looking at animals, we recognize that they have to some extent an understanding as to how other animals are behaving. One animal will be aware that another animal has a prey in its sights. As language developed – as gesture evolved into language – and as our ancestors began to describe things through language, so they acquired a richer source for describing others. What they recognized in others could then be described of them-selves. This is the point at which mental life begins to develop. Sharpe sums up his account as follows:

I have argued that the origin of the human mind lies in our capacity to describe actions and that from this evolves the internalising of such descriptions of ourself. Because I can describe others, I can describe myself. Animals may be able to invite or describe actions in other animals. But self-description is self-consciousness in embryo and here begins the life of the mind.[14]

Sharpe's account centres around a number of important features. First, it argues that public language precedes private thought. Language is a skill, acquired in a social setting. It is acquired like any other skill, by trial and correction. How else could the skill of using language be learnt except in a public setting? It is this publicly acquired skill that is then available for describing our own actions. As a consequence of this, different thoughts will be thought by different groups of people. Societies will conceptualize behaviour in different ways and these are the very concepts that will then be available to members of that society for thinking about themselves.

Second, while possession of a brain is clearly required for mental activity, there is no requirement within this account for a general relationship between a certain thought and a particular configuration in the brain. Sharpe asks us to consider the analogy of music. At one level, music can be described in terms of sounds at given frequencies. If there were not those frequencies, there would be no music. However, we also describe music in terms of more personal qualities. These descriptions are not dependent upon there being certain configurations of notes within the score. Such descriptions 'float free of the empirical base in the sense that no knowledge of the base is required for their accurate use'.[15]

Third, there is no gap between a person saying 'I am thinking' and being self-conscious. That is, the conditions for self-consciousness and the criteria for self-consciousness are identical. If I can say, of myself, that I am remembering, then we have satisfied the criteria for my being conscious of my remembering. 'There are no further deep facts about myself to which this refers and which stand as conditions for its truth.'[16] It may be argued that a machine could be programmed to utter such words. But language use, as was stated earlier, is a skill acquired in a public setting and language develops in a social context. It is also closely linked to the facial and physical gestures out of which language evolved. Until a computer was able to show knowledge of social customs and participate in this common life, and extend its use of language imaginatively, it is unlikely that we would say it had a mind.

Whether a non-realist account of the human mind is thought to be coherent will largely depend upon the discussion of these three points. But suppose that this or some similar account is accepted, what will be the consequences for the religious believer? What advantages are there for the believer?

St Augustine in his *Soliloquies* expressed the intricate relationship between God and the self. 'O God . . . if I know myself, I shall know thee.' How we conceive of the self will therefore determine our spiritual path. Where the self is seen as an immortal and eternal soul imprisoned in a body, then the search for self-knowledge and, by Augustine's path, the search for knowledge of God will almost inevitably mean a withdrawal from the body and the physical world in which everything changes and decays. Where the human being is seen essentially as a conscious, rational mind, then the search for the self and the search for God will involve a rejection of culture and historical change.

Our understanding of the self also affects our understanding of the spiritual life when viewed from the perspective of our ultimate destiny. Where the essence of the self is understood in terms of an eternal and indestructible soul, then the death of the body will be seen as leaving the future of the soul undisturbed. Life is likely to be seen as an endurance test. The spiritual pilgrim will journey through life trying to keep the soul unsoiled by the impurities of the world. Similarly, where the human being is envisaged as essentially a conscious mind imprisoned within a body, then death will bring about a union with other minds and the mind of God, uncluttered by the interference of the body. The spiritual pilgrim will journey through life attempting to avoid the prejudices of culture and historical fashions.

Abandoning dualist ideas of the self means being truly incarnate in the search for the self and God, affirming and rejoicing in our bodiliness, our historical and cultural inheritance, and our mortality. The search for the self and the search for God will not be a journey away from the body, the world and the passing of time, but a journey into the common life of the community whose language creates us. For the radical, therefore, there can be no possibility of isolating the spiritual search from the rest of life. Expressions of the spiritual path in prayer and worship, relation-ships, and the whole ethical life of the community gain a new and urgent perspective.

With the spiritual life seen as a journey into the common life of the community whose language creates us, prayer and worship become one of the main creative influences upon our lives. There is often a sense of embarrassment when radicals are questioned about prayer and worship.

Forced to concede that they set aside the possibility of supernatural intervention in answer to prayer, they rather tamely suggest that such prayer does some good through the power of positive thought, through expressing the values and needs of the community. Forced to admit that they are not addressing anyone in worship, they argue that worship is giving worth. In communion, as in baptism, 'they affirm their fellowship in following the ideals focussed for them in Jesus'.[17]

But there is no need for such embarrassment. If we are created through the language of our communities, then immersing ourselves in the rituals and myths of our faith community creates and recreates us. In communion we will be in the presence of our creator and the word will truly become flesh. Who we pray *with* will be more important than who we pray *for*.

The quality of our relating will therefore be all-important in the spiritual path. Again, dualist philosophies of the self, devaluing the mortal body in the face of the immortal soul, affect the main relationships within our societies. Where such philosophies are linked to human sexuality and the differences between male and female, then those communities become patriarchal and oppressive to women. Augustine neatly makes such a connection when he tells us that

> Where the flesh rules and the spirit serves, the house is in disorder. What is worse than a house where the woman has rule over the man? However, a house is right where the man commands and the woman obeys. So man is right where the spirit rules and the flesh serves.[18]

In much Christian theology, the polarizations between male and female, soul and body, mind and matter, active and passive have been deeply embedded and arise from a dualist outlook. So God is without a body. He is beyond sexuality. For a man to please God, he must dominate and control. A woman must hide her bodiliness and deny her sexuality. The language of domination, penetration and control then enters into the vocabulary of the most intimate of our relationships, the sexual acts.

Non-realists, then, will want to reject a self-centred spirituality. 'We would do better in morality' writes Don Cupitt 'to turn our attention away from the self and towards the ways in which people, things and aspects of the world and our life are valued in language.'[19] This coincides with their more pragmatic view of language and more artistic notions of truth and knowledge. A pragmatist like Richard Rorty, for example, dispenses with the idea of language as a medium. Getting nearer to the truth is not, for him, a matter of making our language correspond more and more to the pattern of a reality beyond language. Knowledge is not 'a matter of getting things right'. Rather, it is a matter 'of acquiring habits of action for coping with reality'.[20] Truth and knowledge are not established by their relationship to non-human realities but by their relationship to the goals and agreements of particular communities. Holding such a view is *not* to say that there is no reality. It is to say that reality, experience and language arise inseparably together.

Putting everything – truth, meaning, the self, even reality itself – into the language of human communities, and seeing these as aspects of our human relating and behaviour, demands that the non-realist brings the ethical into the spiritual. Truth and knowledge are related to the goals of a community and the relationships within it.

What hope, then, of persuading the liberals to take a further step away from dualism towards non-realism? Don Cupitt recently summed up his own view of the self in a lecture to the eighth Sea of Faith conference:

> The answer I have been trying to present in my 'expressionist' books involves giving up completely the idea of the self as a substance, and instead picturing it as a process in time. The self is always both coming to pass and passing away, both becoming itself and losing itself as it pours itself out into expression.[21]

Richard Harries comes very close to summarizing this when he likens the self to a musical composition and talks of 'the music which we are'.[22] But the non-realist will insist that if this is how Harries wishes to speak of people it is how he should speak of the person of God.

Gods are the characters in the stories told about them, as we are the characters in the stories told about us. And as one person may sum up and epitomize a whole generation, so Anthony Freeman may say that God is the sum of our values. But gods lose none of their personal characteristics by being spoken of in this way. And it is such a person that believers will seek inspiration from, meditate upon, and try to make the stories of their God their own.

Nor do gods lose any of their reality. For non-realists will not label people as real or unreal. They will not regard such a distinction as useful. Rather, they will seek to establish what different characters do – and this brings them close to the heart of the task of traditional theology. To say that God is real and not unreal tells us nothing about the way the reality of God impinges upon our lives, nothing about the way the story of God came to be told, and nothing about the way that story is to be interpreted. Equally, to say that God is unreal and not real is to say nothing about the way the stories of the gods shape nations, communities, and people. Rather gods, like all people, will be seen to be more like works of art, needing to be engaged with imaginatively, constantly interpreted and re-interpreted, and whose life and value is to be found in the flux of community life.

Notes

1 Anthony Freeman, *God in Us* (SCM Press, 1993).

2 Walter Schwarz, 'Wide eyed and godless', *Guardian* (4 September 1993).

3 Richard Harries, 'Why God is a god, not just an idea', *Guardian* (25 September 1993).

4 Christopher Mordaunt, 'In the (existentialist) beginning was the last word', *Guardian* (11 September 1993).

5 Richard Harries, *The Real God* (Mowbray, 1994), pp. 2–3.

6 Don Cupitt, *The Leap of Reason* (Sheldon, 1976), p. 114.

7 Scott Cowdell, 'Radical theology, postmodernity and Christian life in the void', a lecture delivered to the second Sea of Faith conference in 1989.

8 Bernard Williams, *Problems of the Self* (Cambridge University Press, 1973), p. 70.

9 Colin Blakemore, *The Mind Machine* (BBC, 1988), p. 257.

10 *The Real God*, p. 59.

11 *The Real God*, p. 50.

12 *The Real God*, p. 47.

13 R. A. Sharpe, *Making the Human Mind* (Routledge, 1990), p. 3.

14 *Making the Human Mind*, p. 122.

15 *Making the Human Mind*, p. 121.

16 *Making the Human Mind*, p. 123.

17 *God in Us*, p. 56.

18 Quoted by Elisabeth Moltmann-Wendel, *A Land Flowing with Milk and Honey* (SCM Press, 1986), p. 85.

19 Don Cupitt, 'Unsystematic ethics and politics' in Philippa Berry and Andrew Wernick (eds), *Shadow of Spirit* (Routledge, 1992), p. 154.

20 Richard Rorty, 'Anti-representationalism, ethnocentrism and liberalism' in *Objectivity, Relativism and Truth* (Cambridge University Press, 1991), p. 1.

21 Don Cupitt, 'Our dual agenda', a lecture delivered to the eighth Sea of Faith conference in 1995.

22 *The Real God*, p. 50.

5

The vulnerability of faith

Graham Shaw

The last thirty years have seen a wide variety of revisionist theologies which mark the unease that surrounds modern theology. These theologies have emerged from within the religious tradition, and however critical or apparently destructive have been intended as a positive contribution to the future of theology, not some purely negative repudiation. For me, the most powerful exponents of this were Thomas Altizer and William Hamilton, the 'death of God' theologians of the 1960s. Their writing encouraged me to explore the difficulties which face contemporary theology, while their example also warned me of the difficulty of doing this in a way which does not invite misunderstanding. More recently, Don Cupitt and Anthony Freeman have addressed these questions using the resources of postmodernist philosophy, and their work has to a considerable extent depended on that philosophical viewpoint. It is however worth remembering that many of the issues were first raised before the widespread influence of French literary theorists, and those theologians who are unpersuaded by postmodernism should not think that they have therefore disposed of the revisionist agenda. At most, they may have criticized one form of it. For myself, I am in philosophical sympathy with the approach of Iris Murdoch in *Metaphysics as a Guide to Morals*, not least in her vigorous repudiation of the structuralist inheritance.[1] With Iris Murdoch and such revisionist theologians as Paul van Buren and D. Z. Phillips, I think it better to look to Wittgenstein rather than to Derrida. In my case, however, all my revisionist theology has emerged primarily from exegesis, from my attempt to understand and interpret the Scriptures and some of the classic texts of Christendom. It may therefore be helpful if I retrace in this paper the path that took me from Paul to Feuerbach.

The need to take responsibility for God

My conviction that believers need to learn to take responsibility for their God emerged slowly as I examined the exercise of authority in the Pauline letters and the Gospel of Mark. In *The Cost of Authority* I began by recognizing that these texts were all concerned with the exercise of power, and that a political interpretation of the text was necessary to understanding it. In that analysis it became clear to me that the arbitrary nature of much religious authority was intimately connected with strategies which disclaimed responsibility. By the end I had concluded that it was impossible to take responsibility for religion without also taking responsibility for God. So I began to think through the possible implications of such an approach for theology itself:

> The emphasis on the function of doctrines, on asking questions about the use to which human beings are putting their religious claims and language, makes possible a new understanding of the reality of God, modified and more intelligible. For the logical consequence of this approach to scripture is that the only reality of God lies in the use of that word by human beings. It does not refer to some supernatural or mysterious or special being; it is instead a word of the creative imagination by which we construct first in imagination and ultimately in reality a new and different world. The only significance of the word 'God' is its purely verbal function; that is not necessarily disparaging, for its function is uniquely precious: it is an integral part of human freedom, a means by which we transcend the given and transform ourselves and the world.[2]

In retrospect, that paragraph might have been more convincing if it had been written more cautiously. It was claiming too much to speak of 'the logical consequence'. It would have been more accurate and perhaps less alarming to say that the approach suggested that the primary reality of God lay in the use of that word by human beings. I then proceeded to indicate those aspects of traditional theology which would have to be repudiated and why:

> All attempts to objectify God, to attribute to God an assured metaphysical reality, have therefore to be abandoned; and that for religious as well as for philosophical reasons. The intellectual difficulties of such objectification

are a commonplace of the modern philosophy of religion. The religious objections are rather different, and lie in the acceptance and evasion of responsibility. A God objectively or supernaturally conceived connives too easily with our attempts to evade responsibility for our constructions, which are thus removed from the possibility of criticism. Moreover the unchanging metaphysical God, whose relationship to the world is fundamentally non-reciprocal, has always been associated with the construction and preservation of equally unbalanced social relationships.[3]

If you believe that God exists in some metaphysical sense, quite apart from human beings, human religious activity is only secondary, indeed in a sense unimportant. Such a God *is*, his existence alone ensures the triumph of his purposes, and is the ground of whatever reward his worshippers seek. Human beings may recognize him and attend to him, through his grace they may participate in his salvation, but they remain radically dependent and will quickly disclaim any initiative or responsibility as being theirs. God alone acts to love and save, and on such a view we at most simply respond. Metaphysical religion is not accidentally passive, it is necessarily so. The existence of God guarantees the possibility of transcendence; we may recognize and adore him, we may love and obey him, but salvation is bestowed. The achievement is said to be entirely God's. The worshipping life of the community may convey a benefit to those who participate in it, but even if the tradition of worship should cease among mankind, that would be our loss; God would remain God. On such a view the secular world may choose to reject God and experience the reality of condemnation, but only the world would be the loser. On the traditional understanding, the word 'God' refers to a transcendent reality, who may comfort and redeem transient human beings, but whose existence remains in its perfection untouched and untarnished by anything we may do. It is a vision with its own brutal beauty, which the music of the well-known hymn only partly mitigates:

Before the hills in order stood,
    Or earth received her frame,
From everlasting thou art God,
    To endless years the same.

A thousand ages in thy sight
    Are like an evening gone;
Short as the watch that ends the night
    Before the rising sun.

> Time, like an ever-rolling stream,
>   Bears all its sons away;
> They fly forgotten, as a dream
>   Dies at the opening day.
>   (Isaac Watts)

Traditional theological rhetoric is rich in such imagery, where the abasement of humanity serves the exaltation of the divine. The credibility of the traditional God is only confirmed by our recurring experience of mortality and its frailties.

Recasting transcendence

The understanding of God that I have tried to put forward is very different. From the outset I was concerned to argue that repudiating much in the traditional conception of God did not necessarily mean the abandonment of the theological enterprise. I tried to give some indication of how I conceived its 'uniquely precious' function:

> The God of the gospel sustains human freedom first of all by providing a vocabulary which readily challenges all human structures of authority and control. This subversive character is not temporary and circumstantial, something which is relevant to one society but not to another; it is one of the intrinsically Christian uses of the word God. The appeal to God negates all existing human claims – it places them in question, and thus enables the individual to resist them. Secondly, it provides a language which enables human beings to transcend the given, to achieve imaginative detachment. Without such a possibility, the scientific description of reality will only reinforce present oppression and inequality. By contrast the language of religion facilitates the creative redescription of reality. Thirdly, this is no substitute for action, but a preparation for it. A religion confined to the imagination, be it the awareness of the mystic or the consciousness of grace, remains in the most negative sense unreal. Once the imagination has been detached from action, the way is open to religious fantasy and every kind of dishonest compensation. The God of the Christian gospel frees precisely because he calls to action. Objective benefits which are passively received easily rob their beneficiaries of initiative. By contrast, the gifts of the Christian gospel are obtained only in use.[4]

The debate is not, therefore, between theologians who still wish to affirm divine transcendence and those who have surrendered that claim. It is between those who believe that only a traditional metaphysic of divine being can adequately do justice to the transcendent, and those who understand transcendence in terms of the human use of language. On such a view it is in prayer and worship alone that transcendence is achieved, and it is a human achievement. The word 'God' is precious not because of some abiding reality to which it refers, but because of the possibility of transcendence which is discovered in its use. A central passage of *God in Our Hands* is headed 'The God who transcends the world':

> We do not value God as God, because he made the world or because he promises its blessings. We find our good in God alone, because only the God who lives in our imaginations can sustain the burden of our hopes and satisfy the depths of our longing. Whatever value we place upon the world – we lose for ever. If the object does not escape us, the joy we associated with it does. In prayer we learn to attribute value only to the God, whom we construct in our imaginations. The value we place upon him, we do not lose, because he is ours. We have only to attend to him to appropriate the glory with which we clothe him.
>
> Prayer on this account is the triumphant art of the human imagination. A person stripped of everything except the power of utterance retains this inalienable dignity which needs no human audience to confirm it. The person who has learnt to find joy in the invocation of God has tasted eternal life.[5]

So transcendence is to be understood not as a metaphysical reality whose existence invites our participation, but as a human achievement made possible by the use of theological language. I believe this account of transcendence, but I recognize that it is much more precarious than the traditional metaphysical understanding, just because human activity is central to it. The reality of such a God is entirely dependent on the continuing human activity of prayer and worship. This gives to those institutions which foster the practice of prayer and the encouragement of worship a central theological importance. For on this account religion is like music, a human activity, which lives in the making. Viewed in this way, a religious community is not simply promising salvation on a take it or leave it basis, it is extending an invitation to a unique form of human creativity which is as vulnerable as any other form of human creativity. Unless the invitation is welcomed the creativity will cease. The metaphysical theist can understand the complacent indifference of secularism as having no relevance to the future of religion, which is guaranteed by the existence of the God who elicits it. Secularism needs neither understanding nor accommodation; all that is necessary is stubborn reaffirmation. On the account that I am suggesting, secularism might be an irreversible human loss. On such a view every worshipping community represents the front line in the struggle for the future of religion. I remain committed not because I believe that there is a God who will vindicate my faith; rather, words of David Jenkins in the 1960s have echoed in my mind throughout my adult life: 'if God is dead then man is dying.'[6] It is the slogan of a religious humanism which has never ceased to fascinate and sustain me.

If my understanding of God has made the future of a worshipping community a central concern, my theological method moves in a direction which makes the whole theological enterprise dependent on its ability to communicate to those outside its circle:

> The believer in the Christian God must subject himself to the discipline of communication, which involves listening as well as speaking. The believer must therefore always be prepared to give reasons, to share his understanding, to listen to criticism and thus to achieve a greater intelligibility; for once he takes refuge in a believing circle his freedom is divisive and becomes an expression and instrument of alienation. The privileged proclamation of the pulpit is no substitute for mutual discussion. The exercise of our freedom, which is also our discovery of the will of God, is necessarily co-operative with others.[7]

It is because the challenge of communication is so important that I have always been very cautious about speaking of the death of God or, more recently, in using the language of non-realism. Stark paradox does not invite understanding and all too easily appears to be merely destructive. I am sympathetic to many of the arguments that non-realists apply, but I remain very unhappy about the term. Like 'the death of God' in the 1960s, it is too paradoxical to be convincing and invites misunderstanding. To concede to the traditional positions the unambiguous accolade of realism is a mistake, and not simply in tactical terms, though I fear that any debate conducted on that ground is unlikely to aid the revisionist cause. The crucial difficulty in embracing non-realism is that it spares its metaphysical opponents from having to face the full impact of a vigorous critique and repudiation of their deeply misleading rhetoric of realism. Those rhetorical strategies must be exposed and abandoned, but the theism which emerges is a realistic one and indeed real in a way that the God of traditional metaphysical rhetoric is not.

Finding the courage for vulnerable affirmation

The most incisive criticism of my position has come from the pen of William Hamilton, who himself in some ways set me off on this line of thought. At the end of a sympathetic presentation of my thought, he makes it clear that he is quite unconvinced by a crucial stage of my argument:

> It is, I suppose, worth wondering whether Shaw's strategy of re-appropriation can plausibly follow his profound act of repudiation. Are there not limits to this project of re-translation? Is it only to play it safe with the authorities that the word [God] is maintained? . . .
>
> Why should the Christian God, effectively killed, be permitted to return with a brand new character, and an old name? Shaw's values – peace, compassion, sharing in the sufferings of this terrible century – these hardly need his imagined God to be validated. His mentor Feuerbach did not need to keep the old word; Shaw's case would lose nothing if he eliminated his new God, along with the old. All his convincing moral vision needs is the man of the cross, victim of corrupt political and religious power and model for our contemporary way of being in the world.[8]

I suspect that the authorities of the Church of England might be surprised to see me as someone 'playing it safe', but the essence of Hamilton's misgiving goes to the heart of the issue and usefully expresses the impatience of many people with the task of theological revision. There is often a curious coincidence of judgement between conservative believers and complacent unbelievers, neither of whom wish to have their respective assumptions challenged, and the revisionist theologian is a threat to both. Hamilton's charge has all the more force, because he cannot convincingly be placed in either of those camps. Nevertheless, I think he is too hasty in the wholesale repudiation of any kind of God for two reasons. First, I do not think it is possible to do justice to 'the man of the cross', while at the same time removing any allusion to God from his lips. Hamilton rightly conveys the central importance in my religious vision of the crucifixion:

> This is the Jesus refusing all privilege, displaying his vulnerability, dying without serenity in the belief that his message was dying with him. The crucifixion enjoins Christians to repudiate all confidence in power, speaking as it does of the best of men killed by systems of religious and political power. 'In a world where every man is either a predator or a victim, only the man of God, sustained not by power but by goodness, can take the decision to be a victim.'[9]

For just that reason I would say that any picture of Jesus in which God plays no positive part is both a travesty and an impoverishment. His God may be very different from the God of those who killed him, but his life and his teaching are saturated with the thought of God and language about God. Neither his life nor his teaching can be affirmed with any integrity if that characteristic is simply removed.

Second, while William Hamilton is quite correct to stress the centrality of the cross, he has overlooked my attempt to speak of Jesus' vindication. My treatment of resurrection may seem very meagre compared with more traditional and literal accounts. It is nevertheless a crucial part of both my vision and my argument:

> I believe that Jesus was vindicated retrospectively, not by a miraculous intervention of divine power, but by the stubborn acclamation of his followers. His achievement was so to educate his disciples, that however falteringly and inconsistently, despite mistake and fantasy, they were able to recognize the figure on the cross as truly the man of God. Their proclamation was at times confused, self-serving, and even vindictive. Nevertheless they justified Jesus' vision of God and came to share it as they affirmed and celebrated the memory of his death. They neither mourned nor forgot him. However much they may have delighted in the prospect of his vengeance, they never repressed the memory of the death which their Redeemer underwent. Far from trying to rewrite history to obliterate his ignominy, their Judge retained the marks of his passion. It was Jesus' achievement that he created followers who refused to let him die. Taught by him to despise the power of men, they ensured that judicial murder would not silence him. Learning from him a confidence which comes from God alone, they refused to allow shame and failure to discredit him. If I deplore and question some of their claims as extravagant and fantastic, I must recognize in their faith their finest tribute to their Master. Only by such a Master could their eyes have been opened to see that the man whom others crucified was nevertheless the man of God.[10]

I have quoted this passage at length because in my view not only is God central to any convincing account of Jesus, but it is precisely the triumph of his understanding of God in the minds of his followers that constitutes his vindication.

Where I suppose I fundamentally part company with Hamilton is in the supposition that God simply provides a validation of our values. For me the drama of the gospels is utterly different. Its excitement and pathos comes not from some model way of life, or exposition of timeless truth, but in the anguished affirmation of the highest human values in a world and a society which is either indifferent or hostile. The haunting transcendence in the gospels is not to be found in the tawdry stories of miracle and healing, but in the way in which, through his God, Jesus is able to transcend the cruel limitations of his immediate environment. Indeed two thousand years later he still seems to be far ahead of his followers. Only a little while ago Marxists would sometimes patronize Jesus by representing him as one of themselves. Today the figure on the cross mocks the powerlessness of modern exponents of ruthless coercion as he did their imperial predecessors.

The vitality of the Christian religion is not simply a matter of articulating, affirming and developing certain human values, though obviously it is engaged in doing this. The crucial function of belief in God lies in the way we continue to affirm those values in a context which often threatens and indeed destroys them. Our experience of life does not consistently nurture kindness, generosity, commitment and love; often these seem to be undermined by accident and illness, the fickleness and cruelty of the human heart, and the suddenness of death. The humbling experience of a parish clergyman is to see how people use their belief in God to transcend their immediate experience, in a way which enables them to retain and indeed to reaffirm those fragile and vulnerable human values. We discover the dignity we share as human beings, not in sheltered lives which consign affliction to other people, but by opening our lives to the reality of others' affliction and by not trying to secure some privileged invulnerability for ourselves. Only at that price can compassion be distinguished from condescension. That is the path to which we commit ourselves when we participate in the broken bread of Christ's body. I am therefore uneasy with an account of theology which simply equates God with human values, without at the same time indicating the difficulty and cost of affirming those values. Religion is not concerned simply to utter the platitudes of a certain ethical idealism. Instead, it invites us to enter a drama, in which we discover that we are as vulnerable as the values we wish to affirm, and it is precisely in that vulnerability that those values are tested and achieved. Perhaps to my surprise, I want to say that this is precisely the Easter faith. I do not look to God to guarantee a certain kind of outcome, I look to God simply to sustain my courage. A century which has seen so much triumphant cruelty is not well placed to declare such a God redundant, for at every stage a carefully nurtured cowardice has colluded and made possible the horrors of our uniquely murderous times.

Notes

1 Iris Murdoch, *Metaphysics as a Guide to Morals* (Chatto & Windus, 1992).
2 Graham Shaw, *The Cost of Authority* (SCM Press, 1983), p. 282.
3 *The Cost of Authority*, p. 282.
4 *The Cost of Authority*, p. 283.
5 Graham Shaw, *God in Our Hands* (SCM Press, 1987), p. 219.
6 David Jenkins, *The Glory of Man* (SCM Press, 1967), p. 65.
7 *The Cost of Authority*, p. 284.
8 William Hamilton, *A Quest for the Post-Historical Jesus* (SCM Press, 1994), p. 35.
9 *A Quest for the Post-Historical Jesus*, p. 36 (quoting *God in Our Hands*, p. 124).
10 *God in Our Hands*, pp. 137–8.

6

The reality of power and the power of reality

Peter Selby

Words are, among other things, instruments of power. They are intended to produce effects, and for better or worse they usually do. So finding out how words work is at least as much a matter of technology as of art. Lives may depend on the working of words, and profits very often do; so the interest in knowing how they work, improving their performance and preventing their failing to function in accordance with our intentions, is felt far more widely than the circle of those for whom philosophy and linguistics are their academic interest. In wanting to know how words work we are asking about the power they have had, and how that power can be maintained or (according to our point of view) confronted.

However, religious believers have become somewhat suspicious of attempts to discover the source of the power of their language. For them, a functional approach to the meaning of religious language can easily arouse the suspicion that questions of meaning and being are about to be circumvented. It can easily appear that statements of religious belief are being explained as *only* or even *merely* 'performances' of some kind rather than propositions with a content, let alone claims to bear witness to the truth about a reality beyond this world. Perhaps religious believers have in fact grown too accustomed to defending their convictions against the positivists' suggestion that they are meaningless, or even answers to questions that cannot legitimately be asked.

This essay, by contrast, for the most part accepts a technological approach to the language of religious faith. It takes seriously such questions as how such language works, what it is meant to do, what gives it its power and (most of all) how it relates to the realities of institutional power within the Church. That is not because I hold the opinion that those questions can substitute for questions of meaning and truth, but because I believe that asking those questions can take us surprisingly close to the heart of the debate which has been occasioned by those who wish to give a 'non-realist' account of the language of God. I shall suggest that the main thrust of their complaint against 'realist' understandings is exceedingly accurate: they point at places where the use of that language by those who most fiercely defend realist understandings contradicts the very meaning which they wish to insist that it has. However, after taking the non-realists' diagnosis with what I hope is due seriousness, I shall seek to argue that in the end their proposed remedy fails to meet the ills which they have discerned.

Grounds for suspicion

There is nothing especially new in suspecting that belief in God is ill-founded, or is maintained and encouraged for sinister purposes. Modern atheism in particular is full of the suspicion that religious belief reflects factors in the individual's structure of psychological need (Freud), or a 'revolt from below' in the form of a cult of inferiority (Nietzsche), or again, the operation of the structures of class domination (Marx). It has become perfectly respectable for religious believers to profess to take those suspicions seriously and suggest that the integrity of Christian belief is made more convincing by doing so.[1]

Thus the vastly expanding practice and literature of pastoral counselling is in large measure a Christian attempt at the appropriation of the insights of modern psychology, beginning with Freud, in the service of religious belief. The religious belief which it seeks to serve is one which would not be vulnerable to Freud's analysis of it as projection and wish-fulfilment. Pastoral theology has among other things sought to rehabilitate belief in God on the basis that it contributes to human health rather than being the expression of psychopathology. In this response, God is not so much argued for against the Freudian critique of religion; rather, God is in a sense excused for what are accepted as the shortcomings of Christian representations of God down the ages. The concession that is made to Freud is to say that Christianity has misrepresented God, and therefore needs to take the Freudian critique seriously in its practice and in its representation of belief. By this means the Freudian critique is in essence bypassed; the argument runs that if Freud had met a form of religion that was productive of health he would not have argued as he did. Thus the 'unreal' God of human projection is displaced by the 'real' God who enables human persons to achieve health and freedom.

The Nietzschian critique of Christian faith as leading to a demeaning of the person has likewise been taken to heart by a number of Christian theologians. There is a readiness on the part of some to own that the Christian tradition has been understood (wrongly) in ways which undermine the stature of human persons. Among the most trenchant and well-known responses is that of Dietrich Bonhoeffer, who says of much Catholic and Protestant theology (and the existentialism and psychotherapy which he describes as its 'secularised offshoots') that it seeks to

> demonstrate to secure, contented, and happy mankind that it is really unhappy and desperate and simply unwilling to admit that it is in a predicament about which it knows nothing, and from which only they can rescue it. Wherever there is health, strength, security, simplicity, they scent luscious fruit to gnaw at or to lay their pernicious eggs in.[2]

In a famous paragraph, he goes on to describe such apologetic as pointless, ignoble and unchristian. He sees it as an attempt to force adult humanity back into adolescence and dependency, exploiting persons' weakness for purposes alien to them, based on confusing Christ with a 'particular stage in humanity's religiousness'.

Again, many Christian apologists have adopted a similar strategy in the face of the Marxist critique of religion. Thus theologians of liberation, for instance, have expressed the belief that a Marxist approach to present-day political struggles can and should be integrated with belief in the God of the Exodus, one who intervenes to liberate the oppressed. In his appearance in the synagogue at Nazareth (Luke 4.16–30) Christ presents himself, through his appropriation of the jubilee prophecy (Isaiah 61.1–4), as the one who is to usher in freedom for a people in bondage. Serious political engagement on behalf of the poor of the earth can create, as Alfredo Fierro sees it, a context in which a 'non-alienated' religion can be professed:

> At bottom it is a question of the credibility of the Christian message. The gospel becomes unbelievable when real-life conditions seem to be completely impervious to all good news. Thus social emancipation and the emergence of new horizons of liberty and justice are basic factors in determining the plausibility of the gospel message and its claims to truth.[3]

In one sense such theologians of liberation have come near to accepting a non-realist position concerning God's existence; for while sometimes God is spoken of as the one whom Christians regard as directing the revolutionary course of history, at other times they come close to saying that the reality of God, or at least the possibility of speaking of the reality of God, is *dependent upon* the creation of certain social conditions. So Fierro sees an analogy between a theology that would 'remain silent about God so long as our fellow human beings had something to reproach us believers for'[4] and the decision of Camilo Torres, the priest-turned-guerrilla, who reflected:

> I shall not say Mass, but I will flesh out that love of neighbor in the temporal, economic, and social sphere. When my neighbor has nothing to reproach me for, when the revolution has been carried through, then I will go back to saying Mass once again.[5]

While the language of liberation theology can sound very far from those whose philosophical and theological struggle is for the 'non-realist' position, we see here a significant point in common: religious faith is recognized as supremely the expression of the choices, the values and the commitments of those who profess religious faith. Both sets of thinkers approach expressions of Christianity with suspicion: in the former case, it is the ideological suspicion that class interests are operating; while in the latter case, non-realists also suspect that religious language is almost always an expression of the power or personal interest of the speaker, using the language for some often undeclared purpose. So Graham Shaw declares 'the appeal to God distracts attention from the human speaker. Heaven is silent, and when men's attention is directed towards it, we easily fail to notice that human lips are moving';[6] while Don Cupitt engagingly defends his preference for a continued debate about truth over a final settlement of the issues on the grounds that

> although I profess to love truth I could not actually endure a One-Truth universe, because even as the angels ushered me into Heaven I would still be nourishing the suspicion that it was all trumped-up, an illusion created by power. I sincerely believe that I would rather contemplate the conflict of two great truths and feel I had a choice between them, because that possibility of choice disperses power a little.[7]

Cupitt believes that this is his preference and that of his readers 'because we are Westerners and not Muslims', and that means that we 'gave up Truth and sold our souls, all for freedom's sake'. A Christian is, he says (without distinguishing a Christian here from a Westerner), 'a peculiar sort of monotheist who unexpectedly likes powerlessness'.[8]

Faith and power – gospel ideals and institutional realities

To approach religious utterances with the suspicion that they are likely to be veiling more sinister or manipulative intentions, however, need not mean that one is bound to have a wholly negative view of what that language offers. Close to the end of what must be one of the most 'suspicious' interpretations of the evidence of the manipulation of authority revealed in the New Testament, Shaw offers an account of the religion of the Gospel. His is certainly an uplifting vision of its subversive possibilities and therefore of the contribution it can make to the realization of human freedom:

> The God of the gospel sustains human freedom first of all by providing a vocabulary which readily challenges all human structures of authority and control. This subversive character is not temporary and circumstantial, something which is relevant to one society but not to another; it is one of the intrinsically Christian uses of the word God. The appeal to God negates all existing human claims – it places them in question, and thus enables the individual to resist them. Secondly, it provides a language which enables human beings to transcend the given, to achieve imaginative detachment.[9]

This statement of religious language and its possibilities significantly follows an interpretation of the use of that language by the New Testament writers which casts their manipulative use of authority and power in an extremely negative light: Shaw's New Testament writers certainly do not live up to Cupitt's commitment to a Christianity that 'unexpectedly likes powerlessness'.

The connection between religious faith and institutional power in every age is something it is hardly possible to doubt. The history of the preservation of orthodoxy is also a history of the use of power. The shock occasioned by Graham Shaw's extremely suspicious account of the exercise of authority in the New Testament period must signify more than a disagreement with the details of his New Testament scholarship, contentious as some of that is. There must also be within the churches a reluctance to accept that the use and manipulation of power has been a feature of the history of the Church from the beginning. Perhaps that reluctance is even greater when it comes to admitting that power is just as much a factor within the life of the Church today. Yet the occasion of this book is itself evidence that it is: granted the general importance of the issues, would this work have been commissioned but for the price Anthony Freeman has had to pay for the expression of his 'non-realist' opinions?

The dismissal of a priest for expressing views that are outside the boundary of what is thought acceptable by his bishop is fortunately very rare. It is, to say the least, an exceptional outworking of any church's need to have some boundaries around its membership and minimum qualifications for holding office within it. But the rare and often highly publicized cases of ecclesiastical discipline or censorship are not by any means the whole of the story.

For this particular and recent episode could well obscure the central role which is played by issues of institutional power in the shaping of religious convictions. For such exercises of discipline have a wider effect than what they accomplish in themselves. In part they happen *pour encourager les autres*, lest others who are appointed to teaching or pastoral offices should feel any temptation to take chances with dangerous opinions. In part also, they are responses to frequent upsurges of insecurity within the Church's membership which in certain moods is glad to see those in authority 'giving a firm lead'. Thus the power that is exercised over an individual can ripple outwards so as to effect a greater compliance among theologians and clergy at large.

There is, however, a more serious effect even than the limiting of freedom of discussion among theologians and clergy: the disciplining of 'unsound' opinions among the Church's appointed teachers also expresses and confirms a view of the recipients of that teaching, their role, and their capacity to make choices among conflicting views. The power structures that exist within the churches, especially when used to decide who is giving true teaching and who not, may present themselves as protection against the ultimate subversion of the Gospel. They may see themselves as intervening against the purveying of falsehoods that threaten the integrity of the faith in a fundamental way. Yet in seeking to do that, what they may in fact be doing (and appearances can easily deceive) is expressing (and thereby confirming) the view that the laity are, in effect, a theological lumpen proletariat. That is, such disciplining by commissions, bishops or whoever can easily suggest that the Church's members are unable to detect the merits of different arguments, let alone take part in them, if they have not themselves been 'theologically trained' (and it is usually the same structures of authority that have the power to decide what constitutes an adequate theological training).

The 'ripples' do not stop at the boundary of the Church either. Not least in an age when news travels fast and millions can be included in a popular discussion through mass media, the use of power in relation to truth is a public event, and makes a public statement. The statement that it makes, whether intentionally or not, is that those seeking to understand Christianity, or interested in discovering a spirituality or a religious meaning for their lives and unsure where to look for it, are to be regarded as *recipients* of what the Church has to say. That is to say, such would-be believers are not seen as participants in an *exploration* in which the churches, their members, ministers and teachers have resources of conviction and experience to offer, and to which those who are not yet believers (or at any rate not yet believers in the sense in which the churches have defined the term) bring questions, commitments, insights, or hints. They are not seen as bringing an essential contribution to the discernment of the meaning of the inheritance of faith which the churches are concerned to guard. To be specific and topical, the exercise of ecclesiastical power to draw boundaries around sound belief declares a view not just that the adherents of the Sea of Faith movement are mistaken in their religious opinions, but that their concerns are not part of what the Church needs to take seriously in discovering for itself more of the meaning of its own tradition of faith.

The guardianship of orthodoxy, therefore, vested in ecclesiastical authority, is not only supported by patronage and the other instrumentalities of power, but provides a transcendent justification for its possession of the power which it has. What this does is to determine the self-perception both of those with power and those without it, to the inevitable destruction of any possible mutuality in exploration. As Richard Roberts remarks in his analysis of the distribution of power within Anglicanism, it is easy for those with power in the Church to engineer the displacement of the conflict that is a part of the search for mutuality. In so doing they also obscure the 'original and final unity, the Alpha and Omega of the Christian rhetoric of salvation' by persuading themselves that the structures of the Church exist to promote and safeguard *its* unity; so 'Christian identity is put entirely and exclusively at the mercy of the informed virtuoso, the writer of Christian character, the Prince-Lord of the Church legislating for the identity of Christianity'.[10] What this makes inevitable is described by Roberts in terms which are even more trenchant than those employed in Graham Shaw's account of authority in the New Testament. Roberts' words certainly reflect the painful experience of many on the fringes of the Church and of its most questioning members. For what is bound to happen when one group sees itself as guardian of truth for another is nothing less than

> the corrupt, obfuscatory manipulation of others through the management of power at the most fundamental and insidious level, that is in the construction of the self-consciousness of the other. It is this 'other' that

dies in the Christian representation of the dialectic as embodied in the structure of *ordo* and *plebs*. This is not normally a violent public act but the quiet ecclesial practice of spiritual abortion, the unprotesting infantilisation of countless millions of embryonic believers upon whose behalf an essential ministry presumes to interpose.[11]

It would be a comfort to be able to assert unequivocally that the case Roberts presents is extreme, that the language of 'corruption' in particular is inappropriate to the conscientiousness with which the responsibilities of the guardianship of truth are generally discharged. Yet it is not necessary to regard such words as a personal attack on particular persons and offices in order to take them seriously.

For what Roberts is essentially portraying is an institutional process. That process may from time to time issue in benign actions by some individuals, and on other occasions in acts which should be condemned; more generally, however, it produces a failure to perceive what is at stake, to notice the role of power in shaping consciousness and to grasp the enormity of what is lost when those on the fringes of the institution or 'lower down' in its hierarchy have their insights and concerns devalued and are told at the same time that their devaluing is all in the cause of unity and truth. The experience of engaging with lay Christians whose experience of witness has primarily to be in the dispersed and often therefore isolated situations of the everyday – in encounters as varied as industrial mission, personal counselling, laity education, spirituality workshops or simply in the course of friendship and acquaintance – makes the force of such analysis all too clear: whatever may be the traditional justification of the churches' hierarchies, they have the in-built capacity to extinguish incipient faith and lay waste areas of enormous theological fertility in the lives of believers and near-believers without so much as noticing. Among those who have found that a non-realist account of faith is liberating are those who have had such experience of the 'real' God through the activities of the real Church.

God of our own making?

Approaching the inheritance of faith and the ecclesial structures that sustain, promulgate and guard it, on the basis of suspicion has therefore yielded much fruit in an honest perception of the situation we are in. It has encouraged an analytical approach to the narratives and texts which describe what got us to where we are, on the basis that it is possible to discern, below the level of what is said, the 'real' motivations and agendas of those who gave us them.

So Graham Shaw, having taken us on a suspicious journey through the New Testament, sees further disturbing signs of such manipulations of power in the songs of Israel, and therefore can see how they are able to be used for such purposes within the Christian community which continues to use them in worship. There is not much about the God so revealed that does not reflect discredit on those who portrayed him:

> The portrayal of God, who knows every action, thought and feeling, and the successful implanting of that belief in the minds of religious people, formed part of a subtle and successful system of religious leadership and control. Just as the doctrine of omniscience must primarily be understood in that context, so the doctrine of divine providence plays an essential part in the same system. While the doctrine of omniscience secured the most intimate sense of accountability, the doctrine of providence provided the sanctions of reward and punishment on which the system depended. Threats and promises are essential to any system of control, and of all the systems devised by men that of religious control has always been the most pervasive, embracing the whole of society and every facet of individual behaviour and disposition.[12]

Shaw is able to be specific about the ways in which the attributes of God as recited in the psalms contribute to the well-being, justice and sustenance of the people. Just as God's omniscience enables the human leaders of the community to evade their responsibility for the decisions they take, so the powers of the royal leadership of the people are seen as derived from the divine court in heaven. God's throne outdoes in splendour all the paraphernalia of the surrounding monarchies, and so vindicates the patterns of authority practised within the Hebrew kingdoms. The celebration of the power of God in the psalms is a reflection of the aspirations of a people who hoped to share in that power; while the justice of God, celebrated in the psalms as vastly more reliable and even-handed than any human justice of which the people had experience, nevertheless vindicated the position of privilege which the people of the psalms had over the surrounding gentile nations. All the celebrations of God's power and justice subserve what Shaw calls a 'tribal providence', the continued goodwill of God towards his chosen people and his continued enmity towards those who invade their territory and defile their holy places.

On his reading, the appeal to the reality of God always masks other purposes, and the purposes are hardly ever good. That is as true in the New

Testament period as in the period before Christ. What happens is that the exposed and humiliated Jesus, reconciled to being misunderstood and betrayed, the victim of those who use religion for power, is himself used for the very different purposes of the early Christian community. By revealing the self-interested character of much appeal to the nature and works of God, Shaw hopes to offer his readers a choice about the 'use of God'; by revealing that God is not the source of human religious sentiment but the creation of it, he hopes to extend to human beings the ability to create a 'religion of peace' that acknowledges their responsibility for God instead of using God as the means of evading responsibility.

On the face of it, Shaw's suspicion of 'God' seems to be well-founded; but what of his trust in the human will? Is all to be left to the realm of personal choice, or might that very choice need to be grounded in the perception that there is a true God and that there are false ones, one who has what it takes to be a God and others who do not? It is significant that among the psalms to which Shaw does not refer[13] is one which draws precisely that contrast. In the theological ferment of the 1960s, when the talk was of the 'death of God' rather than of non-realism, Psalm 82 turned out to be a not insignificant account of how it was that a god might die:[14]

> God has taken his place in the divine council; in the midst of the gods
>   he holds judgment:
> 'How long will you judge unjustly and show partiality to the wicked?
> Give justice to the weak and the orphan; maintain the right of the lowly
>   and the destitute.
> Rescue the weak and the needy; deliver them from the hand of the
>   wicked.'
> They have neither knowledge nor understanding, they walk around in
>   darkness; all the foundations of the earth are shaken.
> I say, 'You are gods, children of the Most High, all of you;
> nevertheless, you shall die like mortals, and fall like any prince.'
> Rise up, O God, judge the earth; for all the nations belong to you.

It is of course possible to 'suspect' this psalm for its concluding exposition of a 'tribal providence' or a 'providence of privilege'; but if so, it is remarkable for the hostage which it gives to fortune, like so much else that is 'suspicious' in the Scriptures. For in the declaration that divinity is tied up with justice and with a concern for the weak, the orphan, the lowly and the destitute, it offered a check against all future attempts to 'claim' or 'use' God in the interests of the powerful. The psalmist lays out here a statement of the structure of reality, about which we may need to decide whether it is true or false.

Any critique of a non-realist view must take seriously the abuses and manipulations to which religious language and claims have been liable, and the self-deceptions which it has encouraged in the hands of those who have employed it. The record is too clear and too devastating to be simply ignored. But the two questions which remain after the suspicions have been uttered are, first, whether human beings will cease their manipulations and self-deceptions simply because they know that they are solely responsible for the 'use' they make of God, or that as Cupitt maintains in his 'theory of God' we have made God out of nothing.[15] The evidence that human beings will exercise responsibility in favour of a religion of peace simply because they know that it is up to them is not altogether encouraging.

But the second question is more serious: it is whether an analysis of 'God' that focuses entirely on the self-interested agenda religion has served will suffice. In particular, will it do adequate justice to the points in the tradition where, often despite itself, it has left traces of a vision and a direction which it would not have been in its interest to reveal – unless they are in fact grounded in a reality outside the minds of those who spoke of them? Francis Watson suggests that the Bible has too global a dynamic to be allowed to be used to subserve the interests of a tribal providence or a parochial self-interest:

> If the triune God brings the world into being for its own sake but above all for the sake of human beings, made in his likeness to engage in dialogue with him, then this beginning must determine the theme and the scope of the story that follows. . . . [A] book which begins with the assertion that 'In the beginning God created the heavens and the earth' establishes, through the comprehensiveness of its scope, the expectation that the narrative will lead eventually to an equally comprehensive goal – as indeed it does, in the creation of new heavens and a new earth at the close of the book of Revelation. The universal horizons of this narrative do not permit the extraction of 'the story of Jesus' to serve as the legitimation-myth of a small community in its self-imposed exile from the world.[16]

Whatever part differing human motivations will have played in the origins of the Scriptures and the development of the Church's tradition, there remains a question whether they can be understood other than as a witness to the activity and self-disclosure of the triune God. It is also that perception of them which stands ready to undermine all present attempts to use the language of religion for purposes of institutional power and manipulation within the community which continues the scriptural narrative. When within that community there are conflicts and confrontations about the uses of the power vested in the institution, it is to more than the chosen values of individuals, power groups or particular communities that appeal has to be made; it is to the One whose purposes are imprinted by the human hands (though it be to their own inconvenience) in the narrative and tradition which contain the Gospel.

So (to take an example that came to mind in the recent commemorations of the fiftieth anniversary of the execution of Bonhoeffer) the German pastors in England, meeting in Bradford in 1933, confronted by the introduction of the Aryan paragraphs, had to base their appeal to the Church governing body in Berlin on nothing less than the heart of the Gospel and the reality of God's dealings with humankind. I say 'had to', because they spoke out of the same cultural formation as those whom they were addressing and were as concerned for the well-being of their homeland as those who were governing the Church within it. What sounds through the patriotism and the reluctance of their statement is that theirs was a stand to which they were compelled by a reality they could not evade:

> The sole basis of our communities is, and has been right from the time of its founding until the present day, the Biblical Gospel of Jesus Christ, the Redeemer, who by His death on the Cross and His Resurrection, has saved the world and will one day bring about its end.[17]

If such a use of language is to be described as 'manipulation', then it is not a manipulation which did much for the self-interest of those who issued that statement. No more has it done for those who in a vast variety of contexts have found within the Christian record a testimony that undermines the pretensions and manipulations of those who have used religion as a shield behind which to manipulate power. To claim the right to use such language against the institutional hierarchies who claimed to guard it has in fact required great courage and exacted a high price.

The power words need to have

This chapter began with the assertion that words are 'instruments of power'. The power religious words have had has indeed been and continues to be of a very ambiguous character. Our examination of some of the analysis of that ambiguity has shown why 'non-realism' seems to some the most attractive option. However, it has also brought us to the point where it becomes most doubtful whether we can do without a view of religious language as calling attention to, grounded in, claiming, struggling for, and in the end obeying, the Reality behind that language, and by the same token contesting its abuse.

If words have had power, it is important that our account of the way they exercise it it does not leave out of account ways in which that power has been used for which we have cause to be grateful. Even more important: we require explanations of the working of religious language that will not prevent it from performing tasks of prophecy and witness we know not when. When Don Cupitt remarks that 'the world is made, poetically, by God, and a little more prosaically, by religious language'[18] we may initially feel, and thousands clearly have felt, released from the power of those who, as God's agents, have used 'God' to mask (from themselves sometimes as well as from others) their own agenda. That is, we may feel released into an arena where we are free to have our dawning spiritual perceptions taken more seriously than the Church has managed to do. In that world it is good news that we are responsible for God and our use of 'God', and our prayers and our action have in them the sense of an authenticity that comes from their having been consciously chosen by us.

But in such a world there is missing, on the other hand, the One we are answerable *to*, and in whose name other gods have to be confronted because they do not have the reality, that is to say they do not have the justice, to be God. What Richard Roberts entertains as a vision for the Church could only be based in the reality of God and the forgiveness of God, because it would require a repentance which those who are clothed in power are not likely to see for themselves; it would require the

> climb into active, stirring consciousness of the *plebs Dei*, God's own proletariat, the people of God . . . and the enactment of a corresponding theological and institutional repentance which served to build structures of anticipation rather than merely to promote regression and conserve hierarchical power.[19]

This essay has not sought to engage with much of the philosophical grounds on which the realist/non-realist debate is carried on. It has chosen instead, in a way which I hope may gain at least the modest approval of some who call themselves non-realists, to receive the full force of their critique of the use to which religious language has been put. That is to say, it has sought to acknowledge what has been shown by their efforts, namely what words are up against in the power structures of those institutions which claim jurisdiction over how they are used.

But confronting those realities is something which I am persuaded words will only have the power to do if the reality behind the words is taken with full seriousness. The reality behind the words is One on whom we need to draw if that confrontation, on which the most powerless within and beyond the Church depend, is to be pursued to the point of repentance and renewal.

Notes

1 See for example Merold Westphal, *Suspicion and Faith: The Religious Uses of Modern Atheism* (Eerdmans, 1993).

2 Dietrich Bonhoeffer, letter of 8 June 1944, *Letters and Papers from Prison*, trans. John Bowden et al. (SCM Press, 1971), p. 326.

3 Alfredo Fierro, *The Militant Gospel: A Critical Introduction to Political Theologies*, trans. John Drury (Orbis, 1977), p. 388.

4 *The Militant Gospel*, p. 391.

5 *The Militant Gospel*, p. 390.

6 Graham Shaw, *The Cost of Authority* (SCM Press, 1983), pp. 15–16.

7 Don Cupitt, *Creation out of Nothing* (SCM Press, 1990), pp. 114–15.

8 *Creation out of Nothing*, pp. 114 and 115.

9 *The Cost of Authority*, p. 283.

10 Richard H. Roberts, 'Lord, bondsman and churchman: identity, integrity and power in Anglicanism' in Colin E. Gunton and Daniel W. Hardy (eds), *On Being the Church: Essays on the Christian Community* (T. & T. Clark, 1989), p. 221.

11 'Lord, bondsman and churchman: identity, integrity and power in Anglicanism', p. 222.

12 Graham Shaw, *God in Our Hands* (SCM Press, 1987), p. 52.

13 Apart from a passing reference to verse 5: *God in Our Hands*, p. 94.

14 I first heard this point made in an unpublished address by Harvey H. Guthrie, in Christ Church, Cambridge, Massachusetts, in 1965.

15 See *Creation out of Nothing*, pp. 113–56.

16 Francis Watson, *Text, Church and World* (T. & T. Clark, 1994), pp. 152–3.

17 *Celebrating Critical Awareness: Bonhoeffer and Bradford 60 Years On*, Conference Papers and Proceedings (International Bonhoeffer Society, 1993), p. 40.

18 *Creation out of Nothing*, p. 194.

19 'Lord, bondsman and churchman: identity, integrity and power in Anglicanism', p. 224.

7

On being a non-Christian 'realist'

Daphne Hampson

In his *Freeing the Faith* Hugh Dawes comments, of myself: 'Hampson is very clear on this matter of the radical discontinuity between past and present.'[1] Well, yes and no. I wish a *discontinuity* where the non-realists persist in an attempt to maintain continuity; while I am convinced of a *continuity* which they do not credit. Hence my title! It is the title moreover which I chose for the lecture I was kindly invited to give at the Sea of Faith conference in 1990. Having now read the 'non-realist' literature I have, however, put inverted commas around 'realist'; and to that I shall come. I shall, then, allow the question of discontinuity and continuity to structure my essay.

If there is to be meaningful debate over the question of the possible continuity with the Christian past, we shall need a more exact definition as to that in which Christianity necessarily consists than the non-realist open-endedness on the matter. Christians have always believed (it seems to me that this is simply a question of historical accuracy) that he whom they call Christ has a uniqueness.[2] Of course this uniqueness has been expressed in different ways in different periods; not all Christians have subscribed to Chalcedonian orthodoxy. Among Christians however the term 'the Christ' has always meant more than that Jesus was the long-awaited messiah. The earliest Christian statement of faith that we have is 'Jesus Christ, God's Son Saviour', which formed in Greek the acronym *ICHTHUS*, fish. To believe that Jesus was a very fine man with an admirable moral teaching, even that he was deeply in tune with God (a theistic position), cannot, I take it, be held to constitute a Christian position. The non-realist position represents a radical discontinuity from what Christians have always confessed: this needs acknowledgement.[3]

For myself, I am convinced that, subsequent to the European Enlightenment, we cannot credit that there could be any such uniqueness. One can only hold to such a uniqueness through a faith which flies in the face of reason; a leap which I see no justification for taking. Thus I am not a Christian. That is to say, I agree with Don Cupitt that around 1690 (his date) something quite new happened in the history of the world, which was to make Christianity as it had been known no longer tenable.[4] People came to realize that the world works according to laws; that history and nature form a causal nexus. The events surrounding Jesus were thus placed in a different context as incommensurate with what human beings now recognized. Søren Kierkegaard, in the 1840s, was the first to point clearly to the incompatibility of Christian claims with the rest of knowledge; though Hegel and Schleiermacher, recognizing the crisis, had each tried to find solutions which would bridge the gap. Karl Barth's proclamation (taking off from Kierkegaard) in the twentieth century of a revelation 'straight down from above' would have been unthinkable and unnecessary in the premodern world.

Christian theology had to become something quite other in a post-Enlightenment age from what it had earlier been. Or at least we may say that this is true of the largely German, Swiss, Dutch and American-German tradition, which was prepared to face modernity. (It is no credit to Catholicism that it has often failed to do so.) Christology in the nineteenth and twentieth centuries may be read as a quest to find some way of speaking which allowed of a uniqueness, while not contravening what was now known of the laws of nature. (This is true not least of modern Anglican theology.) I believe it to be a quest which has failed. In my estimation Rudolf Bultmann takes the prize with his original suggestion that Christian claims should be placed in another sphere of reality (*Geschichte*) from the everyday sphere (*Historie*) of the causal nexus. I have often thought that, were anyone to convince me as to the possibility of Christianity, it would be he; but again I see no reason to take his particular kind of leap. Unlike someone of his generation (and of his sex), it is conceivable to me that I should move outside the Christian framework.

I have before now found myself astonished that even educated people confuse in their minds that 'uniqueness', or 'particularity', which of course we all have (and Jesus too), and that 'uniqueness', or 'particularity', which must contravene our post-Enlightenment knowledge of the world, which Christians (either through speaking of the resurrection as a unique event, or in claiming that Jesus was differently related to God than are all other human beings) must claim for Christ. Nothing moreover, I must contend, has essentially changed (such as to allow the possibility of the uniqueness which Christians must claim for Christ) through the fact that we have now discovered there to be randomness at the sub-atomic level, or the advent of quantum mechanics. These matters I cannot here further discuss. I simply wish to point to the fact that, in regard to these basic axioms as to what kind of a religion is possible today, I take it that my position is also Cupitt's. I sympathize too with his reaction to the discourse of Christians:

> I [want] to ask the usual tomfool questions like, Where is this 'ascended Christ'? I mean, is he a bloke out there? What's heaven, what's glory, what *is* the right hand of God? Until all this talk has been tied into our late-twentieth-century experience, way of life, language and world-picture we cannot do anything with it.[5]

Secondly – and this is a different point – I think Christianity ethically untenable. Again my analysis is that of Cupitt, who alone among British theological writers of whom I am aware (has he perhaps read French feminist thought?) has a clear-eyed and sophisticated analysis of the relationship between the Christian religion and patriarchy:

> [S]o far woman has borne the main burden of culture. Do we understand that woman paid for God? That is, the objectification of God, his enthronement in all his glory and majesty as the supreme power and principle of all things, is the exact counterpart of the subjection of woman. For there to be the one, there had to be the other. . . . [T]he whole system works precisely by putting woman in general and her sexuality in particular at the opposite pole from God. . . .
>
> Thus woman has paid the price.[6]

Yes indeed. Christianity has been the undoing of woman in Western culture. Even in an age in which the secular world has largely escaped its grip, that religion must still serve to legitimize patriarchy.

Let us dwell on this for a moment. The symbolism of this, a Father–Son religion, whether it should have or not, has served to exclude women from the priesthood for two thousand years. Much worse, it has led to a denigration of woman as being 'the other' to the way in which God and therefore the good was symbolized. Women's sexuality has been conceived of as opposed to the spiritual (women have not been allowed to enter Christian sanctuaries), women have been held to invite temptation, while woman *par excellence* has been the daughter of Eve who needed redemption.

At its worst this has led to mass femicide, as for example in a period of about 200 years from the 1490s, during which something like a million[7] women were burnt as witches (at a time when, in 1550, London had a population of 60,000). Precisely, interestingly, the fear was that women were developing their own spirituality (held to be perverted), which was not subject to the male Christian church. Had I lived earlier I should have been burnt without further ado.

But then – I must say to the non-realists, as also to all Christians, though the more particularly to non-realists for they have less reason for clinging to Christianity – there is every reason to leave this religion behind. The fact that the symbols, the metaphors, the creeds of Christianity, are held by non-realists to be not actually true, does not help in the least. For it is precisely that masculinist symbol system which is so problematic. One must assume that a feminist of any description, Christian or not, finds this to be so. Personally I could in no way participate in a church service (albeit non-realist) in which God and humanity, men and women, occupy the respective places which they do within Christianity. Least of all would I be prepared to do this together with a man with whom I had a close personal relation. It would shatter any possibility of equality, and thus the relationship – unless of course he was as horrified as I should be.

Consider then the following statement of the non-realist position. Commenting on the way in which within Christian liturgies creeds 'are dramatically recited and thus embody communal recitations of past history',[8] David Hart compares them to epic poetry. Now epic poetry (and creeds!), we may agree with Hart, bring about a community's and an individual's self-understanding. What then is the construct of 'woman', of 'man', prevalent within epic poetry, or for that matter in creeds? 'We believe in God the Father Almighty . . . and in Jesus Christ his only Son, . . . born of the Virgin . . . ' etc. This is a particular symbolic construal of a world order. It does not help women! Hart continues, of the proposed non-realist Christian service: 'The Ministry of the Word follows, during which the congregation are invited to listen to the sacred history of Israel and the story of the Christ.'[9] That is to say, in a sacred setting, which is potent, men and women are invited to hear about a (male) God and his sons, the more especially about the 'Father' and the 'Son'. Hart comments: 'the effect remains that we hear a number of sacred stories.'[10] Yes I am sure the effect does remain: that is just the point! When a few pages later we discover that Hart wishes to 're-establish the Eternal Feminine'[11] we may well say, of such a non-realism, *plus ça change, plus c'est la même chose*. It sounds to me like ideological propaganda in favour of patriarchy!

But, one might suggest, a bit of tampering will do the trick. Christian feminists certainly seem to think so. Hart tells us: 'Liturgies . . . do need a broadening out, particularly along feminist lines, to release them from an outmoded hierarchism. For the Church of England, a reworked non-sexist version of the Alternative Service Book remains a high priority for the year 2000.'[12] May I ask, are such liturgies and service books to continue to refer to the Father and the Son? Will baptisms still be into this male Trinity? I am failing to see how the Band-Aid procedure will work. Will such ceremonies still be performed in churches with stained-glass windows depicting a man impaled on an executioner's gibbet, while women with covered heads gaze up at him? Not for me, thank you, such liturgies in such a 'place of worship'. The religion is what it is and what it must be, given that Christians believe in a unique revelation in history. They cannot evade making reference to that supposed revelation and reciting the scriptures which tell of it.

Nor is the problem simply the metaphors and the symbolism; the problem commences with the paradigms which that symbol system encapsulates. The non-realists (other than, at times, Cupitt) do not begin to consider this. Anthony Freeman in his *God in Us* suggests that the quest for religious meaning can be built around the Christian creed.[13] Hart tells us: '[W]e do not need to be convinced of the actual truth of the statements of faith . . . We can use them as maps.'[14] And Cupitt: 'You don't have to be a theological realist. You can take a symbolist view of dogma.'[15] But what if the maps lead in the wrong direction and the symbols encapsulate the wrong things? What if the very structuring of the Christian faith may be appropriate to men, or may have been meaningful in our past society, but is not in the least apposite to women today, nor perhaps to many men? To give an example. Christianity, says Hart, 'calls us to deny the self'. No doubt. But I may think it profoundly unhelpful – given the analysis of that state of mind which patriarchy has induced in them – that women, in any straightforward sense, should be encouraged by their religion to deny the self. What women need, as many feminist writers have pointed out, is rather, in the words of Judith Plaskow, 'self-actualization'.[16]

Yet further: if we are rightly to see things for what they are, we must raise the uncomfortable question as to how far the symbol system of Christianity was created (no doubt unconsciously rather than consciously) both in order to explain man's place to himself in a patriarchal world and moreover in order to justify that place. God, man and woman are, in Christian symbolism, mutually held together in a complex order. The man's place is one of sonship: he identifies with Christ in relation to 'the Father'. As God is 'male' in relation to a humanity designated as 'female' (the people of Israel or the Church), so man ('female' in relation to God) is 'male' in relation to woman, who is always designated as the other. Woman as virgin is both a projection of man's imagination, and, as woman, the necessary mediator in the male/male genealogy. The symbolic structure of Christianity will take much exploration. We are only beginning in a post-Freudian, feminist age to think it through. Thus, for example, Cupitt writes: 'We will picture a postmodern eucharist as a ceremonial enactment of the death and dispersal of God. . . . [D]ying [he] communicates his power and creativity to us.'[17] I should think such a sentence in some way to reflect male sexuality. Even were the language and symbols to be inclusive, the paradigms around which Christianity revolves are by no means necessarily relevant to women.

I think then that there is a failure – not surprising considering how long Christianity has reigned – on the part of non-realists, as also liberal Christians, to recognize the depth to which the feminist challenge goes. (Conservatives have often grasped this better.) There seems to be prevalent the sentiment that the Church has got it wrong and that it must, as a matter of urgency, include women. With the ordination of women half the battle has been won; now something has to be done about the Church's language. Dawes writes:

> Accepting that we work with a limited number of insights and principles drawn from our perception of the God of Jesus, along with the best information available to us today, we could for our present time resolve the issue of the dignity and status of the sexes . . . very speedily. Then we could get on to some of those wider themes . . . [18]

But Christianity does not simply consist in an ethic such as Dawes would have us pursue; an ethic (this is a different question) which we might all agree upon. What if the very *raison d'être* of Christianity, as I am increasingly coming to suspect, has in part been the justification of patriarchy, making it seem natural? Then the attempt to patch up the religion is naive at best and ultimately must fail.

Indeed, one might well say the following. Given that a person believes Christianity to be true – he or she holds the bible to be inspired, these metaphors to be God-given, God to have sent his Son; given that a person believes these things, one understands why he or she continues to employ Christian symbolism. If however one no longer holds such beliefs, may it not be morally reprehensible to continue to do so? Non-realists lack any excuse. Cupitt – remarkably – is convinced that language actually forms our world for us. (To a discussion of this I shall come.) Whatever one may think about his particular formulation of the relationship of language to 'reality', it is not to be denied that symbols, metaphors and language carry political import for the ordering of human relationships. Indeed, as we should expect, we find that Cupitt is worried about the hierarchical language of Christianity: 'To radicals, the somewhat Old-Testament, objectified, monarchical Sky-Father idea of God that prevails in Christian worship is very difficult.'[19] Yes indeed. Why then not let it go?

Furthermore the following must be said. As long as men continue with Christianity, if only with its shell, there is no possibility of their being able to repent of what has befallen women in Western culture. Repentance is a complex notion; it is something to which individuals, groups, or nations, must be brought of their own volition. Yet if, as I do, one longs for women and men to find a way forward together, then one ardently wishes (as the necessary prerequisite of this) that men should be brought to dissociate themselves from their past. What we need – as Cupitt without drawing the necessary consequences of this apparently recognizes – is that men should see the enormity of what they have done. Of course one does not hold individuals responsible, any more than one holds the younger generation of Germans (who add so much interest to one's classes in a British theology faculty these days) responsible for the actions of their parents, or more likely their grandparents. Those students must however, by their demeanour and their opinions (as they do), clearly dissociate themselves from that past. Then we can move forward together. Were men to recognize what their religion (let it be categorically stated) has meant for women, then the future could open out. It is the lack of readiness of men, even those who don't actually believe it any longer, to leave the Christian myth behind which strikes one as inexcusable.

What is fuelling the male desire, manifested even by those men who freely admit the 'truth' of Christianity to be an untruth, to stand in continuity with the past? It must seem to an outsider, a woman, that it has something to do with an overriding need to be good sons; to gain legitimacy through being rightful heirs. Such a genealogy is apparently crucial to the male psyche. (That one may be fascinated by European culture and wish to validate that which has been good, even within Christian culture, is quite another matter.) There is a kind of inability on the part of non-realists to be free of something, the Christian Church and religion, which they have loved. It must be important to anyone not to conclude that they have spent years of their life proclaiming something which they now see to be untrue. When one considers how difficult it has been for a woman like myself to make such a break – without doubt the most difficult transition of my life – this becomes comprehensible, though not excusable. Nor is it to cast aspersions on these men's motives to comment that if one's salary and the security of one's family are tied to one remaining an insider it must be doubly hard. One's situatedness inevitably affects what one believes. I do not doubt but that my wishing to be ordained led me to try to take on board (and believe that I had in some sense managed to do so) dogmas which at some level in myself I always knew I could not credit. But such human needs must not serve to disguise from us the necessity of moving on.

I do then think, as Dawes says of me, that there must be a profound rupture with the religion of the Christian West. We have not yet taken the measure of such a discontinuity. If they are to remain effective, symbol systems cannot lag too far behind the social structure of a society. Increasingly Christianity lacks the necessary correlation; and it is feeling the strain. The overcoming of patriarchy must surely shatter the religion. Given that it is not simply an ethic, but a symbol system, embodying certain paradigms and reflecting a certain set of relations, Christianity cannot adapt. What will follow (or whether we should welcome Christianity's demise) is of course an entirely different question. It is I believe difficult for us at present to take the measure of the damage which this religion has done: we are still too close to it. The trouble is that until we undertake a real break with the Christian past, there can be no recognition of what Christianity has meant for half of humanity.

Yet on the other hand non-realists fail to credit that continuity which I, for one, think that we may maintain with the past. Here I skate on thin ice. I shall need to make generalizations. However, the matter is too important for us not to consider. There would appear to be a real difference between, on the one hand, the experience of many women (whether or not connected with the Church and Christianity) and, on the other, the outlook of many men in relation to questions of spirituality. I surmise that men have not really begun to recognize where many women find themselves in relation to spirituality today; which bears perhaps no little continuity with what women have always known. If I am right, the falling away of Christian dogma will consequently mean something very different to men than to women. It is men who have something to learn here. But my experience is that many men find it notoriously difficult to hear these kinds of things!

The difference which I shall try to elucidate has never struck me more forcefully than when I attended the Sea of Faith conference; doubtless that is why it is uppermost in my mind. I think myself to have taken on board a feminist analysis of the world, yet once and again the marked difference between men and women catches me by surprise. It seemed to me that there was a gulf between the agenda of, at least, the dominant men at Sea of Faith and that of many of the women. I remember that it was a matter of intense irritation to some of the men that I spoke of religious experience and spirituality. (That together with the fact that I pointed to the male bias of Christianity, which they seemed scarcely to have considered.) Among the women on the other hand (and some of us came together in a group to discuss my talk) many were looking for a way to move forward as spiritual persons. Some of what transpired in that group was superb. I remember taking away with me some of the thoughts that people had (anonymously) written.

Nor has this been a unique experience. I think of another large gathering of liberal Christians where there was a mood of real anger (among the men generally) about the Church and what was thought to be the rising tide of conservatism and fanaticism within it. This is surely comprehensible. Men who have been ordained (in particular) have given their lives to the Church. As it has become narrower and many have left, they have tried to keep their modern, open faith. They are the people who have hung in there; they have hoped for something more enlightened. Besides which they are tied by invisible bonds to the whole institution, to those with whom they trained, their mentors and men's past history. There is nowhere else to go. By contrast and relatively speaking, it has been easier for women either to leave or to belong to a kind of women's sub-world within the bounds of the Church. A plethora of more or less radical women's and feminist organizations concerned with issues of spirituality and religion have sprung up in recent years. Given the strong ties they have with one another women can let the institution of the Church go its own way. I too was a keen member of the Student Christian Movement in the 1960s; but I have not had to continue in the Church in order to be part of a community of like-minded people.

Moreover there is something else here which we should note. Again I think it is primarily men who need to learn and to use their imagination. Men are inclined to think that Christianity is 'objective' and 'true'; perhaps the fact that its paradigms seem natural to them, or that its narrative tells largely of the doings of men, aids this. Religion becomes something social; it holds together a band of brothers (the male clergy), by extension the Church and even the society. To be religious is to believe this objective system: that God created the world, sent his Son, etc. By contrast the kind of way in which women are inclined to speak of spirituality seems to men to be 'personal', 'subjective', 'emotive', and 'individual'. Perhaps men in our society do not, on the whole, enjoy the kind of personal relations with other people which allows awareness of God to arise? To speak with one's friends of God would involve letting down the barriers too far.

May I suggest that the tables need to be turned? The 'objectivity' of the male religion, Christianity, may be nothing of the sort, but rather a projection of male needs, hopes, fears and sexuality. (It is, after all, a rather fantastic and unlikely story.) It appears to be objective because it has been believed for so long by so many. Moreover it is tied into history, in that it is predicated upon the life of a particular historical person, Jesus of Nazareth. Until the rise of feminism there has been no way in which this story could be relativized and seen for what it is. Of course it is the case that from the Enlightenment forwards one or another part of it has been seen to be mythical. But men have then made that movement side-ways which the non-realists now take to its logical conclusion; they have proclaimed it a 'true myth'. What if Christianity isn't a 'true myth' at all but one which is highly distorting of human relations? To relativize the myth, to understand it to be the product of men living under patriarchy, is to see through it. Cupitt seems to recognize this:

> The main tradition . . . idealized a stable patriarchal order. . . . There was no Otherness [the term he has associated with woman], no unconscious, no exclusion: *no argument*, as they say. But, you will remember, Woman started asking awkward questions and the divine order began to come apart.[20]

Yes: it is coming apart.

Meanwhile many women – including very many women whom I know – have an utter conviction that (to employ a favourite term of mine) there is another dimension of reality. They do not necessarily express this in Christian terms, though I am sure that those who have remained within the Church do. One friend of mine – to whom I mentioned this article which I was about to write – said she used the word 'godding'. By 'godding' she meant that activity by which we make God present to one another; perhaps we should write 'god', or substitute spirit, power or love. She will light a candle so that every time she sees it she is reminded to focus on someone in need. A former student of mine once struck me by speaking of 'God coming into being through us'; again a relational notion. I have not the slightest doubt as to the powers of healing, extra-sensory perception and love which can pass between people. It was William Temple who remarked: 'When my friends pray for me, things happen.'[21] Far from a religious position founded in such a spirituality being 'subjective', it is making a claim (a 'soft' rather than a 'hard', but still an empirical claim) about the way in which things are.

Might not such a religious position have a much greater claim to 'objectivity' than one built on a – highly tenuous – myth?

It is here that continuity with the past lies. For one must surely credit – according to the very axioms which I set out at the beginning of this essay – that the world has a certain constancy: that if there is that dimension of reality which we may call 'God' then this has always been the case. Thus I do not for a moment doubt that Jesus of Nazareth was one who, perhaps supremely in Western history, was able to actualize God in the world. He brought others moreover to an understanding as to how they too might use that power. So I find myself foxed by the apparent dismissal among the non-realists (who are or have been clergymen) of the possibility of any kind of spiritual awareness. Dawes characterizes prayer as 'words uttered into the void'.[22] That is not my experience. For my friends to focus on me in my need is extraordinarily powerful. The fact that there is that which is more than are human beings individually, which passes between human beings, which we can actualize and bring into play, is what I mean by 'God'. What 'God' actually is we do not know. It may be intrinsic to the universe as a whole, perhaps interwoven with matter. These are large questions. Like Cupitt, I suppose that we need a much more 'dispersed' notion of God.[23] Though, unlike Cupitt, I am actually talking about God and not simply an idealized notion of human beings!

Am I then a 'realist'? I had had no doubt that I was! I certainly think the term 'God' to refer. However the way in which those who call themselves 'non-realists' speak of what 'God' would be were there a God (a kind of anthropomorphic being of the male sex) is certainly not a God I think to exist. But then   as I recently commented to David Hart – I am not sure that Thomas Aquinas or Friedrich Schleiermacher are realists according to this definition either! I grant that I may have moved further out than these two thinkers – I live in a different age – but I stand in continuity with what at least Schleiermacher expressed that 'God' might be. I do not doubt, I should have thought, that I conceive of God very differently than did Jesus of Nazareth, standing as he did in the Jewish, monotheistic tradition in a patriarchal world. Yet even this is ambivalent. We all of us lack words for expressing what it is we mean by God. We cannot, can we, think that Gregory of Nyssa (to whom the doctrine of the Trinity in large part owed) really thought that God was actually like the images he conjured up? But then he belonged to a tradition in which all language was recognized as inadequate. To acknowledge this does not mean that the models and imagery which we use are anything other than of supreme importance in shaping what God is for us.

So here we must enter into the debate with Cupitt about language and reality. I do not believe that human beings would have held on to the Christian myth for 2,000 years, however falsely objectifying and however distorting it may have been, had it not, in part, reflected their attempt to express something which they knew to be the case. Though it may no longer be tenable, Christianity in the past has served to bring into focus and to explain their experience to people. When it comes to something so fleeting, if also so actual, as that love and power which we call God, it is difficult for us to grasp in adequate words what we would say. To say this is not to imply that there is pre-linguistic experience for which we (subsequently as it were) find words. Post-Derrida it must seem a dubious proposition that there can ever be such a thing as 'pure' religious experience. Words or imagery, we have every reason to think, pervade our understanding.

To say however that 'all there is' (as Cupitt seems to) is language, seems both superficial and patently untrue. It is certainly not what Derrida himself intends – if I may be permitted to quote him back at Cupitt!

> It is totally false to suggest that deconstruction is a suspension of reference. Deconstruction is always deeply concerned with the 'other' of language. I never cease to be surprised by critics who see my work as a declaration that there is nothing beyond language, that we are imprisoned in language; it is, in fact, saying the exact opposite. The critique of logocentrism is above all else the search for the 'other' and the 'other of language'. Every week I receive critical commentaries and studies on deconstruction which operate on the assumption that what they call 'post-structuralism' amounts to saying that there is nothing beyond language, that we are submerged in words – and other stupidities of that sort. Certainly, deconstruction tries to show that the question of reference is much more complex and problematic than traditional theories supposed. It even asks whether our term 'reference' is entirely adequate for designating the 'other'. The other, which is beyond language and which summons language, is perhaps not a 'referent' in the normal sense which linguists have attached to this term. But to distance oneself thus from the habitual structure of reference, to challenge or complicate our common assumptions about it, does not amount to saying that there is *nothing* beyond language.[24]

Is it too much to suggest that the greater subtlety which deconstruction has introduced into the question of the nature of the relation of language to the 'other' of language may serve us well in theology? For that of which precisely we are in need is more subtle ways of expressing those effects which we call God which are bound up with our human reality.

The most fascinating question here – which for me represents the cutting edge of theology – is whether the new consciousness present among women will give rise to new ways of expressing spirituality. Or perhaps it is no new consciousness, but one which has often been present. Free from the necessity of subscribing to the Christian myth, women today have the possibility of expressing themselves. If it is the case that social relationships, particularly the understanding of selves-in-relation, give rise to language and to conceptions, then it may well be that feminism, representing as it does a very real break with the past, will in time present us with new paradigms for that which we mean by 'God'. For the first time in Western history, we are witnessing the possibility of women, without coercion, being able to think out how it is that they would represent their religious consciousness.

Cupitt's 'Church' of the future is – let us face it – a farce. I quote:

> The historic buildings will still be in use. The gathering will consist of a common meal . . . One of [the congregation's elected officers] will open the meal by standing, banging for attention, and breaking a bread roll, saying: 'the body of Christ' . . . During the meal church business is transacted . . . Tasks are allocated. . .
>
> The chief divisions [of the Church] are Study (courses, evening classes, groups), Training (personal counselling, meditation, yoga), Art (music, drama, the visual arts) and Social Action (including local branches of human rights groups, twinning relationships with overseas congregations, and political action).[25]

Why not, one may ask, let those who are interested in the arts or social work simply meet together without further ado? What end should it serve that a large number of people come together in a great barn of a church and recite together a liturgy in which they no longer have any belief? Cupitt himself, in his latest writing, seems to have abandoned these proposals. Now he tells us, of Jesus: 'He does not join in public worship. When he prays, he prays alone, or with his friends.'[26] Doubtless this small group activity – the benefits of which women have always known – better conforms to the postmodern thesis!

It is the community of women, particularly those who have left behind any kind of orthodox Christianity, who I believe represent the best hope for the future. Cupitt tells us, in a chapter called 'Strategies for Christian survival': 'We need to belong to the church. We have no other place to start from. . . . One-man [sic] religion is madness . . . We've got to work within a tradition; so we've got to belong to the church.'[27] But why? Having left the Church seventeen years ago now I have had quite other 'strategies for survival'. Much of Cupitt's prognosis is bleak. I have a whole circle of friends who speak much as I do of spirituality. Again Hart concludes, of radicals in relation to the Church: 'we should stay and fight our corner.'[28] I am not sure how radical I find this. It sounds like male behaviour in a male club. Far from thinking that women should take their place alongside men in this Church, I wish that men would join women. Through the obvious clash between its philosophy and the ethical norms of our society, the Church would appear to have been tying itself in knots during the past two decades.[29] It has been way behind the secular world in honouring women and their rights. Would it be uncharitable – to extend the metaphor – to suggest that we give it enough rope?

We cannot continue with the religion of the past; nor should we excuse it. Through the Enlightenment and all that has flowed from it there has been a fundamental break with the ancient and medieval worlds. Given that we can no longer believe in the particularity which Christianity must necessarily proclaim, we can no longer be Christian. Since Kant moreover (and this has simply been reinforced by Derrida's attack on metaphysics), we cannot naively credit that there is a 'real beyond', which in time past seemed self-evident and which Christians have conceptualized as an anthropomorphic God. The post-Freudian feminist analysis, raising as it has the spectre that Christianity is in large part a masculinist projection, one which, through its invasion of Western culture, has served to legitimize patriarchy, has driven the nail into the coffin.

What theology can and must do is to respond to the advance both in human knowledge and in human ethical standards. (It becomes unclear how Cupitt's brand of relativism allows us to undertake the necessary evaluation?) I may not doubt but that theology in the West (viz. that ideology which is Christianity) has been a masculinist construct; even that its *raison d'être* has been the disempowerment of women. Yet that people in all ages have known of that power and that love which is God is something that I should never wish to deny. To contend that Christianity is, without remainder, an ideology designed to prop up the *status quo* would be to go too far. Would that men should join women in the endeavour to carry forward that possibility of a spiritual awareness which is our heritage.

Notes

1 Hugh Dawes, *Freeing the Faith* (SPCK, 1992), p. 125.

2 The question of the bounds as to what may be called Christianity is discussed in my *Theology and Feminism* (Blackwell, 1990), p. 50, and in detail, in response to critics, in my *After Christianity* (SCM Press, 1996), ch. I.

3 On the matter of vocabulary, it would be good to point out that endless confusion may be caused by the adoption in recent writing by Don Cupitt of the term 'post-Christian' for a secular position, since this term has now come to be widely used by those, such as myself, who hold a spiritual position in continuity with the Western tradition which has however discarded the myth of Christianity.

4 Don Cupitt, *After All* (SCM Press, 1994), p. 36.

5 Don Cupitt, *Radicals and the Future of the Church* (SCM Press, 1989), pp. 105–6.

6 *Radicals and the Future of the Church*, pp. 94–5; see also pp. 3–4, 92ff.

7 The number given greatly varies. This itself is significant. It was a hidden genocide. At a time when Europe was experiencing the Renaissance, the beginning of scientific thought, and the dawning of Enlightenment ideals, it made no impact on major male thinkers.

8 David Hart, *Faith in Doubt* (Mowbray, 1993), p. 78.

9 *Faith in Doubt*, p. 81.

10 *Faith in Doubt*, p. 81.

11 *Faith in Doubt*, p. 90.

12 *Faith in Doubt*, p. 91.

13 Anthony Freeman, *God in Us* (SCM Press, 1993).

14 *Faith in Doubt*, p. 77.

15 *Radicals and the Future of the Church*, p. 118.

16 Judith Plaskow, *Sex, Sin and Grace: Women's Experience and the Theologies of Reinhold Niebuhr and Paul Tillich* (University Press of America, 1980), p. 3.

17 *Radicals and the Future of the Church*, p. 98.

18 *Freeing the Faith*, p. 81.

19 *Radicals and the Future of the Church*, p. 168.

20 *After All*, p. 116.

21 If any reader has the reference for this, I shall be most grateful for it. I read it many years ago and have carried it with me in my life.

22 *Freeing the Faith*, p. 28.

23 Cf. *Radicals and the Future of the Church*, p. 97; *After All*, p. 23.

24 Jacques Derrida in Richard Kearney (ed.), *Dialogues with Contemporary Continental Thinkers: The Phenomenological Heritage* (Manchester University Press, 1984), pp. 123–4.

25 *Radicals and the Future of the Church*, p. 170.

26 *After All*, p. 22.

27 *Radicals and the Future of the Church*, p. 100.

28 *Faith in Doubt*, p. 76.

29 Cf. Cupitt's analysis: 'The ethical is going to be our Trojan horse.' *Radicals and the Future of the Church*, p. 126.

8

Non-realism for beginners?

Jeff Astley

A lot of it about

Clearly non-realist religion has attracted a number of articulate followers. It is arguable that similar views are shared by sizeable numbers of 'non-devotees' within the less articulate general population, and perhaps even in the churchgoing population, of this country. Quantitative research suggests that the *majority* of the 70 to 75 per cent who claim in surveys to 'believe in God' understand by the term 'God' some impersonal life force, pantheistic notion or even moral principle, rather than a personal God.[1] These less orthodox believers come in a variety of forms, but all of them have taken leave of – or never held on to – the more traditional concept of a deity.

Robert Towler has outlined several 'ideal types' of conventional religion in his, admittedly rather odd, sample of over four thousand who wrote letters to John Robinson after the publication of *Honest to God* (1963). Among them he distinguishes 'exemplarism'. This is a pragmatic form of religiousness, often unchurched and private, that sees in Jesus' teaching, life and death an example for all to follow. For this style of Christian thinking, God is often redundant and the supernatural in general either viewed agnostically or denied: 'exemplarism does not believe in God or in the life after death, in sin or in salvation.'[2] These matters are not regarded by the exemplarists as profitable for ethics or spirituality. Defining it as a 'Christian form of humanism', Towler notes among the doctrines that exemplarism is willing to embrace that of a perfectible humanity. He describes its cognitive style as *hoping*, but purely in the sense of an orientation to a better future rather than any 'as-if' believing directed to a transcendent object whom one hopes for and believes-in, without quite 'believing-that' he exists.[3] Here is a this-worldly eschatology that forms part of a horizontal world view: a faith on the level. Towler offers examples of exemplarism from ecclesiastically tangential groups as well as within the great company of the unchurched, and mentions Don Cupitt as a contemporary exemplarist.

Exemplarism may be said to be a particularly English form of Christianity. Richard Hoggart's account of working-class culture in the 1950s reveals an identification of Christianity with a rather undemanding type of kindness. This corresponds closely with Edward Bailey's more recent studies of the 'implicit religion' of an ordinary English parish.[4] The theology is thin, and kept very much in the background so as to avoid religious 'enthusiasm'. While many of its advocates would agree with Cupitt that 'there must be no more pixie-dust' in religion,[5] most would beg to be excused his more severe inner discipline and his preaching of the way of the cross through disinterested *agapē*. Perhaps there is a reason for this.

A large number of those who admit to a non-realist religious viewpoint have not seriously embraced religious realism first. Their theology, spirituality and (particularly) religious practice are thus likely to be rather different from those being considered in this book. We are concerned here primarily with a Christian *post-realism*, a species of non-realist Christianity that is perhaps not likely to appeal greatly to, or be much understood by, those who have not at some stage seen things very differently themselves. Christian post-realism is a religion for converts, with all that that implies psychologically and socially as well as theologically. To say this, of course, is not to criticize it, let alone to dismiss it. But it may help to draw attention to, and perhaps explain better, some of its features.

Pedagogy and development

Pedagogical issues have a certain relevance here, drawing on the psychology of learning and its facilitation. Teaching often needs to take the form of benevolent lying. Teachers make things clear partly by ignoring their complexity; they adapt the Truth-as-they-see-it, transforming it into truths-as-others-can-see-them. Doctrines of progressive revelation have made similar claims about a kindly, accommodating God who does not teach everything at once, but waits for the individual or the race to achieve

101

the appropriate readiness for new learning. It is quite acceptable, therefore, to teach Newtonian physics or single-factor Mendelian genetics as if they were the whole truth, for unless the students have grasped *that* they will not be able to advance to more sophisticated accounts. The same is true in philosophy. 'Everything is made of water' or 'Only minds and their ideas exist' may seem bizarre places to start, but new students are often more able to cope with such broad-brush positions than with the nuances of much contemporary philosophical discussion. We might make a similar point about the subtleties of modern theology.

But there is an additional problem with some forms of theology. I refer to the danger in introducing 'postliberal' or postmodernist understandings of theology too early in the curriculum, for these are essentially reactions against what has gone before, viz. liberal theology and Enlightenment rationality. How can the learner really get the hang of such movements unless and until she has first grasped, and indeed been enticed and grasped by, the insights, values and thought-forms that they now find inadequate? It seems to me that this is one of the main issues with regard to post-realism. In *teaching about* this form of non-realism, we shall need to start further back and take our time. It would be a mistake to begin with non-realism. Further, we should acknowledge that post-realists are perhaps more readily understood by realists, who can at least appreciate where they have been, rather than by those non-realists who have never visited that foreign land and whose empathy is therefore restricted.

But what of *teaching non-realism* rather than just teaching about it? When we come to consider a person's own beliefs, it should be recognized that the history of those beliefs is important. Thus the relativism of those who have been absolutists is different in kind from the 'adolescent relativism' of people who have never embraced any other view. And the atheism of the once-born atheist for whom God has never been a live option is a world away from the loss of faith – or, better, metamorphosis of faith – undergone by the believer. After all, the death of God is only an item of traumatic news that changes everything to those for whom God was once alive. What does this suggest about the nature of a 'confessional' religious education *into* a non-realistic form of faith? Is that dependent on a preliminary stage of induction into theological realism? Before considering this question further, however, we should explore the suggestion that the shift from realism to non-realism may itself be a product of a psychological change brought about by a *developmental process*, relatively independent of changes resulting from learning or unlearning a particular view of the nature of God.

In many ways *Life Lines* is the most interesting of Cupitt's books, especially for those who find that they cannot walk the whole of the expressivist way with him. The 'kind of Metro map of the spirit' proposed there, with its sixteen stations and web of connecting lines, is intended to accommodate a variety of life-routes of the religious life. Drawn partly from the author's own biography and his interpretation of the history of ideas, it is presented as a series of positions that 'moves (roughly) from birth to death', broadly following 'the traditional Way of Purgation, seen now as a long process of demythologizing'.[6] Cupitt's 'defiant' assertion that the individual's development recapitulates the 'thought-history of the race', much in the way that the developing embryo of a species reveals something of the pattern of its evolution, is suggestive.[7]

It may be helpful to trace some parallels with accounts of the development in individuals of 'human faith' or meaning-making. James Fowler's research into the form, pattern or structures of our faith-knowing and valuing describes changes in the ways in which we understand and relate to that which we take to be ultimate (our 'centres of value and power' and 'master stories'). Although he attempts to separate the content of faith from its form, tracing up to six stages in the development of the latter, Fowler acknowledges that form and content intimately interact.[8] Changes in the way we believe may well be capable of precipitating changes in what we believe, and vice versa. Fowler's account also allows for – and indeed demands – that people rework the contents, foci, images and stories of their faith as they develop in the way they think, make sense of things, relate to others and interpret symbols. Thus, for example, concrete, literal-mindedness often goes along with a particular anthropomorphic image of God; whereas abstract thought, and especially the later development of more complex and inclusive thinking, in turn generate a very different account of the objects of our believing.

Cupitt is more concerned with the contents of faith, but his remarks also relate to some extent to patterns of reasoning and valuing. Thus in the chapter entitled 'Genesis', the developing cognition of the baby is delineated in a fashion that is sometimes reminiscent of Fowler's stage of *primal* faith. Similarly Cupitt describes 'Mythical Realism' as corresponding to the thought world of infancy, and a parallel may be drawn here with Fowler's stage of unordered and impressionistic *intuitive-projective* faith as well as with his next stage of story-dominated *mythical-literal* faith. Cupitt's 'Doctrinal', 'Ladder', 'Designer' and 'Obedientiary Realism' could be said to correspond with the move, usually in late childhood or early adolescence, to *synthetic-conventional* faith and then to the either–or, cut and dried form of *individuative-reflective* faith more typical of adulthood. For Fowler, however, this latter transition is treated as a shift from (psychologically) heteronomous to autonomous faith, whereas Cupitt would not predicate autonomy of any kind of theological realism (apparently as much on logical as on psychological grounds).

Fowler has also described a transition that some undergo later to a more complex *conjunctive* faith: a form of faithing that adopts a more inclusive, both–and approach to other world-views. Interestingly, he claims that this stage change recapitulates a development from Enlightenment rational autonomy (with its over-confidence in clarity) to those less tidy, multi-perspectival post-Enlightenment modes of consciousness that embrace plurality and relativity.[9] The thought-forms of conjunctive faith, we may note, are rarely developed before the age of thirty. One wonders if Cupitt's anti-realism, which is sometimes presented as a form of 'perspectivism' in which 'no one vision of things can any longer be compulsory',[10] is similarly related to cognitive structures – and indeed to age and stage of life. The experience of those chaplains and teachers in higher education who keep in touch with their students confirms that the breezy theistic (or atheistic) certainties of the student years often mutate into something more porous and many-sided. 'Growing up in faith' involves coming to adopt a new openness to others and their viewpoints, and a new ability to keep in tension the paradoxes and polarities of faith and life, as well as a maturity that comes from knowing 'the sacrament of defeat and the reality of irrevocable commitments and acts'.[11] Nevertheless, Fowler insists that this stage of embracing multiple meanings and perspectives does not necessarily develop into the sort of relativism that Cupitt describes. It may eventually transform, however, into the vanishingly rare stage 6 where 'life is both loved and held to loosely',[12] and which is described as a stage of free, universalizing, selfless faith. This could easily take as one variant form the postmodernist, kenotic or Buddhist 'self-giving and self-loss' that Cupitt describes as our proper final attitude – the terminus of 'Good Night', in which 'life can be loved in its transience, and disinterestedly'.[13]

Despite these hints,[14] the scope for claiming that non-realism, even in its post-realistic form, is simply a product of development is limited. It may be that there are elements in the non-realist's psyche that can plausibly be taken as dependent on psychological development. Non-realism is, after all, a fairly sophisticated account intellectually. But non-realism is a world-view, and therefore too broad a phenomenon solely to be determined by such processes of thinking or valuing. This is probably how Fowler himself would understand the matter, non-realism being regarded either as the believers' particular interpretation of the status of the faith-contents in which they believe, or as a change in the faith-contents themselves (from a real God to a symbolic God) – a movement regarded by Fowler as a conversion change rather than a developmental stage change.

Parasitic faith

In arguing elsewhere that Cupitt's non-realist Christianity is best interpreted as a second stage phenomenon, primarily attracting those who are 'taking their leave of a more realist, heteronomous, absolutist position', I asked whether there will be a next generation which has not come from the inside and whether this version of radical Christianity will 'appeal to those who were never insiders at all'. Cupitt's account of religion is certainly post-Christian, and the traditional Christian language and Christian rituals patently still have life and meaning for this style of non-realism. But the questions remain: 'Does the symbol of God help, unless it *originally* referred to a Helper?' and 'Is radical Christian education always a two-stage thing: realism first, *then* the reinterpretation?'[15] For post-realists, traditional theism may be construed as a necessary preparation for the true gospel of non-realist, expressivist Christian spirituality.

In a more recent publication Cupitt more clearly confesses that, and shows how, his non-realism is parasitic on realism. *What Is a Story?* speaks of true religion and spirituality as 'a cure for itself, a therapeutic practice': 'You strive after Heaven in order to learn the wisdom of the return to earth; you try to love something superhuman in order to learn why you must be content to love the human.'[16] Why? Because 'you need to have been jilted by God in order to stir up enough passion for you truly to love your neighbour'.[17] The 'in order to' arrests the eye. It is not just, as he puts it in *After All*, that:

> as things now stand, our lingering anxious desire for fictions of immortality, immutability and absoluteness is itself the problem. True religion now consists not in grabbing at such fictions, but in being cured of the need for them. Selflessly to love the transient and let it go: that is beatitude.[18]

It is also, paradoxically, that the 'quest for the transcendent' of the old religion and spirituality is itself a *felix culpa* – 'a happy fault, a life-enhancing mistake that we need to keep on making'.[19]

The loss of faith in a personal God is seen in an earlier work as an instrument for our own 'de-centring', which incidentally is a process that

Fowler correlates with development through the faith stages. Our dying to God as an object and agent of interpersonal love (egoistic, attached, interested) is described by Cupitt as a dying to self, so that non-egoistic, unattached and disinterested love may live:

> God educates us in love by progressively de-centring himself, withdrawing as an individual personal object of love and leaving behind only pure love, which is his essence. We experience the difficult *command* to love precisely through the withdrawal and vanishing of the God who was a personal object for the involuntary and uncommandable erotic type of love.[20]

Difficulties and dangers can arise from too hard and fast a distinction between *agapē* and *eros*, and many are suspicious of Cupitt's identification of unqualified disinterestedness as the mark of true love. It is true that some theologians have argued that loving God or our neighbour requires us to renounce the desire for the beatitude of God's presence and be indifferent to our neighbour's charms. Vincent Brümmer, however, denies that pure *agapē* ('gift-love') must exclude *eros* ('need-love') for a variety of reasons, including that 'giving without receiving is not love but mere beneficence' and that 'it is only through need-love . . . that I can bestow value and identity on your person and your love'.[21] Objectivity was rejected in *Taking Leave of God* partly because 'external guarantees and sanctions' would inevitably ruin our disinterestedness, and therefore undermine the autonomy of both our ethics and our religion.[22] But we might claim that the guarantee/support for a belief must be viewed very differently from any sanction we might face as people who believe in it, and that the argument from disinterestedness should apply only to the latter. Disinterested realism, on this view, may be a psychologically plausible position. It is noteworthy that Cupitt has elsewhere rejected 'asexual' accounts of *agapē* in favour of a recognition of *human* affection and compassion liberated from self-concern,[23] suggesting that his earlier austere condemnations of a morality and a religion that is good-for-something rather than purely and piously good-for-nothing could be open to some modification.

A focus on disinterestedness may not therefore be very helpful in clarifying the place of realism along the road to non-realism. Is there a more persuasive point to be made? Non-realism sees itself as being on God's side. It is in favour of God, or at least of the moral character of God. Hence it tries very hard to realize – to make real – all of God that it can and should: God's values. A consideration of the place of values in religion is very important for our debate. From the non-realists' perspective, what realism has to offer is an unrealizable search for value. Post-realists used to be realists in love with God. The *point* of that was that they could only fall in love with God by loving what God stood for: God's values. The *danger* of it was not only that their purity of heart was impugned (they would find it, if not impossible, certainly hard to love those values for themselves alone), but also that they might be seduced into giving priority to God at the expense of his values. They might even change the values to fit more closely their inadequate concept of God. And that way madness lies, for ultimate values – that is values that are regarded as intrinsically good – cannot be subordinated.

For Cupitt, non-realist faith came through an 'anti-revelation' of *outside-lessness* and the utter gratuity of empirical existence. 'The message was that there is no message' and this changes everything – 'the here-and-now suddenly became like God'.[24] In Fowler's terms, the transient, ephemeral flux of life is now the 'ultimate environment'. More than that, if there is no power beyond that makes for the righteousness we want, we shall just have to be God for ourselves – and for others. 'The work of God is a work that we have got to do',[25] creating meaning and truth,[26] and particularly creating value by the way we speak and act. 'We've got to do what God used to do for us', revaluing the devalued and ennobling that which is rated too low.[27]

One interpretation of what has happened here is that people have come under the spell of the attractiveness of the spiritual and moral character of God. They have fallen in love with this character – these virtues – in falling in love with God. But then they have changed. Either they have simply ceased to believe that these virtues are instantiated in a supernatural being, or (more radically) they have come to believe that they cannot be instantiated at all: God 'has to *be* ideal to function *as* the religious ideal'.[28] God, for the non-realists, is a personified ideal – a symbol of spiritual values.[29] At any rate they now claim that the ideals themselves are what, and all, we need. *We* always had to realize them; we could never just leave it to God, even when there was a God. Now that it is clear that there is no God, it is even clearer that we have to be God to one another.

But the belief in the real existence of an attractive God was a proper step along the way. We wanted God; that is we deeply desired his holiness, his 'moral attributes' and the effects of his creative, salvific and meaning-making power. We still want all that (quite properly). Perhaps if we had not first become devoted to one who seemed to possess these virtues and perform these acts, we should care less about those things now. It *is* easier to love the real, at least to begin with. Loving the ideal takes a little longer.

It is as though, my mother being dead, I feel impelled to act as she would have done in certain circumstances. I do this not just 'in her memory', but because I value her character. *Because* she is not here to express that character, I will do it 'for her'.

Such an account seems plausible, although I do not pretend that this is all that Cupitt and others understand by giving realism an instrumental role along the way to non-realism. Liberal realists may find echoes of it in the attractiveness of certain Old Testament theologies that retain a motivating force despite being rejected as descriptions of the divine – and indeed have more *regulative* power because they are rejected as *representations*. *We* commit ourselves to intervene in politics, history and the world, modelling our actions on an interventionist, prophetic, even an apocalyptic God whom we no longer expect to act. 'Go and do likewise' is after all the punchline at the end of a parabolic fiction.

This analysis would suggest, therefore, that the preliminary step of realism may be important *psychologically*, in helping people to develop their admiration of God's character and therefore their commitment to a particular set of values. But non-realists should view that as a high risk strategy, insofar as they regard theological realism as oppressive by its very nature or (more convincingly) as open to a subordination of value through an inadequate theology. Since realism can hardly be regarded as a *logically* necessary pre-requisite of non-realism as such (as it is for post-realism), the non-realist must balance the psychological gains against the moral and theological risks before advocating realism to others. Why should people go through a realistic stage? Because it helps strengthen the learner's devotion to the right values. What are the risks? The development of the wrong values. But passionate, right-thinking *once-born* atheists do exist. Some radical Christian educators may therefore prefer to treat them as exemplars and eschew the development of theological realism in their own charges altogether.

Discerning the difference

There is a related issue that both realists and non-realists need to face, not least in an age that increasingly appeals to pragmatic justification, in philosophy and theology as well as politics. What real difference does the adoption of non-realism make? There is a considerable tension between a descriptive thesis that Christianity – properly understood – is basically non-realist,[30] and a non-realism that is presented prescriptively as the way Christianity must now see itself. On this latter view, traditional theistic faith must be 'altogether discarded',[31] and Cupitt at least is out to 'change the definition of what counts as religion'.[32] Not surprisingly, non-realists are sometimes torn between proclaiming the overthrow of realism and the gentler claim that non-realism does not make that much difference because, after all, it is the *symbol* of God that counts.[33]

On the one hand, then, non-realists often assert that non-realism makes all the difference. For Cupitt, realism brings heteronomy and oppression. For others too, the new faith is a liberation and a resurrection because it is seen as a purely human faith.[34] Yet post-realists also recognize realism as the *pedagogue*, the child-tender who brings us to school. Although it is no more than a stage along the way, the post-realist is still loyal to its language and insights, as to a much-loved infant teacher, nanny or even parent, while transposing her tunes 'into an entirely different key'.[35] From the new perspective there may be a recognition that the power of faith is equivalent to the power of God, and that the purpose of God-language was always simply to provide us with a goal.[36] Converts can sometimes be conservatives.

So how much difference does non-realism make? Radical Christianity might seem to differ from the received account most grossly in its denial of the supernatural entities, God and the soul. But these denials are for many writers part and parcel of a rejection of a *debased* Christian spirituality, theology and ethics that finds comfort, support and sanctions in such supernatural realities. In the end, much of the debate is about what people should believe *in*: what spiritual values they should endorse.[37] Despite my reservations about unqualified disinterestedness, I admit that Cupitt has often helpfully pointed up the sharp difference between a spirituality that takes selflessness as a fundamental virtue, and other forms of the 'spiritual life' that are subtly or patently self-serving. Between the two, he would claim, there is a great gulf fixed; and he is surely right. In this way he has reminded us that bland appeals to spirituality (and spiritual education) often gloss over real disagreements over the nature of a truly spiritual spirituality.

Religion for the non-realists is more like morality than anything else. This is perhaps inevitable. Religious concern and commitment is something more than morality, but it leads to morality: 'goodness presupposes holiness.'[38] Religious living is more extreme than merely moral living, but one often gets the impression that it is being encouraged solely for the sake of moral living. Should one complain? Well, morality is not at all a bad substitute for God at the heart of things; some might argue that it should be called on to the field more often even when God is still a player. But most realists would not put morality at the centre. They would say that that place is reserved for God – the really real, the Truth. Here non-realists and realists disagree. However, they could concur about *what makes God central*: not the brute reality alone, perhaps, nor even the necessary existence, and surely not the power. Not just any God will do. By definition my God must be my god, worshipped and acknowledged as worthy of worship. God's character must be valued above all things. And, *in fine*, I must do the valuing.

This sounds like hubris, but it is not. Both non-realist and realist agree that *I*, with my spirituality and my salvation, am not at the centre; or should not be. Cupitt can defend himself against Rowan Williams' old charge that his position was in danger of slipping into an 'ultimate narcissism', embracing the heresy that 'the goal of the spiritual life is to be more spiritual'.[39] At least in his later works, death and the ephemerality of things are taken too seriously for that. There Cupitt has articulated a profound doctrine of selflessness, and rejected an ethic of self-realization in favour of a non-egoistic dying with Christ for a cause – for others and into one's life work – in the 'slipping away' and 'good night' of the truly moral life.[40] Realist and non-realist *could* both adopt these values. There certainly remain real differences between their world-views; but I would claim that the only differences that really matter are any differences over values (and differences over values are equally significant within the ranks of the realists). At the centre of any spiritual account there must be a commitment to values.

Very often what is being offered by non-realism is a particular type of spirituality. How could it be otherwise? Many firmly reject the list of spiritual attitudes and values that Cupitt, for example, provides; and he rejects their lists. These disagreements are themselves instructive, because they raise in a sharp form the question of how we decide between spiritualities. For Cupitt, the answer essentially appears to be a pragmatic one. It depends on whether they work or not: 'When I say that Christianity is true I mean that this particular system of signs and house of meaning is trustworthy and reliable as a medium and a vocabulary in which I can frame my own religious life.'[41] But they work for us, presumably, only if we truly value them. So the question becomes 'Why should we value these attitudes, and not others?' Here Cupitt is necessarily silent, for in the case of intrinsic – though not of instrumental – values the only proper reply is that we just find them to be valuable in and of themselves. Moral and spiritual values, attitudes and virtues cannot be justified by some sort of rational appraisal. The quest for a spiritual education that will educate people into a 'wholly rational adoption' of spiritual values (on what grounds, one might ask?) is clearly a quest for an illusion; values do not have that nature, and they cannot be taught in that way. Spiritual education must rather, and can only, produce a love for them.[42] The value we assign to a thing, Cupitt writes, is 'its only, *and so its true*, value'.[43] Contentious? Yes, but there are no external measures, unless and until we agree to treat them as such – and that implies our valuing their measuring.

If we are to understand salvation in a way that relates to our human world, in terms of coping with life, triumphing over suffering and death, and being truly fulfilled in and through our human valuing, then presumably the point is that we just find these particular spiritual attitudes to be in this way salvific. In commitment to the values of Christian spirituality a new life is engendered that is itself perceived to be intrinsically valuable. It is through our valuing that we find, receive, and give meaning. Concern with spirituality and religion always bring us back to the question of what we truly value.

What is at stake here, then, is indeed the essence of Christianity. I do not mean by that, however, any metaphysical assertion about what is meant by God's reality, but a claim about *what God stands for*. And that is a claim about values. A focus on values is essential in theology, for values are everything. Christianity *is* its values, or it is nothing. Dare we agree on that?

Notes

1 See Mark Abrams, David Gerard and Noël Timms, *Values and Social Change in Britain* (Macmillan, 1985), pp. 258–9, and Michael Svennevig, Ian Haldane, Sharon Spiers and Barrie Gunter, *Godwatching* (John Libbey, 1988), p. 29. In a Scottish survey nearly 14 per cent of (non-Catholic) *church members* declared that 'a sort of distant impersonal power or force' was closest to their view of God: *Lifestyle Survey* (Quorum Press, 1987), pp. 24–6.

2 Robert Towler, *The Need for Certainty: A Sociological Study of Conventional Religion* (Routledge & Kegan Paul, 1984), p. 26.

3 As with Louis P. Pojman, *Religious Belief and the Will* (Routledge & Kegan Paul, 1986), p. 228.

4 Richard Hoggart, *The Uses of Literacy* (Penguin, 1958), pp. 116–19; and Edward Bailey, 'A kind of Christianity: the implicit religion of a residential parish' (unpublished manuscript, 1982), and his essays in Tony Moss (ed.), *In Search of Christianity* (Waterstone, 1986) and in Paul Badham (ed.), *Religion, State, and Society in Modern Britain* (Edwin Mellen, 1989).

5 Don Cupitt, *Only Human* (SCM Press, 1985), p. 200.

6 Don Cupitt, *Life Lines* (SCM Press, 1986), pp. 13–14.

7 *Life Lines*, pp. 202–3.

8 James W. Fowler, *Stages of Faith: The Psychology of Human Development and the Quest for Meaning* (Harper & Row, 1981), especially ch. 23.

9 James W. Fowler, 'The Enlightenment and faith development theory' in Jeff Astley and Leslie J. Francis (eds), *Christian Perspectives on Faith Development* (Fowler Wright/Eerdmans, 1992), pp. 18–27.

10 Don Cupitt, 'Anti-realist faith' in Joseph Runzo (ed.), *Is God Real?* (Macmillan, 1993), p. 51.

11 James Fowler, 'Faith and the structuring of meaning' in James Fowler and Antoine Vergote (eds), *Toward Moral and Religious Maturity* (Silver Burdett, 1980), p. 73.

12 *Stages of Faith*, p. 201.

13 *Life Lines*, p. 200.

14 It is also tempting to look for parallels within Fritz Oser's account of religious development. Oser's research, which focuses on the development of religious judgement, has led to his claim that people pass through a sequence of cognitive stages that are identified by different conceptualizations of the relationship between the divine and the human. However, this development in theological conceptualization does not particularly suggest a journey towards a more non-realist view of God, although in the early stages at least it does trace a movement away from an interventionist, responsive deity and towards a more autonomous religiosity. See Fritz K. Oser and W. George Scarlett (eds), *Religious Development in Childhood and Adolescence* (Jossey-Bass, 1991), ch. 1, and Fritz K. Oser and Paul Gmünder, *Religious Judgement: A Developmental Perspective* (Religious Education Press, 1991).

15 Jeff Astley, 'Review article on Don Cupitt: faith on the level', *The Modern Churchman* XXXII (1991), p. 69.

16 Don Cupitt, *What Is a Story?* (SCM Press, 1991), p.139.

17 *What Is a Story?*, p. 141.

18 Don Cupitt, *After All* (SCM Press, 1994), p. 92.

19 *What Is a Story?*, p. 139.

20 *Life Lines*, p. 111.

21 Vincent Brümmer, *The Model of Love: A Study in Philosophical Theology* (Cambridge University Press, 1993), pp. 240, 241.

22 Don Cupitt, *Taking Leave of God* (SCM Press, 1980), pp. 67–9, 96 and 156–62.

23 Don Cupitt, *The New Christian Ethics* (SCM Press, 1988), pp. 57–8.

24 Don Cupitt, *Creation out of Nothing* (SCM Press, 1990), p. 88.

25 *Creation out of Nothing*, p. 69.

26 *What Is a Story?*, p. 93.

27 *The New Christian Ethics*, pp. 4, 6, 95, 130, 167; *Creation out of Nothing*, p. 154.

28 *Taking Leave of God*, p. 113; cf. p. 96, and *Only Human*, p. 210.

29 *Taking Leave of God*, pp. 69, 85, 94; *Creation out of Nothing*, p. 117, 170.

30 Or is *misunderstood* in the debate between realists and non-realists, the meaning of God's reality or existence only being revealed through a more sympathetic analysis of the depth grammar of religious language. Cf. the writings of D. Z. Phillips, for example 'On really believing' in Joseph Runzo (ed.), *Is God Real?*, pp. 85–108, and Gareth Moore, *Believing in God* (T. & T. Clark, 1988).

31 Don Cupitt, *The Long-Legged Fly* (SCM Press, 1987), p. 147; cf. Don Cupitt, *Radicals and the Future of the Church* (SCM Press, 1989), p. 173.

32 Don Cupitt, *The Time Being* (SCM Press, 1992), p. 13.

33 Cf. Anthony Freeman, *God in Us* (SCM Press, 1993), pp. 24–9, 48–51 and 79–80.

34 Hugh Dawes, *Freeing the Faith* (SPCK, 1992), p. 20; *God in Us*, pp. 12 and 14.

35 David Hart, *Faith in Doubt* (Mowbray, 1993), p. 5.

36 *Life Lines*, p. 103; *Only Human*, p. 202.

37 Cf. *Creation out of Nothing*, p. 117.

38 *Taking Leave of God*, p. 143.

39 Rowan Williams, '"Religious realism": on not quite agreeing with Don Cupitt', *Modern Theology* 1 (1984), pp. 11 and 17.

40 *The Time Being*, pp. 26 and 145; *What Is a Story?*, pp. 60–1; *The New Christian Ethics*, pp. 26–7, 67–80 and 88.

41 *Radicals and the Future of the Church*, p. 55.
42 Cf. Jeff Astley, *The Philosophy of Christian Religious Education* (SPCK, 1994), ch. 9.
43 *The New Christian Ethics*, p. 13; cf. p. 107.

9
Cupitt, the mystics and the 'objectivity' of God

Denys Turner

I

As anyone knows who has ever had to set questions for examination papers, framing a good question is at least as hard as answering one; and as anyone knows who has had to answer examination papers, there is nothing worse than being confronted with an ill-formulated question. I can think of scarcely any question in theology more misleading, that is to say, more likely to lead those who try to answer it into unproductive lines of thought, than the question 'Is the existence of God objective?' Insofar as a theological standpoint called 'theological realism' is characterized by the affirmative answer to this question, this standpoint is, I believe, theologically impoverished. But then, since what is bad about a bad question is that answers *either* way are equally impoverished, there is nothing to be gained over theological realism by a 'theological non-realism' which is defined by its answering that same question negatively.

Though Cupitt's *Taking Leave of God* contains much polemic against theological realisms and objectivisms, his defence of 'theological non-realism' has more to it than can be accounted for by his having simply been misled by a bad question. Be that as it may, I am less concerned in this paper with how Cupitt describes his own theological position than with how he sets about rejecting an alternative, how he characterizes that alternative, and to whom he attributes the alternative he rejects. I suspect that, logically, the case for Cupitt's own position of theological non-realism does not depend upon the success or otherwise of his polemic against 'theological realism', which is perhaps as well, since I regard that polemic as being fatally flawed both philosophically and historically. Nonetheless, since there appear to be supporters of Cupitt's 'theological non-realism' – and possibly Cupitt himself is included among them – who *do* believe that 'theological non-realism' represents the only alternative to 'theological objectivism', it seems worthwhile pointing out that such false dichotomies (as I believe them to be) are the inevitable consequence of attempting to answer a bad question as if it were a good one.

Briefly, then, Cupitt rejects 'theological objectivism': he believes that, for the theological objectivist, the expression 'God exists' refers to an 'actually-existing independent individual being',[1] whose existence or non-existence is determinable in much the same way as it is determinable whether an apparently empty house is occupied or not.[2] He maintains, further, that not only do many Christians in the pew believe that this is what they believe when they 'believe in God', but that many sophisticated ancient, medieval and modern theologians maintained this to be at the core of their Christian belief, among them, Thomas Aquinas;[3] and he thinks that he has, in support of his rejection of this naive theological objectivism, the opinion of Meister Eckhart – or, at any rate, he *appears* to think Eckhart is on his side, for he sets the following quotation from Eckhart's sermon 'Qui audit me' on the title page of his book: 'Man's last and highest parting occurs when, for God's sake, he takes leave of God.'

II

In all this polemic against 'premodern' theologies there are many straw men and one or two genuine, embodied targets. On the score of genuine targets, there does exist, it has to be said, a traditional theological 'objectivism' according to which theology can first of all fix the centre of the universe of discourse upon an 'objective' God and can then deploy the language of religion to speak from that centre. At least since the time of Feuerbach's *Essence of Christianity* it seems to have been supposed by many, Christian believers and their opponents alike, that since that is what you *must* maintain if you are a Christian, the resort of the anti-objectivist lies in the denial of this theocentric objectivism and in affirming, contrariwise, the *human* at the centre. At any rate, Cupitt does. In fact, he does not even think it necessary to argue for this conclusion: he simply takes it as definitive of 'modern thought' that it speaks of a 'modern self', which is 'self-defining, generating its own knowledge and its own destiny of becoming a fully-achieved, conscious and autonomous spiritual subject',[4] adding that this 'modern concern for the autonomy of the individual human spirit' is closely related to the concern for 'the autonomy of purely religious values and claims'.[5] Moreover, such is the relation, logically, between this 'modern' consciousness and that of the theological objectivist that, it appears, they share a common conception of what the issue between them is about: for Cupitt seems to share with his opponents the disjunctions involved, either fideism or reductivism, either an autonomous, objective God or an autonomous subjective and 'atheous' human, for 'as man gains in autonomy God must presumably retire from objectivity'.[6]

This is, of course, pure Feuerbachianism. I mean not that Cupitt shares any of Feuerbach's *answers* – on the contrary, Cupitt's naive individualism is in the plainest contrast with the social humanism of Feuerbach's 'species being' – but that he shares Feuerbach's questions, and so shares with Feuerbach a conception of the dialectics of 'autonomy' with regard to religious language and its objects: *some* being is autonomous, and the autonomies of God and the human are mutually exclusive. Lying behind this conception of how objectivism and non-realism are opposed is, therefore, a belief Cupitt appears to share with his opponents (at any rate those opponents, whether real or supposititious, he polemicizes against) that religious discourse must necessarily name some being at the centre. It is just this belief which lands Cupitt with the theological problematic from which *Taking Leave of God* fails to escape. For though, in the logic of autonomy, there can be only one autonomous being at the centre, unfortunately there are two candidates for the position, God and the human. Necessarily, then, if both are claimed 'objectively' to exist, they compete for the position. In so far as God is centred the human is decentred, diminished in autonomy; in so far as the human is centred God is decentred, and 'must . . . retire from objectivity'. And as one might retrodict from the later work, Cupitt's earlier theology wreaks havoc with classical Christologies which, innocent of Cupitt's antinomies, are nonetheless read by Cupitt – with scant regard for historical context – in terms of them. Indeed, the very concept of incarnation becomes self-contradictory, as Cupitt maintained in his contribution to *The Myth of God Incarnate*, where he spoke of Jesus' 'ironical perception of *disjunction* between the things of God and the things of men'.[7] There cannot, it is supposed, be two autonomous beings 'objectively existing' at the centre; they must be 'over-against' each other.[8] Hence, if Christ is to be at the centre, he cannot be both God and man.

Now it is the main purpose of this essay to argue that, whatever the merits of post-Feuerbachian theologies and their problematics in themselves, Cupitt is simply wrong to draw into the stereotypes they yield the classical negative and mystical theologies of the Middle Ages. In particular, it is only on the grossest kind of misconstrual of the positions of Thomas Aquinas and Meister Eckhart that he can find in the former a defender of his 'theological objectivism' and in the latter an ally for his rejection of it. For what Thomas Aquinas defends amounts to the rejection both of Cupitt's 'theological objectivism' and of Cupitt's 'theological non-realism'; and what Eckhart makes clear is why *neither* is acceptable: to get caught in the antinomies in terms of which Cupitt conducts the argument is itself a, or even *the*, fundamental theological – and for that matter, spiritual – error. Neither answer is a good one because both are attempts to answer a question which is, in itself, a bad one.

III

If we examine Thomas' discussions of the logic of language about God from the standpoint, anachronistically, of Cupitt's problematic, there is a sense in which it can be seen as a wholesale 'decentring' of theology, as an argument for abandoning as idolatrous any human language about the universe which 'centres' either God or the human. For Thomas held that the basic terms out of which theological language is constructed are essentially exoteric, without privileged theological application. Indeed, those root terms form predicates (' . . . exists', ' . . . is good', ' . . . is [an] individual', ' . . . is one') which have no primary significance as predicated of any subject term more literally than of any other. In this, the logical behaviour of such terms differs from that of terms which do have a particular application to a restricted range of objects: a predicate such as ' . . . is red' has a privileged application to objects with two-dimensional extensions, which is why, if we describe something dimensionless such as a person's state of mind as that of 'seeing red', we know we have a sense which is stretched beyond the limits of the literal, ordinary meaning, and so is metaphorical. But predicates like ' . . . is good', being, as Gilbert Ryle called them, 'topic neutral',[9] can *never* be metaphors, for there is no particular domain of objects they principally refer to such that they can refer to other objects only in an extended sense. Anything at all can be a good one of its kind, and it is just as literal a predication to say of a firm, crisp, juicy apple that it is a 'good' one as it is to say of God that she is good. In that sense at least, theological language is already a decentred language: its grammar rules out *a priori* any statement of the problem of God in terms which set her in opposition to 'the things of man', an opposition which we would have to concede if we had to suppose that all language about God was metaphorical; for were the expression 'God is good' a metaphor, then we would have to say it was literally *false* of the creator, being literally true only of creatures.[10]

Of course, Thomas' linguistic democracy runs in parallel with an ontological hierarchicalism. For sure, he maintained, in the causal order of things, God is prior to any creature. The predicate ' . . . is good' is *truer* of God than it is of any creature, because God is the cause of the goodness of creatures and whatever is true of the effect of a cause is truer still of the cause.[11] But it does not follow from this – and in any case, it is not true – that 'God is good' *means* 'God is the cause of goodness in creatures'.[12] Far from it. What we can mean by the predicate ' . . . is good' is entirely dependent on what we can know of goodness in creatures. And that means that we get some meaning for this predicate only from what it is for creatures to be good.[13] In turn it follows from this that we cannot know what it means to say of God that she is 'good'.[14] God infinitely transcends any creature.

In fact, of course, Thomas believes we can know *that* 'God is good' is a true proposition because we can demonstrate that if there were no God there could be no goodness nor anything else in creatures. For 'God' is what we call him who has brought it about that there is anything at all, and so anything good, rather than nothing at all. But, for Thomas, the very argument which justifies our saying that God is good also demonstrates that we could not possibly know what we mean when we say it. That which we show must exist we also show must be utterly unknown to us, so that though we know we must call God 'cause of the universe', the expression 'cause of . . . ' itself transcends our power to understand.[15] And that, the unknown and unknowable cause of all that is, we call 'God'.[16]

This dialectic of 'knowing and unknowing' in Thomas ultimately depends upon some demonstration of the existence of God being valid and for some this is its Achilles' heel. For it is, of course, notoriously easy today to doubt the validity of Thomas' arguments for the existence of God, and Cupitt obtains the usual post-Kantian fun at their expense.[17] But their validity in themselves would have been a secondary matter for Thomas, for what concerns him more is the *demonstrability as such* of the existence of God, less the actual probative power of the arguments themselves. For an argument for the existence of God is more or less successful, and the failure of any particular argument is not instrinsically damaging to faith; but, for Thomas, it is a consideration crucial to our understanding of the nature of faith itself, to maintain the demonstrability of God's existence.[18] It is precisely because an easy, unself-critical fideism would all too readily lapse into the idolatrous illusion that *through faith* we can know what God is, that Thomas wished to show the impossibility of this in principle. Thomas' 'five ways', valid or invalid as arguments, were designed to show just this impossibility *even* for faith: 'we do not know what God is', he insists, '[even] through the disclosure of grace, and so [by grace] we are made one with God as it were with something unknown.'[19]

I do not think that Cupitt's polemic against theological 'objectivism' even begins to get to grips with the resolute apophaticisms of the medieval theological, mystical and spiritual traditions.[20] If by 'objectively existing' Cupitt means 'existing independently of the human mind in the manner of an object', then Thomas cannot conceivably be represented as maintaining that God 'exists objectively'; for Thomas is a close follower of the Pseudo-Dionysius in this as in much more of his doctrine of God, and for the Pseudo-Dionysius, God is neither an object nor not an object, 'he does not possess this kind of existence and not that'.[21] Does it follow that 'God exists' does not name some 'really existent thing'? For Thomas, it certainly does follow: for again, following the Pseudo-Dionysius, there is no kind of thing which God is, 'God is not any kind of thing'.[22] Does it follow, if God does not *objectively* exist, that God exists *subjectively*, simply as the name for that which most fully expresses the 'religious demand'? For Thomas this does not and could not *follow*: for the reason why God is not an existent object is not that God is an item of human-dependent subjectivity, but that God is the cause of all the objects there are, and it would be sheer idolatry to represent God as just another object. For, being the creator of all things out of nothing, God cannot be any part of, still less any one of the things created. There is, in consequence, no description of the sum total of things such that God and creatures can both be said to be members of that sum total. Hence, even if we say that 'God is one', we know that we cannot know what we mean. For God cannot be 'one' in such a way that she is numerable: 'God plus the universe' is not some kind of arithmetical addition, as if, supposing there were a certain number of individual existent things, God's existence added 'one' more individual to that number. There is simply no collectivity of which God is a member. *That* is the sense in which 'an individual' God does not exist 'objectively': but it is no sense from which it can be derived that God exists 'subjectively'. God simply eludes all our categories, including those of 'objective' and 'subjective'.

Thomas' response, therefore, to this Cupittian dilemma is, or would have been, roughly this: our language, perhaps inevitably, distinguishes between 'subject' and 'object'. But this is not a distinction we can make in respect of our knowledge of God, for that distinction fails, and demonstrably so, of that knowledge. For though our consciousness has the nature of subjectivity, God has no nature at all, and so no character of objectivity. It is for this reason also that we cannot give any account of God's existence such that it stands, as object, 'over-against' any supposed autonomy, whether of human knowledge or agency. Any such account is either, for Thomas, plain nonsense, or else vulgar idolatry, or, most probably, both.

It is no wonder that, failing to grasp this fundamental position of 'classical theism', Cupitt misconstrues the Chalcedonian Christology which presupposes it. Cupitt, we saw, rejected that Christology not because it is implausible, which it is, or because it is false, which is plausible, but because it is incoherent, failing, as he thinks, to advert to 'Jesus' ironical perception of *disjunction* between the things of God and the things of men'. But for the apophatic traditions, if our language of similarity between God and creatures necessarily fails, so must our language of contrast and difference. And there is a simple matter of human logic here on which the consistency of the Chalcedonian formulae relies. As McCabe has rightly pointed out, terms and meanings can contrast with one another only within a common territory of meaning.[23] Sheep contrast with goats *as animals*: hence, what is a sheep cannot be the same animal as a goat; circles contrast with squares *as shapes*: hence, what is a circle cannot be the same shape as a square; extensions contrast with colours *as properties of material things*: hence, what has no extension cannot be literally red. But God cannot contrast with creatures even as chalk with cheese. For there is something which chalk and cheese contrast *as*, there is a common universe they belong to, in which they occupy mutually exclusive spaces. But since there is, as Thomas maintains, no collectivity at all to which God and creatures commonly belong, there is not, and cannot be anything at all which they contrast *as*. Consequently there can be no relation of exclusion, no 'disjunction', between what it takes to be a human and what it takes to be God. For we cannot give any content to the expression 'what it takes to be God', since 'God is not some kind of thing'. Hence, it is at least not demonstrably incoherent to say of one and the same person that he – or for that matter she – is both God and human.

Now interestingly, the consequence of this severe apophaticism turns out to be quite the reverse of that which Cupitt himself assigns to it. Cupitt confesses to having tried to combine belief in God with spiritual freedom by means, as he supposes, of a 'negative theology', only to find that 'God had become objectively thinner and thinner in order to allow subjective religiousness to expand'. He even thinks that from this negative theology it 'is only one step further to the objectively atheous position here propounded'.[24] This conclusion ought not, however, to surprise. Cupitt's 'negative theology' contains little in common with classical mystical apophaticism. Cupitt derives from his account the impossibility of reconciling an objectively existing God with the divinity of Jesus: and what would one expect from a fundamentally anti-incarnational theology of God than that it would become 'thinner and thinner'? On the other hand, Thomas' apophaticism is fully consistent with an incarnational Christianity, is fully consistent with the affirmativeness of those theologies which find in Jesus' humanity – and so in all creation – the richest, most complete and most complex revelation of the *Deus absconditus*, who is both revealed in all that is and yet utterly transcends our power to represent her 'as object'.

IV

The speculative mystics of the Middle Ages were fully in command of this apophatic dialectics, whether in their Christologies or in their accounts of the relation between the soul and God. Perhaps the most profoundly and consistently Christocentric of the medieval authorities, Bonaventure, fully realized the force of the revelation of God in the human nature of Christ. For Bonaventure, in Christ is resumed all the *knowability* of God, in Christ is found the fullest human language of God, for in Christ is found the microcosm of all creation which stands in some way as the visible symbol and sacrament of the invisible God.[25] There is, therefore, a heartily cataphatic affirmation of creation in Bonaventure's theology, but it is an affirmativeness which leads, as a ladder of ascent, only into the darkness of unknowing and negation, a *transitus* dramatically signified and effected by the brokenness of the human nature of Christ on the cross.[26] In Christ, therefore, the knowability of God is brought into the unknowability of the *Deus absconditus*, so that if our only access to God is through Christ, Christ is, in an ultimate paradox, our access only to the unknowability of God, in whom all our categories break down – whether of similarity and difference, of time and eternity, or of being and nothingness.[27] Our human categories of 'objective' and 'subjective' are scarcely the last to survive the radicalness of this *transitus*.

And in Meister Eckhart is found this same radical apophaticism, only in him, along with his near contemporary, the Beguine Marguerite Porete, this apophaticism about God is combined with an apophaticism, equally radical, about the self. Here, indeed, Cupitt does share some common themes with the early fourteenth-century mysticism of Northern Europe, in particular in that where, for Cupitt, the autonomy of the religious 'subject' is achieved by the means of a radical impartiality,[28] for Eckhart, the root of the Christian practice lies in a 'detachment' so far-reaching that it outranks even love on the scale of Christian virtue.[29]

For the root of all theological and spiritual distortion lies in the possessive self. The strategy of detachment is the strategy of dispossessing desire of its desire to possess its objects, and so to destroy them. For Eckhart it is not just that, in addition to our other desires, we also desire to possess; as for John of the Cross, possessiveness for Eckhart is pandemic; *all* our desires are infected by it, all that we desire we desire *qua* object of possession; no matter how unpossessible an object may be in itself, possessiveness will convert it into a possible object of possession, will make a property of it, will 'privatize' it, as it were. It is for this reason that the undetached person denatures her world and cannot even properly enjoy it. She cannot meet with reality on its own terms, but only on her own. Detachment, for Eckhart, is not the severing of desire's relation with its object, but the restoration of desire to a proper relation of objectivity; as we might say, of reverence for its object. Detachment is therefore the basis of the true possibility of love, which is why, for Eckhart, it is more fundamental than love, being the condition of its possibility.

After all, as the *Cloud* Author puts it, anyone can love God 'for what he can get out of him'. But such a 'God' is not God. Any 'God' we could possibly love without detachment is not the true God badly loved, but not God at all, the mere godlet of our own invention. What is more, because possessive desire is a form of dependence on its object, the God of our own desire is a form of ego-need, a God on whom we depend not in freedom but in servility, one for whom, therefore, God would have to be master. For possessive desires at once destroy what they desire and are enslaved to what they destroy. The gods of the undetached may be poor diminished little things: but they are, for all that, poor diminished little *tyrants*. The possessive desire for God does indeed create a God who, as Cupitt puts it, stands 'over-against' the human desirer.

Possessiveness is, therefore, the principle of destruction of nature and creation and so of God. Thus far Eckhart and Cupitt share a common theme. But from here on Eckhart's critique of possessiveness takes on a dialectical turn, altogether more radical than anything in Cupitt. For at the root of all other possessiveness is the ultimately possessive desire to be a self: the desire that there should be at my centre not that unnameable abyss into which, as into a vacuum, the nameless Godhead is inevitably drawn, but an identity I can own, an identity which is defined by my ownership of it, an identity, therefore, whose autonomy is defined by its exclusion of all other autonomies. That is the ultimately destructive form that attachment can take, for it is an attachment which seeks to infill that nothingness with images of self and with 'ways' to God. Such an identity must necessarily expel God from the place which it occupies, for a God which is thus made an objective 'thing' (in Eckhart's terms, a *hoc aliquid*) is a rival to the self which is thus made into another thing, a *hoc aliud*. Consequently, any God it does affirm it must affirm in exclusion of the I which affirms it. These are the perverse, inverted dialectics of the undetached, the dialectics of the 'exterior' person who is trapped in the polarizations of interiority and exteriority so as to seek God 'within' *rather than* 'without'. For the truly detached person there can be no such distinction as that between 'inner' and 'outer', though in a typically Eckhartian paradox, only the truly inward person can see this. For this reason too, Eckhart is able to resist the conventional polarization of the active and the contemplative lives and to insist upon the unity of Martha and Mary.[30] That is also why Eckhart is so insistent upon the absolute transcendence equally of God and the self, beings beyond every possibility of being appropriated within some intelligible, meaningful, desirable, possessible structure of selfhood, or of its cognitivity. That is why, for Eckhart, 'my' self is not in the last resort *mine* at all. And any self which I can call my own as if *contrasted with* that of God is a false self, a self of possessive imagination. To be a self I must retain within myself the void and the desert of detachment. To live by detachment is to live without an explanation, without *rationale*, namelessly one with the nameless God.

Hence, the strategy of detachment is not that of focusing created desires upon a God as object. This is, indeed, the 'God' of whom we must 'take leave' for the sake of God. Detachment is, rather, the apophatic critique of desire, corresponding in every detail of its structure and dynamic with the apophaticism of intellect. Just as the dialectics of apophaticism are those of the negation of the negation, so the practice of detachment is that of *opposing oppositions* between one desire and another, between the desire for God and the desire for created things, as if the desire for God was just another created desire for another created object. It is only for the un-detached person that that opposition could exist. To be detached is not therefore to be desireless of creation in order to desire only God, nor is it to desire nothing at all, even God. Rather, it is to desire out of that nothingness of self and God, so that, from the security of this 'fortress of the soul' which nothing created can enter, we can desire all things with a desire truly divine, because it is desire 'without a why'.

There is, in Eckhart's doctrine of detachment, the potential for the critique of an ego-serving spirituality, a spirituality of 'ways to God', which finds 'ways' even in detachment, and so loses God. If there was any kind of undetachment which Eckhart feared above all others for its spiritually distorting potential, it was that of the 'spiritual' for whom means displaced goals. This, among other reasons, should have us pause before answering the question 'What is Eckhart's way?' For his is the way of no ways – or rather, it is the way of any way whatsoever, so long as it is submitted to the critical practice of detachment, the apophaticism of desire. This is not a 'spirituality', but the critique of spirituality. It is practised upon the ordinary 'ways' and means of the Christian life, for there were no others for Eckhart. But without that critique of detachment, even the ordinary ways of Christians can become a deformed, monstrous, anthropomorphic caricature. For which reason Eckhart concludes one of his most spectacularly paradoxical sermons with the question:

> 'Then how should I love God?' You should love God unspiritually, that is, your soul should be unspiritual and stripped of all spirituality, for so long as your soul has a spirit's form, it has images, and so long as it has images, it has a medium, and so long as it has a medium, it is not unity or simplicity. Therefore your soul must be unspiritual, free of all spirit, and must remain spiritless; for if you love God as he is God, as he is spirit, as he is person and as he is image – all this must go! 'Then how should I love him?' You should love him as he is non-God, a nonspirit, a nonperson, a nonimage, but as he is pure, unmixed, bright 'One', separated from all duality; and in that One we should eternally sink down, out of 'something' into 'nothing'.[31]

V

The common thread which may be identified as running between the speculative mysticisms of the Pseudo-Dionysius, Thomas Aquinas, Bonaventure and Eckhart – in spite of their many and very great differences from one another – is to be found not, it must be said, in their critique simply of 'theological objectivism', but rather in their critique of those antinomies of thought and those deformations of spirit for which there can be no alternative to a naive realism except in a naive non-realism. At the level of theological language, those antinomies show up in the naive polarizations of 'objective' and 'subjective', 'realism and 'non-realism', which burden Cupitt's polemic and do, indeed, characterize his thought, as he so frequently insists, as 'modern': 'modern', that is to say, both as contrasted with 'premodern' thought and as contrasted with 'postmodern' thought. For if the medieval mystic and the contemporary critic of modernity share anything in common, it is in the shared rejection of the 'modernist's' assumption of a 'centred' universe, in which God and the human have to compete for the autonomy spot. If, in the end, there are any reasons for asserting that 'God exists' is true, one thing the theist will not be able to say, if they follow the path of Cupitt's 'theological objectivists', is that God's place at the 'centre' of the universe is such that we can fix upon him, or in any way derive from him, a meaning for the universe. It follows from what Thomas has to say about language *as such*, that to assert the existence of God is not to contribute anything to the meaning of things, not even, as some Christians seem to think (with more piety than rigour), to the meaning of evil and suffering. All Thomas will say about the matter is that the difference the existence of God makes to the universe is the difference between its existing and there being nothing whatever. And the difference between there being something and there being nothing is not a difference in the meaning of things for, as Kant reminded us, existence is not a predicate.

This is because though we know what the existence of God *accounts* for – all that there is – we do not and cannot know what this, which accounts for it, is. If we want to say that God exists 'objectively', all we can mean by this is that God's existence is not in any way creature-dependent and that, on the contrary, all creatures are wholly God-dependent, even, in the case of those which possess some 'autonomy', for their 'autonomy'. Those for whom the 'objective' existence of God is incompatible with the autonomies they wish to ascribe to humans, may be able to summon 'modern consciousness' – Descartes, Kant, Hume and Feuerbach – in their support, but they certainly cannot be allowed to claim the support of an Eckhart, and ought not to be allowed so to mis-characterize the thought of Thomas Aquinas as to force his thought into the Procrustean bed of a modernist, and essentially Feuerbachian, antinomy.

For both throw off the theological essentialism with which Cupitt saddles the 'theological objectivist'; and for neither is it necessary to derive from this rejection the consequence of Cupitt's theological 'non-realism'; nor is it possible to derive from it the displacement of divine objectivity by the autonomous human subject. And the reason is: both reject the ideology of the modernist project which is the assumption common to both Cupitt's 'non-realism' and, if there any who avow it, his opponents' 'theological objectivism' – that there is some being who lies at the centre of its meaning and purpose and that we have some language in which to describe it.

My argument, therefore, is that a theological discourse which embodies the insights of the medieval 'mystic' knows itself to be the decentred language of a decentred world, a discourse which is above all a moment of 'unknowing' and mystery in a contingent and semantically unstable world. As such, theological language will be seen primarily as a language of criticism. For in that world humans exhibit the opposed, ideological instinct to stabilize their universe upon absolute sources and referents of meaning, upon idolatrous myths, whether of God or of the human. It is a false theological instinct which provokes a theologian to displace a God at the centre on the assumption that what is opened up thereby is a gap which the human has to fill. This is a false theological instinct not because, after all, it is God who belongs at the centre, but because, although there is a God on whom all depends, there cannot possibly be any language in which to embody the meaning and significance of that centrality of God. Theological language therefore knows itself to consist in failure, for it knows itself in its ultimate 'unknowing'; and in knowing that, it knows all language ultimately to fail, for theological language is but the ultimacy of all language. Hence, also, it knows the name of all discourses, whether of politics, science, theology or spirituality premissed upon a pretentious claim to know, premissed upon *any* privileged 'centredness': it is the name of 'idolatry'.

And so the very best reason why the God Cupitt takes leave of does not exist is that his 'autonomous consciousness' does not exist either. Both are idolatrous illusions, for we do not live in the sort of universe in which either can exist.

Notes

1 Don Cupitt, *Taking Leave of God* (SCM Press, 1980), p. 15.

2 *Taking Leave of God*, p. 15.

3 *Taking Leave of God*, pp. 21–29.

4 *Taking Leave of God*, p. 65.

5 *Taking Leave of God*, p. 85.

6 *Taking Leave of God*, p. 20.

7 Don Cupitt, 'The Christ of Christendom' in John Hick (ed.), *The Myth of God Incarnate* (SCM Press, 1977), p. 140.

8 *Taking Leave of God*, p. 8.

9 Gilbert Ryle, 'Categories' in A. G. N. Flew (ed.), *Logic and Language* (Oxford University Press, 1953), pp. 65–81.

10 For metaphors are literal falsehoods and acquire their power to express truths about the thing metaphorized only on the basis of their literal untruth.

11 *Summa Theologiae* Ia, q. 13, a. 2, corp.

12 *Summa Theologiae* Ia, q. 13, a. 6, corp.

13 *Summa Theologiae* Ia, q. 13, a. 6, corp.

14 Still less can we know what it is to say of God that she is 'she'.

15 '[O]ur understanding cannot know [God] as he is in this life': *Summa Theologiae* Ia, q. 13, a. 1, ad 1.

16 *Summa Theologiae* Ia, q. 2, a. 2, corp.

17 *Taking Leave of God*, pp. 24–6.

18 There is nothing incoherent in an argument for the provability of a proposition which is not itself a proof of that proposition. Such are common in mathematics. To coherently maintain that the provability of the existence of God is in some way crucial to Christian faith it is not required to know of some proof which is unassailable, still less to know of one universally assented to.

19 *Summa Theologiae* Ia, q. 12, a. 13, ad 1.

20 Though he has a passing, and somewhat trivializing reference to such negative theologies in *Taking Leave of God*, p. 13.

21 *Divine Names*, 5, 824B in *Pseudo-Dionysius: The Complete Works*, trans. Colm Luibheid (Paulist Press, 1987).

22 *Divine Names*, 5, 817D.

23 Herbert McCabe, 'The myth of God incarnate' in *God Matters* (Geoffrey Chapman, 1987), pp. 57–8.

24 *Taking Leave of God*, p. 13.

25 *Itinerarium Mentis in Deum*, 1.12 in *The Works of St Bonaventure*, trans. Philotheus Boehner and M. Frances McLaughlin (Franciscan Institute, 1956).

26 *Itinerarium*, 6.7.

27 *Itinerarium*, 5.7 and 6.3.

28 *Taking Leave of God*, pp. 70–83.

29 'On Detachment', in *Meister Eckhart: The Essential Sermons, Commentaries, Treatises and Defense*, trans. E. Colledge and B. McGinn (Paulist Press, 1981), pp. 285–6.

30 Sermon 86, 'Intravit Jesus', in *Meister Eckhart, Teacher and Preacher*, trans. B. McGinn, F. Tobin and E. Borgstadt (Paulist Press, 1986), pp. 338–44.

31 Sermon 83, 'Renovamini Spiritu', in *Meister Eckhart: The Essential Sermons*, p. 208.

10
What's wrong with realism anyway?

Fergus Kerr

I

Philosophers have long been divided between realists and idealists. According to the most recent version of the dispute, you are a realist with respect to a given area of discourse if you believe that the objects referred to by our thoughts in that area are what they are quite independently of what we happen to think about them. This view is vulnerable, many philosophers would think, to the objection that, while the thoughts in question may well aim at representing an independently existing reality or state of affairs, there is no guarantee that they are successful. Indeed, how do we know that our representation of reality ever reflects what is out there? Idealists, or anti-realists as they have been called since Michael Dummett reformulated the dispute in these terms,[1] deal with this scepticism by arguing that it makes no sense anyway to talk about objects or states of affairs that exist independently of our beliefs about them.

The realist holds that understanding an assertion consists in having an idea of what it is for any such sentence to be true or false – independently of any capacity we may have to verify it. There are objects and states of affairs in the world which would be as they are whether we were here or not. In this sense most of us would be realists about trees and stars, for example, although some philosophers might object that they are 'really only' collections of sense data, requiring to be assembled in our heads if they are to count as trees and stars. Many more of us might doubt if goodness, truth and beauty, or electrons and quarks, have any reality independently of our beliefs about them. Realism, anyway, captures the old-fashioned thought that there are more things in heaven and earth than are dreamt of in our philosophy.

The anti-realist, on the other hand, is unhappy about the idea of our being able to understand the meaning of assertions whose truth or falsity transcends our powers to decide. Understanding a sentence must surely involve the essentially practical ability to use the sentence in appropriate ways in response to conditions of whose existence we have knowledge. How, for example, could we learn the meaning of sentences of which the verifiability transcends the available evidence? This picks up the doctrine of the logical positivists, according to which a sentence is cognitively meaningful only if it is either tautological or empirically verifiable.[2] Updated with the later Wittgenstein's supposed theory that 'the meaning of a word is its use in the language', this becomes the doctrine that the meaning of a sentence can never transcend our means of verifying it. We can talk sense only about what we know, as common sense might suggest. This captures, modestly, the traditional idealist doctrine that nothing exists independently of somebody's mind – God's mind, if you like, but in any case our minds.

The anti-realist, as the term suggests, is out simply to interrogate realism, not to promote some supposedly self-standing non-realism that might apply in every area of discourse. For one thing, realism is possible in one area of discourse and anti-realism in another. Iris Murdoch, believing that moral conduct is rooted in natural desire for truth and goodness, conceived in Platonistic terms as transcendent realities which we have to discover, with effort and training, endorses realism in ethics. But she favours non-realism in theology because she cannot believe in an objectively existing quasi-personal being who might become incarnate in our history.[3] More commonly, no doubt, as with A. J. Ayer, non-realism in theology rides tandem with non-realism in ethics (variously labelled non-cognitivism, emotivism and projectivism).

In moral philosophy, as it happens, the dispute is particularly lively at present. Realists such as David Wiggins and John McDowell believe that some things and situations have moral properties whether or not human beings realize this at a given time or in a particular society. Anti-realists in ethics, such as Bernard Williams and Simon Blackburn, are inclined to hold, on the other hand, that moral values are invented or projected by us.[4]

Philosophers usually speak of anti-realism, regarding it as a cluster of arguments that probe the strengths and weaknesses of realism, dialectically, without closing the debate. While it seems obvious that we cannot talk meaningfully about things beyond our ken (the anti-realist's intuition), it seems equally platitudinous that there is far more to reality than we can ever know (the realist's conviction). These intuitions are not easy to reconcile. Philosophical work at its best is dialectical, seeking to maintain the tension between *prima facie* incompatible positions.

But there is always a temptation to find a solution by eliminating one or other of the antithetical intuitions. In some recent philosophy of religion, for example, realism is often taken to be such an absurd and obsolete position that talk of anti-realism is giving way to talk of non-realism. Realism in religious discourse, understood as meaning that there is a self-subsistent transcendent deity independent of human thought, is assumed to be so implausible that nobody is interested or motivated enough to argue against it. Theological statements are supposed to depict objects and states of affairs in a supernatural realm, God is thought to be an objective entity whose existence is establishable by neutral enquiry, and so on. Over against all such attempts to represent supernatural objects in descriptive and quasi-scientific language, the non-realist in theology[5] insists on the symbolic – and that means the non-cognitive and conventional – character of language. The non-realist as regards religious language operates with the logical-positivist dichotomy between factual-descriptive and evaluative-expressive language (as in Ayer). If realism in religion means, say, that we regard God as an object of knowledge which just happens to escape our existing cognitive powers, it is understandable that an anti-realist might want to insist on the non-cognitive character of religious utterances – on their non-factual and non-representational character.

But this is to take the pains and pleasures of dialectical argument out of philosophical work. It is strange that philosophers of religion should be adopting non-realism at the very moment when realism is making a comeback in philosophy at large, especially in ethics, precisely under the challenge of anti-realism. Non-realism, in religion in particular, is of course at odds with ordinary people's beliefs, in the West at least, whether they personally are religious or not. It has been suggested that, in his later work, Wittgenstein is in favour of global non-realism – 'Everywhere', we are assured, he 'is a thoroughgoing constructivist and voluntarist.'[6] Wittgenstein, however, never suggests that ordinary people's ways of talking and thinking either should or indeed could be revised by philosophers. On the contrary, his work aims at liberating us from the confusions of philosophical theorizings. It will be suggested here, then, that his later writing is always so dialectical that he cannot be read as plumping for either realism or anti-realism. The lesson of anti-realism, for theologians as for moral philosophers, may reside in a more hardly-won realism rather than adoption of wholesale non-realism. Indeed, Wittgenstein may even be suggesting that where a dispute in philosophy seems so cut and dried, there must be some assumption that is common to the two sides, the removal of which will lead to the disappearance of the dispute.

II

There are passages in the later Wittgenstein's writings which lead good philosophers to regard him as an anti-realist. In his writings on the philosophy of mathematics in particular, as Michael Dummett has argued,[7] Wittgenstein reacts so strongly against the idea that the truths of mathematics have always already been objectively there, in some celestial realm, waiting for us to discover (realism), that he may seem to go to the other extreme, suggesting that we simply create them (constructivism). Dummett speaks of Wittgenstein's 'full-blooded conventionalism'.[8] The proof of this, it is claimed, lies in the way that he believes that 'logical necessity is created by the rules governing language'.[9] And the rules that govern language, it seems, are created at will by those who speak the language. Far from being a set of eternal truths which human beings hit upon as an explorer might discover a hitherto unmapped mountain range, mathematical propositions seem more like pragmatic inventions which could easily have been quite different.

This interpretation has been challenged, but it remains quite widely held that Wittgenstein's later work authorizes radically anti-realist inclinations, at least as regards mathematical propositions. Some philosophers – though not Michael Dummett – have then been tempted to extend Wittgenstein's supposed endorsement of constructivism in the philosophy of mathematics to other realms of discourse. But the lengthy and complex reflections on the phenomena of rule-following, which are central in Wittgenstein's later work, far from endorsing some kind of voluntaristic conventionalism, are surely aimed at liberating us from any such doctrine just as much as from its opposite.[10] Far from being a recommendation of global non-realism, applicable also in religion, the philosophical interest of these considerations is surely that Wittgenstein is trying to do justice to the conventional (hence revisable and arbitrary) element in regular behaviour and thinking – without denying that there is an irreducible given element as well (for example, the consistency of a set of conventions is not itself a convention). Given our natures and forms of life, so he surely seeks to show, many aspects of our behaviour cannot intelligibly be described as 'conventional' in the sense of being arbitrary and revisable at will – which does not mean, on the other hand, that much else, perhaps hitherto regarded as natural and immutable, might not be open to questioning and revision.

Far from legitimizing non-realism in the sense of voluntaristic constructivism in every domain, including that of religion, Wittgenstein arguably was doing his best, in G. E. M. Anscombe's phrase, 'to avoid the falsehoods of idealism and the stupidities of empiricist realism'.[11] To repeat: philosophical work at its most characteristic is dialectical, and the fascination of Wittgenstein's later work lies, not in his espousing one doctrine rather than the other, but in his indefatigable endeavours to steer a way between the two antithetical intuitions.

III

Wittgenstein is not the only major philosopher of our time to seek to do justice to these antithetical intuitions without eliminating one or the other. Much recent European philosophy (deconstruction, postmodernism, etc.), which greatly fascinates theologians of a non-realist persuasion, stems from the work of Martin Heidegger. But he too, paradoxically, dismissed the dispute between realism and idealism as resting on a mistake – in particular, on neglect by both sides of the place of our minds in the world.

In lectures given in 1927 and recently translated, Heidegger argues that, instead of having to clarify these two rival philosophical doctrines, let alone plump for one or other as the only solution, the way forward is to see that neither is tenable except on the basis of a certain negligence.[12] His suggestion is that each of the two views tacitly presupposes conceptions of 'subject' and 'object' which are precisely what require to be exposed and investigated. The whole point of his insistence on phenomenological description of our existence as always already being 'in the world' is that the concepts of subjectivity and objectivity with which the realism/idealism dispute silently operates need to be unmasked as the products of metaphysical fantasy.

Idealism moves in the right direction, Heidegger believes, in the sense that idealists recognize that what we mean by reality becomes clear only when we remember that we are always already participants on the scene – 'only when being, the real, is present and encountered'.[13] Realism is right, he thinks, to the extent that it respects our natural common-sense recognition of the independent existence of entities in the world – but it

immediately goes astray in assuming that their character, and the relationships between them, can be explained neutrally in terms of some causal
theory which leaves out our involvement as beings with intentionality.

In *Sein und Zeit*, his most famous book, published in 1927, Heidegger
dispenses with lengthy discussion of the realism/idealism dispute, ascribing
it to neglect by both realists and their opponents of any serious reflection
about the place of our minds in the world.[14] What he means is that for the
problems generated by the realism/idealism dispute to have any backing in
ordinary everyday phenomena, we must be able to find grounds for them in
phenomenological description of our place as cognitive agents in the world
– and, according to Heidegger, we shall find no such grounds. Certainly,
he adds scornfully, no such grounds will be secured by tinkering with the
concepts of consciousness and the subject. We just have to move right away
from all philosophy of consciousness – all philosophy, that is to say, that
privileges the first-person singular.

One of the reasons that Heidegger's dismissal of the realism/idealism
dispute is less familiar than it might be to Anglo-American philosophers
is, of course, that it is buried in appallingly unattractive terminology.
'Along with *Dasein* as being-in-the-world', he says, 'entities within-the-
world have in each case already been disclosed.' That recapitulates what he
has attempted, and surely achieved, in the preceding 200 pages of *Sein und
Zeit*. What it means, translated into more familiar terms, is that, when we
remember that, instead of being isolated centres of consciousness, we are
always already agents in the world, acting and reacting, we see also that the
world is well furnished with middle-sized dry goods of many kinds. We
bump up against them all the time – the real is always already encountered,
as he would say. This might seem like good old-fashioned realism, he
concedes, in the sense that 'the external world', speaking somewhat
portentously, would be regarded as being 'really there' – independently of
us. The 'results' of realism are right, if you like – but Heidegger cannot go
any further with realism, for the following two reasons.

In the first place, realism as traditionally conceived leaves itself open to
scepticism. Realists hold that the existence of the external world (as of other
minds, we may add, in terms of more familiar Anglo-American discussions)
is demonstrable. Instead of dismissing sceptical objections, in other words,
they try to answer them, thereby conceding that the existence of the
external world (say) needs to be demonstrated. They try to close the gap
between our minds and the world – a gap which, according to Heidegger,
simply does not exist. Once we remember that we are always already 'in the
world', as he puts it, the scepticism about our knowledge of the external

world (or of other minds) that seems to threaten the realist position simply collapses. For Heidegger, when we think about it, we see that our way of being is engaged agency from the outset. From our infancy we are embodied and embedded in a whole network of relationships – which sometimes break down, leaving us in the lurch, perhaps even prompting moments of despair and loss of faith in the trustworthiness of our surroundings. Of course Heidegger does not deny that we find ourselves in situations where our picture of this or that relationship turns out to be misleading or illusory. Things are not always what they at first seem, and so on. But his argumentative strategy is to remind us that, for all its precariousness and vulnerability, our relationship to the world in the open-ended system of the conventions and practices which constitute our way of life is always already – *immer schon* – a way of 'being-in-the-world' – *in-der-Welt-sein*. There is no gap between self and world, subject and object, mind and reality, which needs to be bridged. The scandal that Kant noted is not that philosophers have not provided a successful proof of the reality of the external world – but that philosophers ever thought that such a proof was needed.[15]

But, secondly, realism tries 'to explain reality ontically by real connections of interaction between things that are real'. The phrase 'connection of interaction' – *Wirkungszusammenhang* – provides the clue for those more at home in Anglo-American philosophy. As above, but in even more unattractive jargon, what Heidegger means is that realists attempt to deliver accounts of the world in terms of causal theories of reference and the like – leaving us as cognitive agents out of the picture. In effect, realists pretend to be able to see the world from above, as it were from a God's eye point of view.

Compared with that, idealism, 'no matter how contrary and untenable it may be in its results', has the advantage at least of bringing in the human agent: 'idealism emphasizes that being and reality are only "in the con-sciousness".' But as long as idealism fails to clarify how consciousness of reality is possible, the picture that it offers is empty. 'Being cannot be explained through entities' – that is where realism goes wrong; but the fact that 'reality is possible only in the understanding of Being' – which idealism gets right – 'does not absolve us from inquiring into the being of consciousness, of the *res cogitans* itself'. Indeed, if idealism were pushed right through, then 'ontological analysis of consciousness' would prescribe itself as the unavoidably first task. The advantage of idealism, in the history of modern philosophy, is that it compels us to return to the question of the place of our minds in the world.

If what idealism amounts to, then, is that the world can never be explained by items within it as if we were not participants on the scene, then idealism opens the only way forward, so Heidegger thinks. But if idealism means referring everything to a subject or consciousness (divine or human, we may add) which remains indeterminate, or at best characterized negatively as 'un-thing-like' (*undinglich*: 'immaterial'), then 'this idealism is no less naive in its method than the most grossly militant realism'.

This discussion of the customarily unexamined presuppositions of both realism and idealism shows, Heidegger concludes, that we had better move to different ground altogether – to what he calls 'existential analytic of *Dasein*', which may be translated as description of the place of agents always already involved in the world. We should not picture ourselves as transcendental subjects confronting contextless objects upon which we subsequently confer intelligibility. On the contrary, things around us, including other people, are always already significant in some way or other – whether they are attractive or threatening or whatever. We are involved in countless practical ways in the world and with one another – long before we can stand back and regard anything as it were from above. For Heidegger, the realist/idealist dispute depends on the supposition that there is an unbridgeable gap between us as minds and things around us, such that the outcome is subjectivism in some form or another. The dominant form, he would think, is the view that the subject makes the world intelligible by means of representations. This opens up the objection that there is no way of knowing in the end whether the representations mirror the world truly or are merely pragmatically useful fictions. The only way to free ourselves from representationalism is to remember how complicated our participation in the world is. We are always caught up in a 'hermeneutic circle', as Heidegger would say. Our general sense of things depends on what we encounter in the world (the realist intuition); but we discover things as significant in this or that determinate way only because we have been initiated into the practices and customs of our culture (the idealist emphasis). For Heidegger, the fact that things come to us only within the network of our conventions is entirely compatible with a full-blooded realism that insists on the self-standing reality of what shows itself.

IV

Wittgenstein and Heidegger worked independently of one another and in very different terms, but their moves as regards the realism/idealism debate were quite similar. Wittgenstein too sought to bring realism and idealism together in such a way that the dispute would become pointless.

When he returned to philosophical work in 1929, for example, Wittgenstein wrote a good deal about solipsism. In the *Blue Book* (dictated 1933–34), for example, his focus is on the sort of claim that might be expressed as follows: '"I can only know that *I* have personal experiences, not that anyone else has."'[16] He counters that feeling with a little mockery. Suppose, for example, that I am in pain – 'Does a realist pity me more than an idealist or a solipsist?' That is to say, what difference does it make whether you subscribe to realism or anti-realism? The common-sense man, Wittgenstein insists, is 'as far from realism as from idealism'. The realist philosopher, however, thinks that 'there is no difficulty in the idea of *supposing* . . . that someone else has what I have' (my emphasis). That is to say, it is a supposition, a kind of hypothesis, we could demonstrate it. 'But the trouble with the realist is always that he does not solve but skip the difficulties which his adversaries see, though they too don't succeed in solving them.' This supposed 'supposing' opens the way once again for doubts about our having knowledge of anything. As regards our knowledge of other minds (or of the world), the realist fails to see the depth of the sceptic's difficulties – and yet, for Wittgenstein as for Heidegger, idealism is no solution either.

'There is no common sense answer to a philosophical problem', Wittgenstein says. There is no point in merely restating the views of common sense – what we have to do, rather, is to cure philosophers of the temptation to attack common sense. When the philosopher whom we call a solipsist tells us that 'only his own experiences are real', this does not mean that he disagrees with us about any practical matter. He does not say that we are pretending when we complain of pains, he pities us as much as anyone else. He just wants to restrict the word 'real' to what we should call his own experiences. '"I can't know what he sees when he (truthfully) says that he sees a blue patch"', the philosopher might say.[17] The idealist wants us to see how inadequate our form of expression is – how it misleads us. He wants to introduce a certain rigour into our understanding of commonplace expressions.

The difficulty here arises, Wittgenstein suggests, from our being inclined to identify 'knowing what he sees' with 'seeing that which he also sees' – not in the sense in which we both have the same object before our eyes, but in the sense in which the object seen becomes an object in our minds. 'The idea is that the same object may be before his eyes and mine, but that I can't stick my head into his (or my mind into his, which comes to the same) so that the real and immediate object of his vision becomes the real and immediate object of my vision too.' That is to say, by 'I don't know what he sees' I mean 'I don't know what he is looking at' – and I am assuming that what he is looking at is something hidden, a private object that is floating before his mind's eye. The only way to rid oneself of this tempting thought, Wittgenstein suggests, is to investigate the conceptual difference between saying things like 'I don't know what he is seeing' and 'I don't know what he is looking at', 'as they are *actually used in our language*' (my emphasis).

Heidegger, with his 'existential analytic of *Dasein*', offers a fairly systematic exposition of the always already existing conditions of our being placed in the world as we are, in terms of being thrown into it, having to make it our own, being affected by it, and so forth. Wittgenstein, on the other hand, prefers an assembling of reminders for a determinate purpose.[18] But his target too is a certain conception of the self that springs from neglect of aspects of things that are hidden because of their simplicity and familiarity,[19] but of which we can be reminded. His much more disseminated polemics, his 'album' of sketches, this investigation that compelled him to 'travel . . . criss-cross in every direction',[20] is nevertheless rightly classified as remarks on the philosophy of psychology. His philosophical psychology, like Heidegger's existential anthropology, is a painstaking description of how our minds are actually placed in the world.

In effect, Wittgenstein, like Heidegger, believed that the famous dispute between realists and idealists, while it has been at the centre of much philosophical attention at least since the time of Kant, should be set aside in favour of sober description of our place in the world as cognitive subjects and moral agents. Once we had moved a certain distance into *Daseinsanalytik* and philosophical psychology, so each would have thought, the dispute would cease to seem interesting. As so often in philosophy, a dispute between two parties loses its interest once something that both sides have overlooked or repressed has been brought to light.

Much of Wittgenstein's later work is devoted to breaking the hold of certain obsessive pictures that, so he thinks, generate what then pass for extremely important philosophical problems. 'From the very outset', he writes in 1929–30, '"Realism", "Idealism", etc., are names which belong to metaphysics.'[21] That is to say, he goes on, the parties believe that they can each say something specific about the essence of the world. They take for granted, he is suggesting, that we are the ones whose distinctive contribution is to describe the world. The realism/idealism dispute unwittingly depends on the picture of us as subjects over against objects which it is our principal activity to represent.

Michael Dummett puts it as follows:

What the realist would like to do is to stand in thought outside the whole temporal process and describe the world from a point which has no temporal position at all, but surveys all temporal positions in a single glance. . . . The anti-realist takes more seriously the fact that we are immersed in time: being so immersed, we cannot frame any description of the world as it would appear to one who was not in time, but we can only describe it as it is, i.e. as it is now.[22]

The anti-realist, having silently inherited a good deal from Hegel among others, recognizes that our descriptions of the world cannot be other than coloured by our historical situation. Anti-realists, in other words, move in the direction of historicism, cultural relativism, and so forth. Realists, on the other hand, hanker for a description of the world that would be unstained by the human observer's contribution. They believe that there is, in principle, one true theory about the world, although it may always elude our powers to discover. Either way, however, the decisive point is that they all assume that our relationship with things in the world is primarily and paradigmatically one of *representation*.

But what if describing the world – representation – is not so central to our way of being in the world? The opening discussion in Wittgenstein's *Philosophical Investigations* is devoted to reminding us that describing the world, designating objects by name, referring to things, and suchlike, are far from the most distinctive human activities. 'Think how many different kinds of thing are called "description"', Wittgenstein admonishes us.[23] It is tempting to reduce all assertions to descriptions – even to descriptions of one's inner life – which would be solipsism. Narrating, story-telling, recounting, and suchlike, certainly belong to our natural history – but no more and no less so than commanding, questioning, chatting, walking, eating, drinking and playing games.[24] We need to keep the multiplicity of language-games in view. But this is not just Wittgenstein's way of advising us against raising metaphysical questions. By implication he has already started his philosophy of psychology. He is reminding us of how varied the activity of referring actually is – and of how interwoven it is with so many other activities.

'"We name things and then we can talk about them: can refer to them in talk."'[25] But why assume that talking about things comes inexorably from naming them? Naming is not just a preparation for referring; learning someone's name is not sufficient for being able to talk about him or her. Furthermore, when we reflect about it, we see that there is no one thing which counts as talking about something. 'We do the most various things with our sentences', Wittgenstein reminds us. Asking 'What is that called?', a question which takes it for granted that one already understands what it is to be given the name as well as how to understand a gesture of pointing something out, is something to which we are 'brought up, trained'. In other words, even as common an activity as referring is already pretty sophisticated. For there to be referring, designating, describing, representing, and so on, a good deal else has to be in place. It may be tempting to regard pointing with one's finger as an absolutely basic, untaught and utterly unambiguous gesture. But once we have allowed Wittgenstein to assemble reminders of the obvious for this particular purpose,[26] we begin to doubt whether the picture of ourselves as the ones who go in, in some culture-free and foundationalist way, for describing the world, has much to do with the realities of the situation. The man who is engaged in some privileged way in representing reality begins to look, if not a mythical creature, then certainly a somewhat contextless one. A philosophical dispute that turns unwittingly on this picture begins to seem much less gripping. The subject whose principal activity is representation of objects that present themselves in the world is just not as central to our lives as philosophers have often led us to believe.

Heidegger and Wittgenstein, in quite different ways, struggled to bring about an understanding of ourselves as engaged agents, as embodied and embedded in a culture. The great temptation that Wittgenstein strives to expose is the inclination to take naming as a primitive, self-sufficient operation – forgetting that a great deal else has already to be in play in the conversation before the mere act of naming is to make sense.[27] In both cases, the argumentative strategy is to bring to the fore the skills, activities, and so on, overlooking which creates the fantasy of representation as the paradigmatic move on the human agent's part.

V

Questioning the dominance in philosophy of the subject's representation of objects has parallels elsewhere. In art, for example, non-representationalism has made great headway. In many scientific investigations the effects of the observer's participation are factored in. It is not difficult to think of artists who dismiss representation completely in favour of thoroughgoing expressionism. It would not be difficult to find philosophers of science (though not many scientists!) who dismiss the ideal of our eventually attaining the one true representation of reality in favour of the belief that the best we can ever do is to project a variety of interpretations upon the world which may be equally valid in practice and yet incommensurable with one another at the theoretical level. But neither for Heidegger nor for Wittgenstein is such constructivism the only option. Abandoning a certain picture of the self in the world, and of the conceptions of subjectivity, objectivity and representation that go with it, need not mean abandoning the notions of subjectivity, objectivity and representation altogether. Neither Heidegger nor Wittgenstein throws the baby out with the bath water.

On the contrary. As Hilary Putnam shows, in his recent writings,[28] Wittgenstein's questioning of the privileged status of reference to an objective world by a transcendental subject also puts an end to the version of realism according to which reality divides itself up into objects and properties in one definite unique way, as if our concepts were dictated to us by the world. That is the myth of the ready-made world, as Putnam calls it.

But to deny that there is such a ready-made world is not to say that the world is our invention:

> [I]f anyone believes that certain concepts are absolutely the correct ones, and that having different ones would mean not realizing something that we realize – then let him imagine certain very general facts of nature to be different from what we are used to, and the formation of concepts different from the usual ones will become intelligible to him.[29]

Our concepts are not 'arbitrary'; we cannot choose them 'at pleasure'. Putnam, following Wittgenstein's lead, argues that while what we say about the world certainly reflects our interests and conceptual choices (and these can vary over a considerable range), its truth or falsity is not determined simply by our interests and choices. The world is not the product of our will, neither biologically nor culturally, nor of our disposition to talk in certain ways either.[30]

It is futile, Putnam argues, to try to divide the factual and the conventional from one another absolutely. Of course, even when we look at something as simple as a stone or a tree, the possibility of the perception depends on a whole conceptual scheme – on our having a language. But, equally, it is not a matter of arbitrary convention that something is a stone or a tree. What we call language or mind enters so deeply into what we call world or reality that the very idea of picturing ourselves as observers of something independent of language or mind is fatally compromised from the outset.[31] But recoiling against that into some kind of voluntaristic constructivism according to which we 'make up the world' leaves us immured in the same mistake. Once again we are picturing the world as a product — if the realist pictures it as preconceptualized reality (some kind of raw material that awaits our intervention), the non-realist views it as a creation *ex nihilo* (all his own work).

The picture we need, Putnam suggests in a famous phrase, is that the world and the mind make up the world and the mind. Reality is always from our point of view (the Kantian anti-realist point) — but that does not mean that there are no objective facts of the matter (the realist's concern). Indeed, after many years spent questioning metaphysical realism, Putnam is now engaged in opposing the slide into relativism, which he finds even more worrying. In ethics in particular, he very much wants to show what is wrong with moral subjectivism.[32] He even goes so far to contemplate 'a rebirth of a full-bodied, red-blooded metaphysical realism if that were the way to get people to accept the objectivity of ethics'[33] — pretty well what Iris Murdoch's revival of Platonism has offered.

But, in a typically Wittgensteinian move, he argues that metaphysical realism and moral subjectivism, far from being opposites, are deeply connected tendencies. It is because we see physics as the one true representation of the way the world is, Putnam suggests, and not simply a rationally acceptable description suited for certain problems and purposes, that we tend to be subjectivistic about judgements in ethics and aesthetics that we cannot reduce to physics. What is required is that we become less realistic about physics and less subjectivistic about ethics, so Putnam concludes.[34]

Of course, nothing suggested here rules out the possibility that religious discourse should be treated non-realistically. In philosophy at large, it is certainly not established that realism is an obsolete doctrine (I). On the contrary, many philosophers are torn between the attractions of the two opposing intuitions that give rise to the realist/anti-realist dispute. Good philosophers find anti-realism in Wittgenstein's work on the philosophy of mathematics but, even if that interpretation is correct, it is arguable that he should not be made responsible for the spread of non-realism into every other domain (II). Indeed, it may be suggested that philosophers should not be plumping for either realism or anti-realism. Heidegger, at least as important for theologians as Wittgenstein, argued that the whole realism/idealism dispute was rooted in a false picture of the place of the self in the world (III). In very different terms, but in a quite analogous way, in particular by dislodging representation from its status as the most characteristic activity of the subject with regard to objects in the world,

Wittgenstein also sought to incorporate the insights of realism and idealism in a way that breaks the grip of the supposed dichotomy (**IV**).

With Hilary Putnam, one of the most discussed philosophers at the present time, much indebted to a reading of Wittgenstein's work which certainly does not take it as propagating anti-realism, we find ourselves deeply engaged, as regards moral philosophy in particular, in working our way between realism and anti-realism in search of what he labels *realism with a human face* (**V**). The mind and the world cannot be described as if from a God's eye view (realism at its most exorbitant); but that does not entail our succumbing to the abyss of relativism and voluntaristic constructivism (non-realism at its dandiest). But the fact that realism is regarded by many respected philosophers as not so wrong that nothing can be salvaged from criticizing it does not show that, in the philosophy of religion, non-realism may not be the only option. That many good philosophers are engaged in arguing for realism in moral philosophy might, on the other hand, give philosophers of religion something to think about.

Notes

1 Michael Dummett, *Truth and Other Enigmas* (Duckworth, 1978), pp. 1–24.
2 A. J. Ayer, *Language, Truth and Logic* (Gollancz, 2nd edn, 1946).
3 Iris Murdoch, *Metaphysics as a Guide to Morals* (Chatto and Windus, 1992).
4 See G. Sayre-McCord (ed.), *Essays on Moral Realism* (Cornell University Press, 1988).
5 E.g. Don Cupitt, *Taking Leave of God* (SCM Press, 1980).
6 Don Cupitt, *The Sea of Faith* (BBC, 1984), p. 222.
7 *Truth and Other Enigmas*, pp. 166–85.
8 *Truth and Other Enigmas*, p. 170.
9 *The Sea of Faith*, p. 222.
10 See S. Holtzmann and C. Leich (eds), *Wittgenstein: To Follow a Rule* (Routledge, 1981).
11 G. E. M. Anscombe, *From Parmenides to Wittgenstein: Collected Philosophical Papers*, Vol. I (Blackwell, 1981), p. 115.
12 Martin Heidegger, *History of the Concept of Time*, trans. Theodore Kisiel (Indiana University Press, 1985), p. 222.
13 *History of the Concept of Time*, p. 223.
14 Martin Heidegger, *Being and Time*, trans. John Macquarrie and Edward Robinson (Blackwell, 1962), p. 207.
15 *Being and Time*, p. 205.
16 Ludwig Wittgenstein, *The Blue and Brown Books* (Blackwell, 1958), p. 48.
17 *The Blue and Brown Books*, p. 61.
18 Ludwig Wittgenstein, *Philosophical Investigations*, trans. G. E. M. Anscombe (Blackwell, 1953), #127.
19 *Philosophical Investigations*, #129.
20 *Philosophical Investigations*, p. ix.
21 Ludwig Wittgenstein, *Philosophical Remarks*, trans. Raymond Hargreaves and Roger White (Blackwell, 1975), p. 86.
22 *Truth and Other Enigmas*, p. 369.

23 *Philosophical Investigations*, #24.
24 *Philosophical Investigations*, #25.
25 *Philosophical Investigations*, #27.
26 *Philosophical Investigations*, #127.
27 *Philosophical Investigations*, #257.
28 Hilary Putnam, *Renewing Philosophy* (Harvard University Press, 1992).
29 *Philosophical Investigations*, p. 230.
30 Hilary Putnam, *Realism with a Human Face* (Harvard University Press, 1990), p. 29.
31 *Realism with a Human Face*, p. 28.
32 Hilary Putnam, *Reason, Truth and History* (Cambridge University Press, 1981), p. 143.
33 *Realism with a Human Face*, p. 37.
34 *Reason, Truth and History*, p. 143.

11

Theological materialism

Graham Ward

It was Kant's analysis of the operation of reasoning that led to the creation of the two main joists of twentieth-century anti-realism. For Kant, on the basis of an analysis of certain judgements such as 'all bodies are heavy', concluded that we have no immediate access to things in themselves. Our perception of the world is always a creation of certain dispositions and faculties which create and order the concepts which constitute our consciousness of things. Judgements are *made*. And within this philosophical framework both the sociology of knowledge and linguistic idealism were developed. A word about these notions. Sociology of knowledge claims that all we 'know' is a social construction – that is, there are no universal, timeless truths to which we can point. Any and every judgement is conditioned by the time in which it is made, the person who makes it and the society in which they live. Our knowledge is as historically specific as it is historically contingent. Linguistic idealism claims that there is nothing outside language. There is no Nature, no Order of Things, no Reality, no Out-There which is not a representation, a chain of signs. Our language constructs a culture, a *habitus*, an order out of symbols, and this unending symbolic field is simply an all too human net thrown across the chaotic and unformed.

Much postmodern theology to date has hung its anti-foundationalism from these two philosophical joists, the sociology of knowledge and linguistic idealism. This is Don Cupitt in a recent exploration of his philosophical presuppositions: 'In the movement of words we come to feel and understand that moving energies, formed into words, are what everything's made of.'[1] This is Mark C. Taylor: 'The death of God, the disappearance of the Father, is the birth of the Son, the appearance of the Word – the appearance of language as sovereign.'[2] On one level, their work (and the work of other so-named postmodern theologians like Charles Winquist, Thomas Altizer and David Ray Griffin) expresses the apotheosis of liberalism: God is dead, truth is created, all standpoints are provisional, flow with the flux for only in doing that is there freedom.[3] But this is liberalism without egos – for the human subject as an entity, as a perceiving consciousness, is also a part of an extensive textual reality. Personal identity is constructed by the social, historical and linguistic conditions in which any human being is located and through which he or she is defined. Thus this 'theology' argues for a radical antinomianism, a bacchanalian nihilism, without a determinative concept of agency and, therefore, without an ethics. In doing so it advocates a mode of life dangerously open to the manipulations and exploitations of pragmatists equipped with institutional forms of power. The intellectual difficulties of this anti-foundational theologizing are both philosophical and theological.

Philosophically, the difficulty with this anti-realism is that it is massively counter-intuitive. The deconstructed Cartesian ego still retains the 'sense' of agency. Culturally specific interest groups – the policy makers at the Adam Smith Institute, local gay activists, pressure groups of all kinds – still 'work' with a sense of the non-provisionality of knowledge, notions of 'truth', beliefs in their possible social effectiveness and therefore in a certain freedom and potential liberation. You will notice my language of qualification – 'sense of', 'work with', 'notions of', 'possible' and 'potential'. But to qualify is not to erase. We still need to ask why these possibilities still remain, why intuitively the life I live is not in accord with the anti-realist, anti-foundationalist world-view. As has frequently been pointed out, these theologians still write sentences, still argue for a case, make judgements, rationalize, abstract, deduce. They too still retain a sense of agency. They promulgate a certain cultural politics – liberalism's *laissez-faire* – and believe it is the 'right' cultural politics. We should not accept this discrepancy between what these theologians propose and the self-assertive manner in which they propose it[4] as illusory. Rather, we need to examine a distinction it opens up. It is a distinction described recently as:

> The fact that every object is constituted as an object of discourse has *nothing to do* with whether there is a world external to thought, or with the realism/idealism opposition. An earthquake or a falling brick is an event that certainly exists. . . . But whether their specificity as objects is

145

constructed in terms of 'natural phenomena' or 'expressions of the wrath of God' depends upon the structure of a discursive field. What is denied is not that such objects exist externally to thought, but the rather different assertion that they would constitute themselves as objects outside any condition of emergence.[5]

The implications of this recognition that despite the sociological and linguistic constitution of an object the external existence of the object cannot be denied, need to be examined theologically. For the theological difficulty of anti-realist 'theologies' is that theology requires some notion of realism. For theology to be *theo*logy its discourse must, in some sense, be saying something about God and God's relationship with the world which is true. If this is not the case, if theological statements are simply expressing our own states of mind, our own politics, our own cultural situations, then 'theology' is a misnomer and theologians are anthropologists, sociologists, psychologists and ideologues. Theology is then a cultural science trafficking in opiates and mysteries, illusions and panaceas which only encourage bad faith. Theology *as such* must be subsequently demythologized and seen for what it is, at best – a means for self-development through the expression of an ego-ideal. And so say the postmodern theologians listed above. But theology if it is to have validity as *theo*logy, cannot dispense with realism. It is the grounds for its realism that are problematic. For theology cannot dispense with representation either. We have no unmediated access to God. If we did have, then God would simply be an object among all the other objects of the world. Theology *is* mediated; and the transcendence of God (or the otherness of God) is maintained by this mediation. Something *is* only something *as* it is represented. This has to be accepted. If there is no direct apprehension of the world, then there is certainly no direct apprehension of God who, as its creator, is other than the world. The immediacy of revelation, like the immediacy of sensuous experience, depends upon its mediation: concepts, metaphors, discourse. Furthermore, any language is constantly changing – through time, through a diversity of cultural contexts. Meaning is never fixed, never independent of histories, societies, subjectivities, the bones and sinews of language itself. As a result of research into comparative linguistics we have come to recognize the cultural specificity of any language, the cultural specificity of 'reality' as it is not only portrayed but constructed in and through any language. Any mediated revelation of God must also then be historically contingent, sociologically embedded and linguistically specific. To argue, therefore, for a theological realism it is necessary to demonstrate that despite the ubiquity of language, our appreciation of the real is not completely language-dependent. We have to argue for the limits of a sociology of knowledge and a linguistic idealism.

The question remains, then, that there may be nothing outside textuality that we can intellectually grasp and possess, but is there that outside of textuality which can be inferred, the recognition of which provides the basis for any knowing at all? The question to be examined, therefore, is the relationship of realism to representation; the position to be avoided is the extreme of either the correspondence view of language (word directly relating to the empirical object) or the identity of reality with its representation (words constructing their object).[6] What I wish to argue for, in this essay, is whether when we step back (the extent to which we can step back will constitute part of the analysis) from knowledge as discourse we do not have to infer a theology which makes discourse possible at all. In other words, I wish to argue that language does create reality (and hence our grounds for a foundationalist realism flounder upon the immanence of representation) but that language itself attests to a 'transcendence' (yet to be defined) which is ineradicable.

There is a further question which follows: by what method can we attempt to formulate *both* an anti-foundationalism *and* a realism? Anti-foundationalism issues from the conviction that there are only pragmatic starting-points, no position from which objectivity might conduct an examination, no subject who is not himself or herself caught up in larger fields of symbolic power and interest. Realism would disagree and base its judgement upon the availability of such an objectivity enabling any investigation to proceed. Thus, for the realist, any argument might be concluded for the subject as enquiring agent is able to make correct and intellectually honest judgements (or intend to do so). Since the operation of language (i.e. discourse as language in use, rather than language in the abstract) is the focus for my concerns then the method I adopt is one of intratextuality – that is, examining, within language, the processes of language, the economy of signification as it functions both immanently and transcendentally. A complex operation emerges composed of three different sets of analysis. First, an analysis of the seeming objectivity of propositions and statements. Second, an analysis of the distinctive context within which this statement occurs; an analysis of the specific relations and interests (social, historical and biographical) bearing upon the maker of this statement. Third, an analysis of the rhetoric employed (metaphors, analogies, suggestive language) which causes an excess or deflection of meaning above and beyond the logic of the statement itself.

At the risk then of simply reviving the old nominalist/realist debate, I ask what is the character of language as an operation? We will proceed slowly, examining a communicative practice. In a seminar in the Lightfoot Room in the Divinity Faculty at Cambridge, while giving an account of Derrida's notion of *différance*, I am told that Derrida is evidently confused (and confusing). For when one taps the table (which dominates the room) and states 'This is a table', no one in the room acquainted with the English language is remotely in doubt about the meaning of the phrase and its relation to the object around which we sit. 'This is a table' would classically be termed a 'referring expression' by analytical philosophers. The word 'table' refers – it does not differ, it does not defer – to that empirical object independent of both the word and the speaker of the word. It mediates meaning, relating object to the subject's concept of the object. Hence, philosophical realism is assured on the basis of the positivist validation of the object there in front of us, made known to us through the medium of language. Bertrand Russell's famed criterion for a referring expression is justified: 'Whenever the grammatical subject of a proposition can be supposed not to exist without rendering the proposition meaningless, it is plain that the grammatical subject is not a proper name, i.e. not a name directly representing some object.'[7] This is only a short step away from those defenders of theological realism who employ a similar representational view of language. Let me outline three such defenders and three varieties of representational views that their work unveils: cognitive, critical, and expressionist realism.

The first we will deal with quickly because it is already dated and has few advocates. Here is R. B. Braithwaite, writing in his essay 'An empiricist's view of the nature of religious belief':

> The meaning of any statement, then, will be taken as being given by the way it is used. The kernel for an empiricist of the problem of the nature of religious belief is to explain, in empirical terms, how a religious statement is used by a man who asserts it in order to express his religious conviction.[8]

Braithwaite distinguishes between expression and conviction. Religious beliefs for him are expressions, representations using a religious vocabulary, of moral convictions, assertions about how one intends to act. Thus the meaning of any religious expression can have empirical verification – even though the intention may not find realization in any act. The expression itself is a metaphorical description but with empirical reference. Therefore, religious assertions are empirical propositions. They have an empirical referent which validates their meaning. In cognitive realism words are clear-glazed windows upon the world.

Janet Martin Soskice's early work on models, metaphors, and the ineliminably figurative nature of theological language defends a similar position. She sets out to give an account of how the use of metaphors in theological discourse can tell us something *about* God. Like the scientific realist, the theological realist wants to preserve models and the metaphors issuing from them 'not as convenient fictions for the ordering of observables but as terms which somehow provide access to states and relations which exist independent of our theorizing about them'.[9] It is that 'somehow' of which an account must be rendered. But it is a somehow accounted for on the basis of language as 'reality-depicting', not reality-conscripting. Representation and reality, expression and reference, having been broken apart, the humpty-dumpty of this theological realism rests upon putting them back together again. Two points become vital to establish this realism. First, reference is dependent as much on context as content. So 'valve' will mean something different if used in an operating theatre, or a garage, or a TV repair shop. Second, reference can be indirect. I can speak of 'electricity' through speaking about its effects, rather than its visible properties. Meaning in metaphors, then, is indirect and relates to the communities within which the metaphors have emerged as significant ('a context of agreement'[10]). Religious metaphors speak indirectly of religious experience and are understood and developed by a community sharing that descriptive vocabulary and working with a particular interpretative tradition. Thus, there remains the possibility for speaking about God – without which the firm ground for theological realism is impossible. Language-users construct symbolic representations of their worlds (or, at least, their experience of those worlds). In critical realism words remain windows on the world but the glass is now coloured and the light therefore filtered.

We can distinguish this critical realism from expressionist realism (also founded upon the metaphoricity of religious language) by the much more non-cognitivist conclusions of the latter. Thus Sallie McFague, in her influential book *Metaphorical Theology: Models of God in Religious Language*, begins by emphasizing that there is *not* a distinction between ordinary language and metaphor. Cognitive and critical realism would both insist upon the distinction. For McFague all language is metaphorical, and metaphors are 'constantly speaking about the great unknowns – mortality, love, fear, joy, guilt, hope and so on'.[11] Metaphors emerge from 'our sensuous, affectional, and active lives at the most primordial level',[12] giving expression to that which lies too deep for words, the ineffability of our existential condition. This enables McFague to conclude that 'a metaphor is an assertion or judgment of similarity and difference between two thoughts in permanent tension with one another, which redescribes reality in an open-ended way but has structural as well as affective power'.[13] What metaphor 'refers' to cannot be identifed, for it is semantically open-ended. It asserts in its judgement, it is structurally tensile and it has affective power. To appreciate its assertion then cognition is necessary, but the power and operation of metaphor exceeds the ability of reason to contain and define it. Since it bespeaks our fundamental human condition in the world, it expresses more than we can think or know, passing through but then beyond consciousness. Hence the burden of such metaphorical utterance is non-cognitive. In expressionist realism religious words remain windows on the world but attention cannot focus upon that world, for it is transfixed by the stained glass artefacts which elicit aesthetic and emotional responses.

Sallie McFague builds upon the work of the philosopher Paul Ricoeur, and Ricoeur argues that ultimately metaphors have an ontological and transcendent import. They move us beyond ourselves to a place where human existence is rooted in a universal Being. Only in this sense can we say they 'refer'. Metaphor eclipses ordinary reference 'in order to reach the mythic level where its function of discovery is set free'.[14] In this way we can still speak of truth, of the reality to which metaphors point us and, in that pointing, the truth they enable us to glimpse. But linguistic idealism only takes this position one step further by emphasizing that that 'reality' glimpsed is as much a product and invention of metaphor as its discovery. The 'world' is simply artifice, figure and simulacrum. Therefore, Ricoeur's account of metaphorical reference is circular – it only discovers that which it creates. Nietzsche waits in the margins of such an account of metaphor and reference, flagging his assertion that truth is 'A mobile army of metaphors, metonymies, anthropomorphisms'.[15] The difference, then, between the realisms of Braithwaite, Soskice and McFague and the linguistic idealism of Mark C. Taylor *et al.* is that the latter deny and the former assert a division between experience and language, truth and expression, reality and representation.

Having said as much let us return to the specific context I have set up, the Lightfoot Room at the Cambridge Divinity School, and enter again the lists of the debate concerning the statement 'This is a table'. What is quite evident is that it is not the language itself which is doing the referring here. The demonstrative pronoun 'this' requires the supplement of a physical gesture – the movement of the head, the eyes or the finger which allows the phonetic unit 'this' to be in contact with the table itself. If there was no such supplement then the announcement 'This is a table' would require us to negotiate for a supplement by asking 'What is a table?' If the speaker then pointed to a door or a window or the ceiling or another human being, that would not alter the contents of the phrase itself; it would simply defer the meaning of the supplementing gesture until the speaker elaborated further (giving us yet another supplement to the initial assertion). He or she would now need to explain in what sense that door, say, could be described as a table. If no such supplement was given then we would not be able to understand the meaning of the sentence, though its correct grammar would indicate that it was a sentence. 'This is a table' would then be a subset of those phrases beloved by analytical philosophers of language and linguists examining phrases which can be created without transgressing the rules of syntax and yet which remain nonsensical. Now let us examine further the nature of this supplement and deferral of meaning. For what I am indicating here is that no sentence has meaning outside of context – and then the question must be asked: where does context begin and end? To what extent is there a difference between text and context? Another way of asking this question would be to ask: where does the requirement for supplementary information stop? What is the context, then, which enables the phrase 'This is a table', as it is spoken by someone around that enormous table which dominates the Lightfoot Room, to be rendered meaningful? A note must be made here. If I list the various forms of context for that sentence the order in the listing is not hierarchical, nor chronological; it is simply as they come to mind.

First, there is the context of linguistic competence – that is, a knowledge of the language (by speaker and audience) which enables the production of a grammatical unit asserting that this is a table. The phrase is made up of a seemingly simple assembly of a demonstrative pronoun, a copula, an indefinite article (specifying number) and a noun. But we have been taught and internalized this grammatical construction, the order of elements in the phrase, just as we have been taught to use the grammatical categories themselves. An assertion cannot, in English, have the form 'Is this table the' or 'Table this is the'. We have internalized our learning, through repeated use, without, for the most part, being able grammatically to characterize what we have been doing. Saussure called the structure of any language out of which any assertion issues *la langue*, while the particular linguistic instances of language-use he called *la parole*. He drew attention to the way meaning is produced in discourse through a differential system. So, with our phrase 'This is a table', the meaning of the phrase issues from the fact that syntactically a noun differs from a verb, a verb from a pronoun. He called these 'syntagmatic relations'. Furthermore, a table is not a chair, it is not a stool, or a sideboard. Nor, though these other words might be suggested by 'table', is a 'table' a 'label' or a 'cable' or a 'tablet'. He called these 'associative relations'. The first set of relations are present in the text, the second are absent. The meaning or semantic value of 'table', then, issues from this differential context in which present and absent relations play a constitutive role in communication. Semantic value does not consist in the term's association with another object in the world as its referent, as all those who divide representation from reality, expression from content, believe (Braithwaite and early Soskice among them). This differential system Saussure developed upon the basis of his observation that the relation of sign (the phonetic and graphic markings of 'table') and the signified (the concept table) is arbitrary (there is no natural, only conventional, association between them). The relationship between them is oblique, not direct nor transparent. The identity of 'table' (or 'is' or 'this'), then, can never be fixed or finalized. For its appearance, or repetition, will always occur in particular contexts, in particular differential webs of semiotic relations. Its necessary iteration (for only repeated social usage establishes its conventional value) means that its final and definitive meaning is always deferred – and in being deferred will only refer us to other signs and how it differs from them, as in a dictionary, where the meaning of one word endlessly points towards other words. We observe a large rectangle of polished oak on four bolster legs and call it 'table'. In another context, we observe a circle of reinforced white plastic on a three foot tripod and we also call it 'table'. We perceive these objects as tables. But there is no essence of or universal table to which these all relate. In each case, the meaning of the word issues from the differential web of its context. We have not grasped what a table *is*; we have simply learnt how to use the sounds or visible markings which make up 'table'.

Second, there is the social context to which the meaning of the noun phrase 'This is a table' is related. By 'social' I allude to the political, historical and economic forces which have given rise to and permeate the situation within which the phrase 'This is a table' has been spoken. By 'social' I also allude to the psychological and biographical forces from within which we all speak. If the phrase was not part of an argument against the coherence of Derrida's notion of *différance* its meaning would be altered. The same phrase might be used in the beginners' classes at a school teaching English to foreign students, and its meaning would then be not that a table exists as part of the furniture of the world, but 'This is the

English word for a table', or 'This is how we construct a simple noun sentence in English using a demonstrative', or whatever part of the syllabus is being taught that day. We might, then, pay some attention to the psychological dynamics of the context of the debate in the Lightfoot Room, and ask why the speaker needs to make this assertion, from what regions of the unconscious it issues, and what it betrays about the personality of the speaker. We could develop this psychological account (and a psychological account is available for every utterance and action we make) with all kinds of Freudian depths and Jungian extensions. But the point, I hope, is sufficiently made. Psychology presents us with another possible meaning for that utterance; another framework for interpreting it. We could, alternatively, place the statement within a historical and political context – the debate among English analytical philosophers on the role and importance of Derrida's work, and of continental philosophy as a whole. The interjection 'This is a table' now takes on another meaning such as 'I am a member of the British analytical school of philosophy', or 'I am one of those who believe Jacques Derrida to be a philosophical cowboy'. We might even then find a context for our noun phrase in the Britain/EC tensions of the 1980s and 1990s – British empirical analysis versus continental idealistic speculation. The context now becomes ethnographic and political.

The point is that no one speaks or acts outside these contextual fields – psychological, historical, political, ethnographic. Derrida's work also issues from a specific context. The French sociologist Pierre Bourdieu points to how the radical nature of much post-structuralism and deconstruction arises from those on the margins of respectable academia.[16] Perhaps in choosing to expound Derrida's notion of *différance* I am wanting to make a political gesture. Perhaps it constitutes a personal act of iconoclasm. What is at stake is that the meaning of the phrase 'This is a table' cannot be fixed. Its meaning is neither simple nor single. Its meaning is disseminated through and endlessly deferred by expanding networks of contextual relation, so that where the text ends and the context begins is impossible to locate. A new word is needed, such as intratextuality, to indicate that all investigation continues in, through and by means of contexts.

But what does all this description of contexts amount to? It amplifies the insight that meaning is not stable, that the truth-value of a phrase cannot be equated with its semantic value without also recognizing that it has a semiotic value – a value, that is, as a sign in relation to a differential network of signs. Whether we all see the same object, whether we would all agree that convention has taught us to classify such an object as a 'table'

– the fact remains that the meaning of that noun phrase is multiple, and modified with every new iteration or repetition because it is context-dependent and all the fields of possible context cannot be delineated. 'We can call "context" the entire "history of the world"', Derrida writes.[17] Nor do we each occupy the same contexts (even though we may all be in the same room and around the same table). The assertion is iterated within a context where its past and possible future reiterations have a context *for us*. With the diffusion of contexts a further problem arises, the problem of destination. For to whom is this demonstrative assertion addressed? To me as the expositor of Derrida, to those others in the room who may wish to join in the debate, to both, to Derrida, to the edifice of postmodernism, to the father the speaker never knew? Or on whose behalf is it voiced? The speaker's, theology's, God's, the institution's? And does it reach its destination? Is there a pure delivery of information via this statement that does not, necessarily, leave other questions, other meaningful possibilities, silent, marginalized? Of course, there are depths of ambiguity and contextual limits can be enforced (restricting the context to those in the Lightfoot Room, rather than the Lightfoot Room in the Divinity School and the Divinity School as a Faculty in the university, etc.). But where does the scale exist that can measure and chart various depths of ambiguity? Assessment of depths and ambiguousness depends upon establishing differences, through comparisons, and this will only engender further contextual negotiation. And contexts are never stable. They are motile because always *in actione*, shifting because ceaselessly performative. Hence the limitations of contexts are like so many nets cast upon tidal waters. This raises the question of the violence and trangression of meaning and interpretation, the ethics and politics of naming and defining.

If assessing the slipping and sliding of meaning for terms like 'table' results in so much complexity, then how much thicker would a description have to be for what William Empson would call a 'complex word' (Shakespeare's use of 'will'), or when a proper name has no verifiable object (like 'God' or 'gravity'), or when a proper name only has a verifiable object for some people from some perspectives (like a rainbow or certain sound frequencies)? When to 'table' we append an adjective like 'solid' or 'beautiful', or another noun like 'talk', then we are more evidently involved in interpreting a rhetorical phrase and the complexities of rhetoric's relation to assertion.

The hornets' nest of relativism has now been stirred. According to the analytic tradition, demonstrative expressions such as 'This is a table' 'appear to require the audience to think of the referent in a quite specific way, not obviously allowing room for counter-examples to the principle that communication requires that a speaker and his audience have the same thought'.[18] But, as I have shown, the speaker, the one to whom the assertion is addressed, the others in the room listening to and ready to participate in the debate and the language of the assertion itself are each situated in webs of context in which there is no single and final under-standing of what is said. The communication is not, of itself, a vehicle for communication. It requires the supplement of a physical gesture in order for there to be a common object between the speaker and the others. Demonstratives may appear to require that each have 'the same thought'. But that requirement is an effect of the rhetoric. There is no objectivity, no stepping outside the rings of context, no metalanguage possible which can calibrate how similar are the thoughts engendered by the production of that sentence. The presence of a stable meaning, a uniform identity for the assertion 'This is a table' is a linguistic effect – a trace of a presence, a reality, independent of language and language-users. It is this trace or the language effect of truth which makes stability and identity (however provisional) possible.

It is time to reintroduce Derrida, whose work on language focuses upon 'the essential predicament of all speech and all writing, that of *context* and *destination*'.[19] It is in one of his earliest works, *Of Grammatology*, that Derrida makes his infamous statement: '*il n'y a pas de hors-texte*'. This has been understood to mean 'nothing exists that is not a text', although, more accurately, the French reads 'there is no outside-text'.[20] Later, in the same book, he writes: '*il n'y a rien hors du texte*' – there is nothing outside of the text[21] – which appears to come closer to those who wish to see him as a linguistic idealist, a relativist and a nihilist. But let us put the first of these remarks into its immediate context:

> if reading must not be content with doubling the text, it cannot legitimately transgress the text toward something other than it, toward a referent (a reality that is metaphysical, historical, psychobiographical, etc.) or toward a signified outside the text whose content could take place, could have taken place outside language, that is to say, in the sense that we give here to that word, outside of writing in general. That is why the methodological considerations we risk applying here to an example are closely dependent upon the general propositions that we have elaborated above; as regards the absence of the referent or the transcendental signifier . . . [22]

In other words, the statements that there is no outside-text and that there is nothing outside of the text are inferences from 'the general propositions' which issue from Derrida's insistence upon 'the absence of the referent'. The human situation, and all communication within that situation, traffics in and exchanges signs; and dependence upon signs (which are substitutionary, or supplementary) indicates absences. This is so even if the effect of communication is to establish the existence or presence of the referent. There is, therefore, something rather problematic, *par excellence*, about a demonstrative. For if the object was present in its self-evident manner, then why does this need alluding to? Why is the language not enough? Why is a further, supplementary sign required – the pointing of the hand, the nod of the head in the direction of the object? These absences, which provide the possibility for, in fact necessitate textuality, do not mean that nothing is ever present, only that we traffic in mediations. In fact, presence, the promise of the transcendental signifier, the referent outside the text, is *also* a necessary condition for the possibility of textuality. There may be no immediacy, but mediation bears witness to the absence of that immediacy. This Derrida terms the 'trace' – the trace of finalized and absolute identity which haunts language, that propels the economy of *différance*, in which meaning is deferred (not annulled). In his work throughout the 1980s he called this the promise of the yes, but since it is never immediate, and is always caught up in its absence and therefore the supplementarity of signs, Derrida termed it a 'Yes, yes'.[23] It is for this reason that certain commentators have championed Derrida's work as a form of negative theology. Derrida has protested loudly that he is a philosopher, not a theologian, and negative theology begins from an after-the-event analysis of the experience of the full presence of God, even when, subsequently, God is then absent. But Derrida is nevertheless aware of parallels between the textual strategies involved in deconstruction and mystical theology.[24] The main point in so far as this essay on theological realism and anti-foundationalism is concerned is that Derrida's understanding of language does not replace plenitude with nihilism, undecidability and freeplay – 'Greatly over-emphasized in the States [is] this notion of "freeplay".'[25] The basis of his understanding of discourse is a system of differences and oppositions. Nihilism, like relativism, issues from the irrelevance of difference – from indifference itself. Derrida examines the contamination of presence by the undecidable. The ubiquity of the sign puts all meaning into play, but it does not eradicate meaning. His examination of discourse *both* challenges representative models of communication *and* also challenges the linguistic idealism, indeed the relativism, with which he has been charged. Thus, if

Derrida's analysis of discourse rescues the philosophy of language (and theological realisms argued for on the basis of such a philosophy) from the scientism which holds sway in Braithwaite and Soskice, it does not allow us to abandon ourselves to the nihilistic free for all which provides the philosophical starting point for much postmodern atheology. As he himself acknowledges, in one of his most clear discussions of *différance*, what is pointed to is not the indeterminancy of meaning, but any finalized decidability:

> I say 'undecidability' rather than 'indeterminacy' because I am interested more in relations of force, in differences of force, in everything that allows, precisely, determinations in given situations to be stabilized . . . Which is to say that from the point of view of semantics, but also of ethics and politics, 'deconstruction' should never lead either to relativism or to any sort of indeterminism.
>
> *Différance* is not indeterminacy. It renders determinacy both possible and necessary.
>
> I have never 'put such concepts as truth, reference, and the stability of interpretive contexts radically into question' . . . I have − but this is something entirely different − posed questions that I hope are radical concerning the possibility of these things, of these values, of these norms, of this stability . . .
>
> I say that there is no stability that is absolute, eternal, intangible, natural, etc.
>
> The ties between words, concepts, and things, truth and reference, are not *absolutely* and purely guaranteed by some metacontextuality or metadiscursivity.[26]

I quote Derrida's own words at length to emphasize that this is not simply (although it is also) my interpretation of what deconstuction reveals. The immediate context of these remarks is a letter to Gerald Graff, who was editing the debate between Derrida and the analytic philosopher of language, John Searle.

Where does this leave us − or at least me and those like me − who believe that it is important that theology accepts *both* its anti-foundationalism (a correlative of the freedom, magnitude and alterity of the divine) *and* (in order for it to remain theology rather than some subset of anthropology) a realism concomitant with traditional notions of revelation and incarnation?

It leaves us with what I suggest might be termed a *theological materialism*. Our webs of words and power relations, the differential grids within which we live and through which the significance of our lives is both given and received, bear witness to our finitude and fallibility (sin, perhaps). The immediacy of things in themselves remains inaccessible. Language does not mediate in the sense of acting as a third order, as a vehicle for the expression of these things. But language is not a totality. It presents the aporias, the effects of an alterity which has preceded and gone on ahead of it. This alterity we can neither capture nor tame. But neither is this an other which is so other that we know nothing about it. It is an other, a negative plenitude, which makes possible all our mediations and promotes the endlessness of supplementation – as the empty margins enable the text to be positioned. Deconstruction, as Derrida has recently remarked, is an aporetics[27] – an analysis which continually alerts us to that which exceeds our grasp, to that which remains enigmatic, mysterious, outside and yet bordering what is known. Language, by its operation, the fulfilment and plenitude it both chases and prevents, the excess and aporias it inscribes and attempts to forget, is then, ineluctably theological – in so far as it raises theological questions (questions even Derrida has to account for). Theological questions necessarily circulate about the body of a text, the texture of what is textual – what, in French, is also the word for biological tissue. With post-structuralist or deconstructionist thinkers such as Derrida (but also Jean-François Lyotard, Luce Irigaray and Julia Kristeva) theological and metaphysical horizons are opened up – not, as with forms of empirical representationalism or linguistic idealism, closed down. Deconstructing the hierarchical binaries of outside/inside, mainstream/marginal, transcendence/immanence, mind/body describes and affirms the very possibility of metaphysics. This is the operation of what Derrida would term a 'quasi-transcendence', an opening into that which is other and non-totalizable. As a philosopher, Derrida will not name and define the aporia to which he constantly bears witness. But as theologians, it is with this intimation of transcendence that we begin. With enigma (a word frequently used by Emmanuel Levinas to express the same excess), and hence awe and wonder, located in the very historical, economic, social and physical matrices of our living (materalism as understood by Marx and Engels) we are, I suggest, as theologians, being offered a new model for incarnation.

Notes

1 Don Cupitt, *The Last Philosophy* (SCM Press, 1995), p. 47.

2 Mark C. Taylor, *Deconstructing Theology* (Scholars Press, 1982), p. 91.

3 See my essay 'Postmodern theology' in David Ford (ed.), *The Modern Theologians*, second edition (Blackwell, 1996).

4 Mark C. Taylor has gone much further than most of them: see the language games he employs in 'GNICART TRACING: *Inter Alios*', the final section of *Deconstructing Theology*, pp. 107–26.

5 Ernest Laclau and Chantal Mouffe, *Hegemony and Socialist Strategy: Towards a Radical Democratic Politics*, trans. Winston Moore and Paul Commach (Verso, 1985), p. 108.

6 There is, in fact, a spectrum of correspondence theories of language ranging from one word corresponding to one object (Locke and Royal Society empiricists like Sprat) to language as an external symbolic form which represents the internal experience (Saul Kripke and Hilary Putnam). All these forms distinguish, with varying degrees of correspondence, an internal and cognitive aspect and an external reality. Language in all correspondence theories acts as a medium, a third order. They are all representational views of language.

7 A. N. Whitehead and Bertrand Russell, *Principia Mathematica*, vol. 1 (Cambridge University Press, 1927), p. 66.

8 R. B. Braithwaite, 'An empiricist's view of the nature of religious belief' in Basil Mitchell (ed.), *The Philosophy of Religion* (Oxford University Press, 1971), pp. 77–8.

9 Janet Martin Soskice, *Metaphor and Religious Language* (Oxford University Press, 1985), p. 110.

10 *Metaphor and Religious Language*, p. 114.

11 Sallie McFague, *Metaphorical Theology: Models of God in Religious Language* (SCM Press, 1982), p. 15.

12 *Metaphorical Theology*, p. 37.

13 *Metaphorical Theology*, p. 42.

14 Paul Ricoeur, *The Rule of Metaphor*, trans. Robert Czerny (Routledge, 1978), p. 247.

15 Quoted by Janet Martin Soskice, *Metaphor and Religious Language*, p. 78.

16 Pierre Bourdieu, *Homo Academicus*, trans. Peter Collier (Polity Press, 1988).

17 Jacques Derrida, *Limited Inc.*, trans. Samuel Weber (Northwestern University Press, 1988), p. 136.

18 Gareth Evans, *Varieties of Reference* (Oxford University Press, 1988), p. 41.

19 *Limited Inc.*, p. 112.

20 Jacques Derrida, *Of Grammatology*, trans. Gayatri Chakravorty Spivak (Johns Hopkins University Press, 1976), p. 158.

21 *Of Grammatology*, p. 163.

22 *Of Grammatology*, p. 158.

23 See Jacques Derrida, *Ulysse Gramophone: Deux Mots Pour Joyce* (Galilee, 1987).

24 See Jacques Derrida, *'Différance'* in *Margins of Philosophy*, trans. Alan Bass (University of Chicago Press, 1982).

25 *Limited Inc.*, p. 115.

26 *Limited Inc.*, pp. 148, 149, 150, 151 and 151.

27 Jacques Derrida, *Aporias*, trans. Thomas Dutoit (Stanford University Press, 1993), p. 15.

12

Non-realism in art and religion

George Pattison

Introduction

Many modern theologians are persons of culture, participants in the musical, dramatic, literary and artistic worlds of the ancient or metropolitan cities where, for the most part, they live. Yet in relatively few of them does this participation show itself in what they write – beyond, perhaps, a passing allusion to some great work of art in order to illustrate or add colour to a particular point being made. There are, of course, exceptions. Roman Catholicism, not surprisingly, has produced a number of theologians for whom engagement with art has been part of the shaping spirit of their work. These include some of the most significant figures of twentieth-century Catholic theology: Jacques Maritain, Etienne Gilson and, more recently, Hans Urs von Balthasar being prominent examples. Protestantism, where a strong an- or anti-iconic undercurrent can still be felt, can offer fewer names, although the outstanding achievement of Paul Tillich in this respect shows that a Protestant theology of culture is not a contradiction in terms.

There is, minimally, a case to be made for including Don Cupitt amongst those for whom art is not merely an occasional source of illustration but integral to the shape of his theological project. This is because, for Cupitt, the world of art does not just provide a useful analogy to what is going on in religion: it actually shows the kind of religion – and, indeed, the only kind of religion – that a postmodern world can get along with.[1]

A particularly telling instance of this comes in the chapter 'We are grateful to art' in *Radicals and the Future of the Church*. Cupitt's argument is vividly concentrated in his remarks on Mark Rothko:

> I have chosen to emphasize especially the case of religious art because nobody can deny, first that works of art are just human constructions, secondly, that great religious art, such as the late paintings of Mark Rothko, can still be produced, and thirdly, that such works as Rothko's can be quite new and independent of existing religious groups, their teachings and iconographies. I want to say that Rothko (for example: he is by no means the only one) just invented works of art that are great religion. Indeed, I maintain that the major artists of Modernism and after – roughly, since the mid-1860s – can be viewed as the prophets of a new religious order. From their dedication to their task, their creativity and their works many people now get the sort of charge that earlier generations once got from icons and the cult of saints.[2]

Moreover, he goes on to say:

> Painting in particular is super-charismatic, in that it was the first of the arts to begin living . . . in that queer post-modern condition in which it has to operate by continually reinventing itself. We don't get anywhere. . . . We keep restarting. The establishment of a settled tradition is impossible, and although dozens or perhaps hundreds of little groups are formed, each of which solemnly issues its manifesto, they can stick together and work in a common style for only two years, or five years, or so.[3]

These comments not only tell us a great deal about how Cupitt sees what a religion that could truly claim to be a religion for our time would be like; they also tell us a great deal about how he understands art. So intimate, indeed, is the interconnection between the two that an examination of what he has to say about art will, purely in its own terms, provide important material for reflection on his understanding of religion.

Three main themes can be extracted from the quotations just given: art as fulfilling a religious function, the artist as creator, and the impossibility of tradition. To these I shall add one more, found in a number of Cupitt's writings about art, such as his remarks about Richard Long in the catalogue for 'The Journey', an art event sited in and around Lincoln in 1990 and dedicated to exploring the frontiers between art and contemporary spirituality. Here Cupitt wrote:

To be truly religious, [art] must be 'flat', entirely of this world and quite unconsoled. The Abstract Sacred gets its religious weight from its very repudiation of the supernatural, a point eloquently made in the work of Richard Long. When people compare Long's works of landscape art with megalithic monuments, the comparison only draws attention to the uncompromising horizontality of Long's work. From Babylonian ziggurats and Stonehenge to Victorian spires, through almost five millennia, religion had pointed upwards towards a higher world. Long's chosen materials, rocks and mud, stood at the bottom of the old Chain of Being. They could not be more than a launch-pad for the soul. Long, however, really does want us to stop at them. Sacred stays on the land surface, and we should stay there too.[4]

Art, then, the postmodern art that is best suited to generate the symbolic order of a viable contemporary way of being religious, is strictly horizontal, 'on the level', all surface and no depth.[5]

I shall, then, take these themes in the following order: art as religion, surface and depth, the artist as creator, the breakdown of tradition. I shall argue that, in every case, Cupitt's view of what art is and how art functions, whilst by no means trivial (indeed, as I shall amply illustrate, it reflects a broad and powerful stream of Romantic and Post-Romantic thought), is seriously lacking and that this lack necessarily feeds through into his under-standing of religion: what it is, how it functions, and what sort suits us. I should add only that in concentrating on the visual arts, and, above all, painting, I am following Cupitt's own lead – not only with regard to the examples he uses but also in the light of his specific singling-out of painting as 'the first of the arts to begin living after the end of its own history'.[6]

Art as religion

It is perhaps almost a commonplace to say that for us, today, art has taken the place of religion. To enter a major gallery is to enter a space that has all the trappings of the sacred. There is a special kind of hush in the air. We speak, if we speak at all, in whispers. We pause, standing or sitting, before the objects of our devotion in postures of reverence, hands folded, heads bowed, lost in contemplation. Some consult their catalogues or study the gallery's inscriptions with an intensity and earnestness that marks out a disciple in search of an authoritative 'word' as to the truth of what is being seen. We have come to a place apart, a place which, even if it does not overawe us with its architectural grandeur (as not only the older museums – temples of culture – sought to do, but also newer buildings such as the National Gallery's Sainsbury Wing achieve with a less obtrusive dignity), nonetheless has rules of conduct and deportment that are quite distinct from those of the world outside. Even if we take on board André Malraux's point that, for the modern world, the totality of global culture, produced for the most part under the spell of a myriad of differing religious beliefs, now stands open to us as a museum without walls, that merely extends the scope within which these comments can be applied. For in the museum without walls the monuments of the past are all essentially equalized: a statue in a museum, a cathedral building, a medieval castle, ancient earthworks – all alike elicit 'museum'-type behaviour. The world of the gods has metamorphosized into the world of culture, of humanity's self-representation, approached with the profound reverence of a newly learned self-respect.

We could multiply the behavioural and social analogies between the worlds of art and of religion almost indefinitely: compare, for example, the crowds who flock to the great blockbuster exhibitions in metropolitan galleries and museums with medieval pilgrims. (Not least striking in this respect is the compulsion not to leave without some relic as a tangible token of the blessing received – even if it is only a T-shirt or chocolate box!)

Yet however successful we are in applying the analogy there remains the further distinct theoretical issue: that modern artists (or those critics and manifesto writers who have functioned as their publicists) have themselves claimed to be doing for their time what religion did in the past.

In the first wave of Romantic writers life, love and art blended together into a visionary enthusiasm for which only the language of religion seemed adequate. Friedrich Schlegel's fictional Julius, the hero of his programmatic Romantic novel *Lucinde*, recounts how the mysterious voice of fantasy speaks to him in a vision: "'The time has come when the inmost essence of the Godhead can be revealed and shown, all mysteries be disclosed and fear cease.'"[7] He goes on to say how this voice has inspired him to a renewed enthusiasm for art, to find and to create symbols and letters with which, in the service of fantasy, to represent the eternal truth about the world. The artist takes on the part of prophet. He is, in his poetry, the servant of a new religion of love.

But if the artist was already being endowed with the status of prophet circa 1800, a further revaluation of the artist's role in the condition of modernity – and one that is directly relevant to Cupitt's own work – was to be offered in the writings of Friedrich Nietzsche. For Nietzsche it was not only the God of the Christians who had died. It was any 'God' created by the all-too-human longing to ground our self-understanding in an absolute value or system of values. In a truly godless world the sentimentality of Schlegel's vision is still too pathetic, still too charged with nostalgia for the lost horizons of transcendence. Values can no longer be ascribed to the decrees of either a Christian or a Romantic God. Values are the creation of human beings themselves. Above all they are the creation of the artist. Only the artist has the power – in the face of the unconsolable abandonment of a purely earthly reality – still to win us for life, to make us believe that life is worth living, that it is beautiful, entrancing, lovely:

> Art and nothing but art! It is the great means of making life possible, the great seduction to life, the great stimulant of life.
> Art as the only superior counterforce to all will to denial of life, as that which is anti-Christian, anti-Buddhist, antinihilist *par excellence*.[8]

In this regard, then, art is the great redeemer of life for our time: it is the redemption of the man of knowledge, the redemption of the man of action, and the redemption of the sufferer, 'as the way to states in which suffering is willed, transfigured, deified, where suffering is a form of great delight'.[9]

Thus, although Nietzsche does not want to see the reinstatement of new gods, he regards art as fulfilling tasks in some way analogous to those previously filled by religion. Art gives meaning, purpose, dignity and delight to life – fully conscious that all of these are its own invention, the creatures of what Schlegel called fantasy's magic wand.

Whether in terms of the anthropology of culture or in terms of the programme of modern art, then, art can be seen as filling a place left empty by religion.

Yet this function is profoundly ambiguous. Judgements will inevitably differ, but there would be many who would regard the history of modern art – that is, of art that has cast itself in this quasi-religious role – as the best argument for the case that art needs religion more than religion needs art. Those who regard modern and postmodern art as increasingly prolific in the production of banal, vacuous and merely manipulable images (a situation in which meagre talents, such as Andy Warhol, can be puffed up into major figures in the international art-world) might well be tempted to see in this fall the fruit of Romantic and post-Romantic attempts to use art as a substitute religion.

Something like this was certainly the view of the late English critic Peter Fuller, who, despite his avowed atheism, remarked that 'it is a moot point whether art can ever thrive outside that sort of living, symbolic order, with deep tendrils in communal life, which, it seems, a flourishing religion alone can provide'.[10] Tellingly (with regard to Cupitt's use of Rothko), this view led Fuller to a revaluation of a number of widely-held pieces of popular critical wisdom, including the status of Rothko himself. Although (as far as I know) he went much further in conversation than he ever did in print in this respect, the comments on Rothko in his last writings indicate a line of critique that would be unsettling for a Cupittian view. Thus, Rothko is described as symptomatic of the 'nihilistic' background of modern art,[11] and is compared – at first glance, perhaps, bizarrely – with Winifred Nicholson, whose work was coincidentally shown at the Tate at the same time as a major Rothko retrospective. Fuller conceded that 'Winifred Nicholson was undoubtedly not such a "great" painter as Rothko', but, he goes on to say, 'her lack of a sense of self-importance gave her strengths which he did not possess'. He concludes: 'Perhaps if Rothko had suffered less from a need to create masterpieces and had shared Winifred Nicholson's love of the blooms of particular things, he would have drawn even closer to the expression of those fundamental truths which preoccupied them both.'[12] This does not, of course, imply any necessary denigration of Rothko, but it indicates a reserve that renders questionable the obviousness, assumed by Cupitt, of Rothko's ability to create works of art that are 'great religion'. There are further aspects to this reassessment that touch on issues to be discussed below. For the present, these reflections aim to do no more than to keep open a question with regard to the claim made on behalf of art by Romantics modern and postmodern that art is fitted, of itself, to provide a paradigm of what contemporary religion should be.

Surface and depth

We have heard Cupitt's words on Richard Long, an artist who rearranges natural materials, sometimes simply photographing them *in situ* and then leaving them to their fate, sometimes reassembling them in galleries and museums. For Cupitt, we recall, Long stands as a prominent example of postmodern art's horizontality, the creator of a new sacrality that is strictly 'on the level'.

The view that painting itself has, in Cupitt's words, 'become flattened out upon the canvas . . . no longer trying to create an illusion, or to have us looking away from itself, at all [but] content to be itself, its own colour, and its own surface'[13] is widely shared in surveys of modern painting. Georges Bataille described the transition from the previous dominance of an art of illusion, an art in which a painting was evaluated according to its capacity to make us believe that we were confronted by the represented object itself, to an art 'on the level', in Cupitt's sense, as 'the passage of painting, from a language which narrates . . . to a language which is bare'; and he credited the accomplishment of this transition to Manet, to whom, he said, 'we must attribute in the first instance the birth of this kind of painting devoid of any signification other than the art of painting itself which is "modern painting"'.[14] I shall take this as a cue to focus my questions regarding horizontality on Manet's own painting.

We may well be tempted to see in this nothing but the painting of a purely secular consciousness, illustrative of Baudelaire's call to modern art to concern itself solely with 'the ephemeral, the fugitive, the contingent', the world of the man of the crowd, 'the perfect *flâneur*'.[15] Look at a painting such as Manet's 'The Concert in the Tuileries', where we see Manet himself and Baudelaire too, along with other members of the Parisian artistic élite relaxing in the Sunday afternoon crowd beneath the spring foliage and distant blue skies. The top hats and walking canes of the men, the billowing dresses and bonnets of the ladies, the air of refined and casual pleasure – the whole scene is superficial in every sense. There is no great issue at stake and no great passions are aroused.

But is that all there is to Manet's art? Even with respect to a painting such as this we might do well to reflect on Baudelaire's comment on the frock coat that was the ubiquitous garb of the Parisian gentleman: 'Is it not', he asked, 'the inevitable uniform of our suffering age, carrying on its very shoulders, black and narrow, the mark of perpetual mourning? . . . All of us are attending some funeral or other.'[16] Look again at Manet's *flâneurs*. What funeral could they be possibly be attending?

In attempting to answer this question I shall accommodate myself to the popular wisdom that all judgements in art are purely subjective and offer the merely anecdotal evidence of my own encounter with Manet's work. Of course, I had always known of Manet, but somehow he had never touched me. This changed in December 1990 at the turn of a stair in the Museum of Fine Arts in Boston, Massachusetts. The particular painting I chanced upon at that time and place was the portrait of Madame Brunet and, a short while later, I found myself in front of another portrait (this time using one of Manet's favourite models, Victorine Meurand), 'The Street Singer'. In the eyes of those portraits I saw something quite different from what the textbook talk of Manet's 'discovery' of the two-dimensional picture plane had taught me to expect. It was not simply the absence of sentiment or feeling in the Romantic sense, but *the interiorization of feeling* to the very lowest threshold of visibility. In other words, in its very understatement, it nonetheless expressed the 'metaphysical shock', described by Paul Tillich as 'the shock of non-being', that is the wordless recognition that each and every step we take is encompassed by possibilities of death, extinction, oblivion. The modern artist, as Baudelaire well understood, does not invest his paintings with the grim reminders of mortality nor yet with the symbols of a better life in the hereafter that were part of the stock-in-trade of an earlier art. Nor is he comforted for long by the heroic defiance of a Byronic refusal of metaphysics. But everywhere he goes in his frock coat he is on his way to 'some funeral or other', knowing himself to be, in the very act and work of artistic production, an 'infinitely suffering' being who nonetheless has no other materials in which to express that suffering than those of the unheroic, ordinary bourgeois world of the modern urban environment.

Let us try to name this loss more precisely. Manet painted two overtly religious paintings. The first – and probably the most important – of these was the 1864 'Dead Christ with Angels'. In the blunt words of one typical critic of the time, this image was an utter and virtually blasphemous humanization of Christ: 'We have never seen such audaciously bad taste, the negation of scientific anatomy, spoiled color, lampblack abased and applied to the face of the most beautiful of men, carried so far as by Manet in the "Dead Christ".'[17] For this critic, the painting was nothing less than a visual equivalent of Renan's reductionist *Life of Jesus*. It was simply a portrait of dead flesh. Nothing more. As such it showed, in a manner unacceptable to the piety of the time, the utter death into which Christ descended. A Christ who could be as dead as this had no divinity in reserve. As Dostoevsky's Prince Myshkin said of another 'Dead Christ' (by Holbein, in the novel *The Idiot*), '"Why, a man's faith might be ruined by looking at that picture"'.[18]

Here is the one point in Manet's painting career where his implicit religious assumptions come into view: the horizontality of his work is revealed as nothing less than a painterly expression of the death of God, an event that was to take philosophy (in the name of Nietzsche) another generation to name. This is the funeral that modernity is attending.

The flatness of Manet's picture surface is not then the plane of a play without depth. It is itself the revelation of the deepest melancholy, the deepest pathos. Therein is its power. Manet is no 'one-dimensional man' (Marcuse). Rather, his painting, precisely in its melancholy 'depth', is a powerful critique of a world that is otherwise flat only in the sense of 'a characterless flux of essentially identical elements'.[19]

Of course, these reflections on Manet cannot of themselves be taken as determinative for the whole phenomenology of flatness or horizontality in modern and postmodern art. Nonetheless, the pivotal role of Manet in the emergence of this artistic orientation may give us pause for thought as to whether it is unproblematic to assert without further ado that flatness is all. Maybe, beneath the very flatness of modern art lies the infinite tension of a dead God – and this, precisely, is the most powerful source of modernity's characteristic pathos. Perhaps, as Cupitt declares in *The Long-Legged Fly*, it is time to declare that the mourning is over.[20] Yet even an example such as that of Richard Long, a man who walks alone across the solitary places of the earth, places of emptiness, devoid of human artifice, may offer more than a simple and direct injunction to embrace the present as that present is presented to us in the experience of modern urban horizontality.

If the questions of God and of the death of God thus lie not so far beneath the (apparent) surface of the modern, that is not the only, indeed not the most immediate, direction in which the culture of horizontality is more problematic than it seems. Specifically with regard to art there are issues of environment and context that require another and, dare we say, a deeper look. We shall approach these issues through the question of creativity: how far can the artist truly be spoken of as a 'creator' of values?

Creation out of nothing

We have seen that Cupitt, in close and conscious alliance with Nietzsche, sees in the artist an exemplary role model for how the religious person can create values to live by in the wake of the death of God. As with the theme of art functioning as a substitute for religion, this idea too is profoundly rooted in the culture of Romanticism. Repudiating the view of the artist as a 'mere' imitator of reality, the Romantics insisted that the artist is essentially creative. The artist does not merely (as Plato had charged) copy something that is already there. The artist creates. Indeed, this creation is not simply the creation of a new form for an already existing material, it is – at least in the most extreme forms of Romanticism – absolute. Schlegel could claim that 'artistic production (*das Dichten*) . . . does in a certain sense produce its own matter'.[21]

For an early critic of Romanticism, such as Kierkegaard, this theme provides a clue to the ultimate failure of Romanticism as a view to live by. As he saw it, this doctrine of absolute creativity is interwoven with the apotheosis of irony in such a way that although the Romantic ironist is indeed, in a certain sense, absolutely free, that freedom is merely the avoidance of responsibility. The ironist is only able to maintain his peculiar stance in the face of life by virtue of an 'acosmism', a 'Docetism'[22] that effectively ignores the claims made on him by reality. The reconciliation of life's contradictions in the harmony of art is, as far as the Romantics are concerned,

> a kind of reconciliation, but it is not the true reconciliation, for it does not reconcile me with the actuality in which I am living; no transubstantiation of the given actuality takes place by virtue of this reconciliation, but it reconciles me with the given actuality by giving me another, a higher and more perfect actuality.[23]

The Romantic claim to absolute creativity is a flight from reality, not a conquest of it.

Kierkegaard himself is specifically concerned with the tension between artistic creativity and ethical life, but even within the field of specifically aesthetic considerations there is considerable scope for questioning the values of creativity. We may already take preliminary bearings from Fuller's comparison between Winifred Nicholson's flower paintings and Rothko's bleak, nihilistic abstractions. Although it was Nicholson's aim, in Fuller's words, 'to see beyond the veil of appearances into the spiritual essences of forms and things',[24] she was prepared to submit to the engagement with 'the blooms of particular things', to allow her eye and intellect alike to be trained by the visible surface of nature.

Although it is not only Romanticism that has denigrated the classical view of art as essentially mimetic, certain forms of Romanticism (such as those of Schlegel or Nietzsche) have carried the repudiation of mimesis to an extreme. An alternative approach is that which Fuller finds in Ruskin. This is the view that all art is dependent on *theoria*, that is, on the contemplation of the visible forms and structures that God has, as it were, built in to the very fabric of the created order so as, through the eye, to train our spirits in the apprehension of divine things. *Theoria* does not apply to each and every observation of 'what things look like' but, in its strict sense, is confined to the 'moral appreciation of ideas of beauty'.[25] Nonetheless, this profoundly moral act of contemplation can only be arrived at through patient and constant familiarization with the simplest and most everyday perceptions of visible forms: the tones of colour in the sky above, the patterned profusion of the vegetation under our feet, the outlines of distant

169

hills on the horizon, the sense of lightness as we run up a sand dune on the other side of which lies the sea. All these, and many other examples, make up the stuff of Ruskin's *Modern Painters*. Landscape itself is morally significant, for it is, like Scripture itself, a medium of divine self-revelation. God has chosen the world to have the shape it has in order to draw us to himself, through a sequence of affinities that run through the whole of the created order.

It was only too evident that, as Ruskin saw it, the hand of man could only ever diminish and never improve on this revelatory power. Industrialization is not only constricting the native beauty of the land 'into a narrow, finite, calculating metropolis of manufactures',[26] but is sapping our very sense for colour and shape.

If Ruskin offers the most outstanding example in modern times of an aesthetic founded upon the requirement of attention to the external, visible form of the created world,[27] he is by no means unique in recognizing the incalculable role of 'what is there' to the artist. Thus, although he prefers the language of creation to that of imitation, Jacques Maritain speaks of the artist as responsive to the 'eternally mysterious and disturbing . . . logic of the structure of the living thing . . . the intimate geometry of nature'.[28] Similarly, interpreting the medieval understanding of beauty, Umberto Eco has spoken of 'a structural grace of things'.[29] We might also in this context mention Nicholas Wolterstorff's concept of 'fittingness' as a requirement of all good art.[30]

In these and many other ways we are dealing with the situation in which the artist is not working in a vacuum, but face to face with nature, a situation that is no less true if we extend the concept of nature to embrace that of abstract and multi-dimensional form. It is by no means necessary or appropriate to limit what has been said to 'landscape' or 'figurative' painting in any conventional sense.

Once more, we conclude with a question: is it really self-evident that the artist is best understood as 'creator'? Isn't it just as plausible – isn't it even compelling – to see art as essentially responsive to the givenness of colour and form? And isn't it perhaps the case that art is not only at its best but at its most religious when it does just that?

One further point for reflection. Isn't it precisely at this point that art offers the best analogy for a spirituality of our time? For isn't the return to earth, the acceptance of situation and location in time and space, the precondition of such a spirituality?

The end of tradition

Modern art has been extravagantly iconoclastic in its attitude to tradition. The modern artist is one who has internalized into the very programme of his art what the critic Robert Hughes called 'the shock of the new'. 'Newness', doing what's never been done before – isn't that just what art is about when it's at its most typically 'modern'?

But if that is true, then modern art spells the end of art as tradition, as the handing down from master to pupil of a store of learned skills and techniques. Art no longer grows from one generation to the next, it leaps in sudden and startling forward and backward spurts. The world of modern art seethes with newness and the buzz of what's happening. Now it's Paris, now it's New York, but wherever it is it's always just about to move on.

Such rootlessness is, of course, intertwined with the declared horizontality of modern art – it never stays long enough to grow roots – and with the modern artist's aspiration to create out of nothing, for he has always already left behind the world of his upbringing. It is also, as we have seen, used by Cupitt at least in characterizing the 'style' of postmodern religiosity. Such religiosity will have no use for timeless institutions or perennial philosophies, but will be happy to ride the shifting tides of change and chance, making itself up as it goes along.

But is this situation as good for art as it would seem? Isn't it also one of the areas in which modern art is profoundly problematic and self-destructive? It is striking, for instance, that the value of tradition is one of the recurrent motifs of Peter Fuller's later writings on art. Not that he believed that art could be acquired by the handing down of ready-made objectifiable skills. That, in any case, is not what tradition means. Tradition in its proper sense allows for the inclusion of subjectivity and the variability of individual and local circumstances. It is, ideally, flexible and changing, self-transforming in every generation. But it does not, as Fuller sees extreme modernism and postmodernism doing, sweep away all elements of continuity. Rooted in and face-to-face with the givens of visual form, artistic tradition develops as a language within and through which to make sense of the individual experience of those givens. These themes come together when, for example, Fuller speaks of 'a Romantic tradition' in British cultural life, 'whose twin characteristics were a belief in the human imagination and a close, empirical response to the world of natural form. I believe that this tradition . . . persisted in England and gave rise to some of our best art in the twentieth century' – and he goes on to cite Paul Nash,

Henry Moore, Graham Sutherland, David Bomberg and Peter Lanyon as examples of this tradition.[31]

A similar emphasis can be found in his essay 'Rocks and flesh: an argument for British drawing',[32] and in many other places. He is scathing about what he regards as an unholy collusion between left-wing critics such as Peter Berger and the Thatcherite right in assaulting the public museums and educational means by which this tradition is concretely realized. The celebration of Gilbert and George as significant artists is the ultimate and banal *reductio ad absurdum* of this retreat from tradition.[33]

Maybe, then, art needs tradition for its own sake – and, as we have seen, maybe it needs religion as much as religion needs art, maybe it needs depth if it is to make the earth move for us, and maybe it needs to pay attention to the world about it rather than relying solely on its own powers of creation. All these are 'maybes', that is, questions, and the view we arrive at will depend on a complex set of responses to particular works and to whichever lines of criticism best interpret those responses. There is a lot of work to be done that cannot be done merely by following arguments or setting quote against quote. All I hope to have achieved here is to draw up a list of questions to set against Cupitt's assumptions about what art is, what it can do, and how it does it, principally (but not exclusively) using Peter Fuller as exemplifying an alternative approach.

But, given the close connection Cupitt makes between his understanding of art and the project of postmodern religion, does it follow that a view such as Fuller's, in which the dependence of art on religion, on tradition, on the givenness of its matter and the depth of its subject is affirmed, automatically and immediately leads us back to the faith of the Church? By no means. Fuller himself remained constant in affirming his atheism to the very end: 'For myself', he wrote shortly before his death, 'I remain an incorrigible atheist; that is my proclamation of faith.' And yet, he continued, 'there is something about the experience of art itself, which compels me to re-introduce the category of the "spiritual"'.[34] Moreover, he endorsed George Steiner's assertion that '"where God's presence is no longer a tenable supposition and where His absence is no longer a felt, indeed overwhelming weight, certain dimensions of thought and creativity are no longer attainable"'.[35]

There is therefore no direct route 'back' from the abandonment of modern and postmodern art to the faith of the past – and no reliable route forward into some spirituality still to come either. What we can say, though, is that the kind of modernist aesthetics espoused by Cupitt as illustrating the situation of contemporary religion only distracts us from the real opportunities and openings that the experience and the making of art has to offer the spirit. It also fails to do justice to Cupitt's own keen sense for art. It is not in the glittering performance of surface-skimming acrobatics but in waiting and watching, and discerning the depths, that we prepare the way for such epiphanies of the sacred as may yet be vouched to our time. So art and religion alike and together attend the God who is yet to come.

Notes

1 For a critical survey of Cupitt's writings on art see Charles Pickstone, 'We are grateful to Don Cupitt: Don Cupitt on art', *Modern Believing* XXXV (1994), pp. 10–17.

2 Don Cupitt, *Radicals and the Future of the Church* (SCM Press, 1989), pp. 25–6.

3 *Radicals and the Future of the Church*, p. 26.

4 *The Journey* (Usher Gallery, Lincoln, in association with Redcliffe Press, 1990), p. 102; cf. 'Seen and unseen' in the catalogue *Art and Worship* (Worcester, 1991).

5 For a further exploration of this motif of 'horizontality' see Don Cupitt, *The Long-Legged Fly* (SCM Press, 1987).

6 *Radicals and the Future of the Church*, p. 26.

7 Friedrich Schlegel, *Lucinde* (Reclam, 1963), p. 24 (my translation).

8 Friedrich Nietzsche, *The Will to Power*, trans. Walter Kaufmann (Vintage, 1967), p. 452.

9 *The Will to Power*, p. 452.

10 Peter Fuller, *Images of God: The Consolations of Lost Illusions* (Hogarth Press, 1990), p. 189.

11 Peter Fuller (ed. John McDonald), *Peter Fuller's Modern Painters: Reflections on British Art* (Methuen, 1993), pp. 26–7.

12 *Peter Fuller's Modern Painters*, p. 116.

13 *Art and Worship*.

14 Georges Bataille, *Manet* in *Oeuvres Completes*, vol. IX (Gallimard, 1979), p. 131 (my translation).

15 Charles Baudelaire, *The Painter of Modern Life* (Phaidon, 1964), pp. 13 and 9.

16 Charles Baudelaire, *Selected Writings on Art and Artists* (Cambridge University Press, 1972), p. 105.

17 Quoted in R. Hamilton, *Manet and His Critics* (Norton, 1969), p. 60.

18 F. M. Dostoevsky, *The Idiot*, trans. Constance Garnett (Dent Dutton, 1914), p. 207.

19 H. Ferguson, *Melancholy and the Critique of Modernity: Søren Kierkegaard's Religious Psychology* (Routledge, 1995), p. 80. Ferguson's book is an intriguing study of melancholy as a factor enabling the critique of modernity, with particular reference to Kierkegaard.

20 *The Long-Legged Fly*, pp. 150–9.

21 Quoted in Walter Benjamin, *Der Begriff der Kunstkritik in der Deutschen Romantik* in *Gesammelte Schriften* 1:1 (Frankfurt, 1972), p. 63 (my translation).

22 Søren Kierkegaard, *The Concept of Irony*, trans. Howard V. Hong and Edna H. Hong (Princeton University Press, 1989), p. 273.

23 *The Concept of Irony*, p. 297.

24 *Peter Fuller's Modern Painters*, p. 116.

25 John Ruskin, *Modern Painters*, vol. II (Dent, 1906), p. 166.

26 *Modern Painters*, p. 161.

27 For a full discussion of Ruskin and his influence upon Fuller, see my *Art, Modernity and Faith* (Macmillan, 1991), pp. 54–77.

28 Jacques Maritain, *Art and Scholasticism* (Sheed and Ward, 1933), p. 52.

29 Umberto Eco, *Art and Beauty in the Middle Ages* (Yale University Press, 1986), p. 76.
30 Nicholas Wolterstorff, *Art in Action: Towards a Christian Aesthetic* (Eerdmans, 1980).
31 *Peter Fuller's Modern Painters*, p. 45.
32 *Peter Fuller's Modern Painters*, pp. 49–68.
33 Peter Fuller, *Theoria: Art, and the Absence of Grace* (Chatto and Windus, 1988), pp. 211–15.
34 *Images of God*, p. xiv.
35 *Images of God*, p. xviii.

Index of names

Index of names